Special Edition

In Search of Ruritania
The Life & Times of
IVOR NOVELLO

By

David Slattery-Christy

&

My Life

By

Ivor Novello

1933

Paperback Edition: ISBN 9781838136550

Copyright © 2022 David Slattery-Christy

All rights reserved.
Hardack Edition
ISBN-13: **9781838136529**

Mossovells
" Aldwych
London.

City 166).

In Search of Ruritania

Published by Christyplays Books. First published by AuthorHouse 2006

www.christyplays.co.uk @DSCAuthor

Copyright. The rights of David Slattery-Christy as author has been asserted in accordance with the Copyright, Designs and Patents Act 1988. All rights reserved.

A CIP Catalogue record for this book is available from the British Library, London.

Design : Christyplays
Book cover designed by Ed Christiano at Deeper Blue Designs
www.db-md.co.uk

This Special 4th Hardback Edition published 2022
By Christyplays Publications.
All Rights Reserved

IVOR NOVELLO

> "We shall see great changes and feel it here – times of unrest and anger and hatred in the world – and these things are strong. We shall almost forget to laugh and make music, but we shan't quite forget, and some day we'll wake up, as from an evil dream, and the world will smile again and forget hate, and the sweetness of music and friendliness will once more be important…"
>
> Ivor Novello as Rudi Kleber in The Dancing Years, 1939.
>
> These words are sadly as pertinent today as they were when Novello wrote them in the late 1930s. Nothing has changed.

Ivor Novello

In Search of Ruritania

CONTENTS

Part One
My Life by Ivor Novello – 1933
Part Two
In Search of Ruritania
The Life & Times of Ivor Novello

	Acknowledgments	i
	Author Foreword	
1	Lavender & Lilacs	8
2	Spring of The Career	29
3	Roaring Through The 1920s	45
4	Noel, Alfred & Elsie	67
5	The Land That Might Have Been	110
6	Gosford Park & Red Roofs – Myth & Reality	126
7	A Russian Émigré And A Glamorous Fight	158
8	End of An Era	188
9	Let's Face The Music!	206
10	A Duo, A Drag Queen And A Movie	240
	References	265
	Index of Songs, Films, Plays & Musicals	265
	Further Reading	286
	Index of Newspaper Reviews	290
	Credits for Photographs & Index	292

Also by David Slattery-Christy

Books:

Traveller's Tale: The Making Of A Fairground Showman

Mildred on the Marne: Mildred Aldrich Frontline Witness 1914/18

Edwardian Beauty: Lily Elsie & The Merry Widow

The Mistletoe Haunting – Legend of Minster Lovell

Plays:

A Marvellous Party! Novello, Noel & Friends

Naturally Insane! The Life of Dan Leno

Flyte or Fancy? The Road to Brideshead

Ghost Lights: Ivor Novello & His Leading Ladies

Elvira & I – Puccini's Scandalous Passions!

Forever Nineteen – WW1

The Post Card – Titanic Play

After The Tone

www.christyplays.co.uk

@DSCAuthor

ACKNOWLEDGMENTS
With Thanks to:

Theatre Royal, Drury Lane, Archives. Magdalen College Archives, Oxford.
Doris Bentham, Capitol Films, Dr. Robin Darwall-Smith, William Differ
Gordon Duttson, Mary Ellis, Douglas Fairbanks Jnr, Lord & Lady Fenton
Nicholas Gaze, Graham Greenwood, Nicholas Hassall,
Col. Michael Hickey, Donald Macleod, Matthew Lloyd, Sir Cameron
Mackintosh, Lilly Moore, Lynn Nortcliff, Betty Paxton, David Potts,
Sarah Potts, Ian Richardson, Maroussia Richardson, Rosy Runciman,
Rob Sedman, Lee Stephens, David Walters, Luke Whitlock,
Sandy Wilson, Michelle Woodman,

Special thanks to the following and cast members, and Capitol Films and
Robert Altman for their kind permission to reproduce their images in stills
from Gosford Park

Robert Altman
John Atterbury
Kelly MacDonald
Dame Helen Mirren
Jeremy Northam
Dame Maggie Smith
Geraldine Sommerville
Dame Kristin Scott Thomas
Frank Thornton
Natasha Whightman

Special thanks to BBC Radio 3 and Composer of the Week
Dedicated to Ivor Novello, Christmas 2016

Producer: Luke Whitlock
Presenter: Donald Macleod
Featuring: David Slattery-Christy, Rosy Runciman
& William Differ
December 2016

Reviews

"As latecomers to Gosford Park, we were intrigued by the more than passing references to Ivor Novello. This book is a delightful look into the life and work of the composer of 'Keep The Home Fires Burning' and will surely keep your interest on a coast to coast flight.

Phil Stevens – Los Angeles 2016

"David Slattery-Christy is a writer very much in tune with British society during the first half of the last century…it has served him brilliantly with his two well-researched biographies [on Lily Elsie & Ivor Novello]. David has an amazing gift for bringing back to life the bustle and allure of London's West End in the days of Daly's and beyond."

*Raymond Langford Jones –
Sardines Theatre Magazine 2014*

"David is the absolute authority on Novello, and this new edition including Novello's own My Life is a bit of a must."

*Alexandra Coghlan
The Sunday Times
July 2023*

Reviews

"An absorbing and thoroughly engaging read, and a must own for fans of Altman's work looking to learn more about Novello and his work…straight from the film's Ivor Novello Consultant."

Tara O'shea – Chicago USA

"This new biography delves much deeper into Novello's life than its predecessors. While this may have alienated those who prefer to remember Novello as fragrantly as his famous lilacs, I found it to be well-researched and thought-provoking…the writer often uses a compelling style – the description of his first visit to red Roofs is akin to something out of Rebecca."

David Wheeler – The Gaiety Magazine

"A biography which is the result of extensive research…I found this an intriguing reappraisal of a former theatre idol whom I had tended to dismiss."

Tom Howard – Rogues & Vagabonds

William Haines, Joan Crawford, Douglas Fairbanks Jnr and Ivor Novello attending the premiere of Fairbanks's film Union Station, 1930.

Author's Foreword

It is extraordinary to think that it is eighteen years since this book was first published, and even more so when I consider the changes that have occurred in that time and the recognition that Ivor Novello has enjoyed in the years since Gosford Park and then Sir Cameron Mackintosh's decision to rename the West End's Strand Theatre in honour of Ivor to the Novello Theatre. Even the music award that bears his name now uses his full name and are referred to as the Ivor Novello Awards. The man himself would be thrilled indeed.

My Life
By
Ivor Novello
1933

My decision to create this special hardback edition for 2022 came about for several reasons. For many years I have had on file an autobiography that Novello wrote in 1933 covering his life and career up to that point in time. Due to copyright issues I was unable to use the material. Now that Novello's copyright has ended I wanted to make sure this unique document is preserved for future theatre historians. It is written by Novello in a chatty way and you really get the sense of him and his voice – the reason I decided to include it unabridged in this edition rather than chop it up into quotes. Doing that would have lost the spirit of the writing and his voice.

A marvellous discovery I made when the most recent census was released astounded me. My paternal grand mother, Florence Emily Phipps, from an Oxford family, was a house-mother to the young boy choristers at Magdalen College and was there at the time Novello attended. He was a boy soloist soprano of note.

I had a desire to update the book to include the wonderful changes and opportunities that have arisen during the intervening years. My adaptation of Glamorous Night was finally staged the the Buxton Opera House in 2008, proving a great success. I was also delighted to be a part of a BBC 4 documentary on Novello titled The Handsomest Man in Britain and also the BBCs Great War Centenary season with a BBC Radio 2 programme titled Keep The Home Fires Burning that was presented by Don Black and produced by Jonathon Mayo – this was a two part special that included a special Friday Night is Music Night dedicated to Novello's music presented by Ken Bruce.

I was contacted in 2016 by Luke Whitlock, a producer for the BBC Radio 3 programme Composer of the Week, who asked me to be a script consultant on a planned set of programmes dedicated to Ivor Novello – the first time Composer of the Week have featured him in its seventy year history. In addition to that, Luke asked me to be the guest interviewee for the week – interviewed by the show's presenter Donald Macleod. An honour indeed.

The recording of the programme was a joyful day for many reasons. I had put Luke in touch with Rosy Runciman, archivist for Sir Cameron Mackintish and Delfont Mackintosh Theatres, who had kindly agreed that part of the programme could be recorded at the Prince of Wales Theatre, where Novello had his first success as a playwright in The Rat, and also the Novello Theatre. We started off in the Waldorf Bar of the theatre, it is where the pictures of Novello's musical Glamorous Night I donated are displayed. Rosy Runciman was interviewed in this area. We then moved to what was Novello's flat that sits on top of the theatre, now used as offices. It was a memorable time to be in "the flat" and to remember all the famous people who had passed through that special place.

In the years after I first published this biography I have been surprised and amazed at the reactions it generated from people. Mostly the feedback was positive but there were a few that felt I had betrayed Novello by talking about his sexuality and also his prison sentence. Rather than be upset or offended by the vitriol and hate mail, it made me realize that Novello still inspired such loyalty from so many and that the few that were still alive were willing to voice their disapproval. I never intended to cause any offence to anyone, but alas I did, but as much as I understood their reasons, I would not change anything as a result. For me, looking at all aspects of Novello's life was so important if a true study of the remarkable man was to be created. My respect and admiration for Novello knows no bounds and I like to think that all my efforts over the past thirty years and more have somehow helped to give him the profile he now has – instead of the obscurity in which he languished for too long.

There have been sadnesses too. Mary Ellis, Elisabeth Welch, Sandy Wilson, Alan Bates and Robert Altman have all passed away during the intervening years.

Whilst talking to Donald Macleod for the Composer of the Week show he said to me that it is amazing that nobody has ever attempted to make a film of Novello's life story. I agreed with him and it has to be said that his life is such a rich seam of drama, and covers some of the most innovative years of the first half of the last century, that it must be worth serious consideration. Perhaps I will be lucky enough to get the chance to work on that film – it would be a blockbuster indeed. Robert Altman had the idea in his mind, but it was not to be.

It is impossible for me to say that this edition is definitive. I have accepted that Ivor Novello is now such a part of my life that I feel that I know him quite well and he is thus a permanent fixture. A posthumous friend – and long may he continue to be so. I thank him for all the special and magical experiences I have had on my journey of discovering his life. In turn those experiences have enriched my own immeasurably.

David Slattery-Christy
September 2022

David Slattery-Christy & Donald Macleod – BBC Radio 3
Broadcasting House, London, October 2016
Composer of the Week – Ivor Novello

In Search of Ruritania

Part One

David Slattery-Christy, Rosemary Ashe & Roy Hudd OBE
Unveiling a Blue Plaque in memory of Lily Elsie on her former Hyde Park home,
London, August 2019.

"The attendance I danced on the Widow was urged by the passion I had for Lily Elsie – a passion which has lasted until this day; in fact, the glamour she has for me increases every time I see her!"
Ivor Novello (1933)

For Ivor...

Lily Elsie & Ivor Novello
1928

My Life

By

Ivor Novello

*This partial autobiography was written by Ivor Novello in 1933.
It covers his life and career from his birth in 1893 to that date.*

Transcribed and edited by
David Slattery-Christy
2022

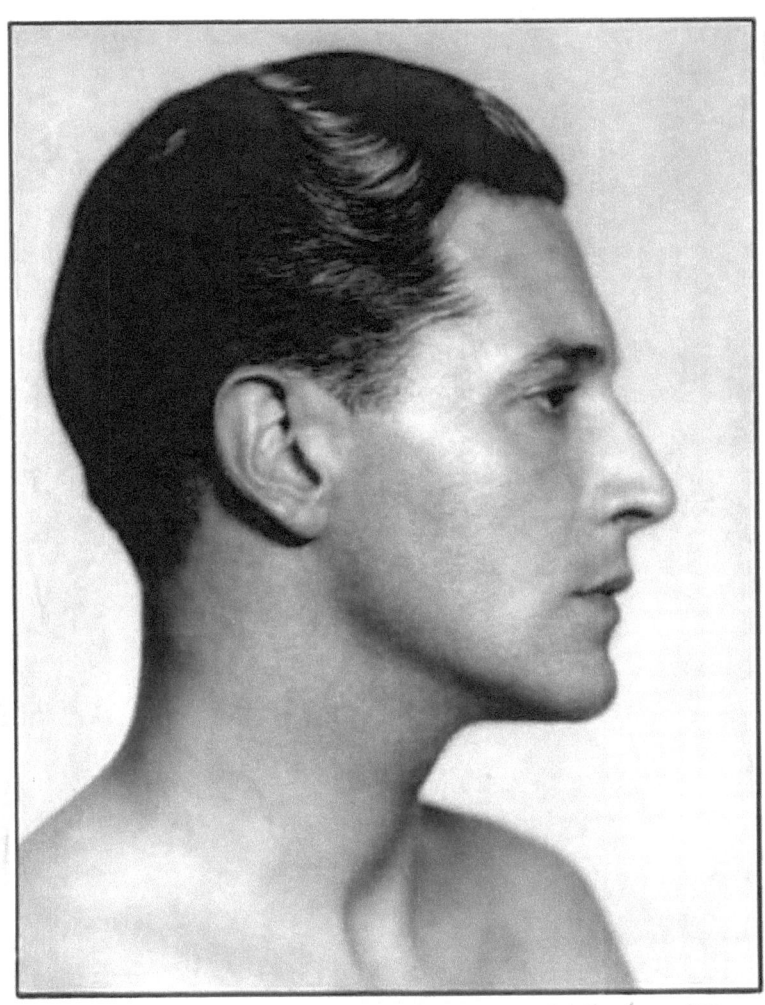

Ivor Novello – 1920s

Composer, Film Star, Stage Actor, Playwright

"*The handsomest man in Britain*" [*New York Times*]

For Graham
1953-2021
Love is Eternal

Christyplays Publications 2022
Special Hardback Edition including My Life by Ivor Novello and
In Search of Ruritania – The Life & Times of Ivor Novello by David Slattery-Christy

ISBN: 9781838136529

*Novello's lyricist Chrisopher Hassall
Painted when he was at Oxford in the early 1920s*

Biographer's Note

For many years I have had in my files a typed copy of an autobiography that Novello completed in 1933. It outlined his career both in films and theatre, and as a musician, along with more personal memories growing up with his famous mother, Clara Novello Davies, herself a successful musician and singing teacher. Its intentional use in 1933 was for magazine serialization.

Due to copyright issues I was never able to reproduce this document when I completed an early edition of my biography of Novello titled: In Search of Ruritania – The Life and Times of Ivor Novello. In later editions it was unviable still – even when we did the 10th anniversary edition to coincide with BBC Radio 3 commissioning Novello's music for Composer of the Week in 2016, where I was script advisor and guest for the five hours of programs, dedicated to his prolific musical genius.

In 2021 Novello's copyright came to an end after 70 years, he died in 1951, and that enabled me to make the decision to create a full unabridged version of his partial autobiography to ensure it is saved for posterity and future theatre historians. I decided to publish it unabridged as it gives a clue to Novello's voice and character, written in first-person, so dismantling it into quotes to insert into his existing biography would have taken away the spirit of it. I have only added comments to clarify in [brackets] where really necessary as I didn't want to detract from the flow of Novello's voice.

Sadly his autobiography only goes as far as 1933. His life and career changed from that point and the last seventeen years of his life he focused on his spectacular musical creations starting with Glamorous Night in 1935 and ending with Gay's The Word that premiered a week before his death in 1951 aged 58. Much has been written about these musical years, so this autobiography of his sets out his life and career that led up to that gear change in his career.

There will be a special hardback edition where it is incorporated in whole as an appendix in a new edition of In Search of Ruritania – the Life and Times of Ivor Novello. It will then have a separate stand alone version published at a later date.

David Slattery-Christy - 2022

Ivor Novello's bronze bust by Clemence Dane in the Grand Saloon of the newly refurbished Theatre Royal, Drury Lane, in London's West End.

Novello's musicals saved the theatre's fortunes in the 1930s
Glamorous Night (1935) – Careless Rapture (1936) – Crest of the Wave (1937) –
The Dancing Years (1939)

Ivor Novello & Isabel Jeans in The Rat 1925

Ivor Novello and cast of Fresh Fields during the opening night party at Criterion Theatre in London's West End 1920s

Chapter One

"I never could remember things in their right order; if I write these impressions of my life chronologically they would make dull reading."

Most people write their reminiscences far too early; what, after all, of real interest can happen in the short activity of twenty years? Time and again I have said that nothing would induce me to join the group of 'memoirists'. When the idea of writing my story has been mooted I've put it off and edged it away, vaguely suggesting that ten years would be time enough! Then I suddenly thought: 'But supposing, when I come to write, no one cares two hoots then whether I do or don't – or even if they do, perhaps my memories will be blurred; there will be a temptation to eke them out with lies and embroidery, and I shall write something that will have little or nothing to do with the real me. It will be just another 'Story of my Life; a series of egoistical inventions.'

What is there of interest in my life? Well – I earned my keep when I was none; made a fortune before I was eighteen and spent it by the time I was twenty; I have had three careers all going at the same time; I have been applauded and derided, praised and scoffed at, discouraged and spurred on.

I have realised every ambition I set out to realise – I have even flown an aeroplane when I hadn't the faintest idea of how it kept up in the air (and indeed it didn't), I have played on the stage with nearly every beautiful actress in England and am still unmarried! I have run my own theatre since I was twenty-six, and I have adored life – how I have adored life! – every minute of it.

My existence can surely never be so exciting again as it is at present – I've got two plays and a film running in London and a third play in New York – so now, perhaps, is the time to jot down impressions of my life, a life which has, by turns, been sad and happy – mostly happy, thank goodness – and always thrilling. Not, however, by way of thumbing my nose at those who will undoubtedly say 'What conceit! What's he done to write about?' but rather for those friends, all over the world, who are constantly asking me for more information than can be found in books of reference; who want to know 'what happened then?'

Well, this is what happened then…

I never could remember things in their right order; if I write these impressions of my life chronologically they would make dull reading. Things that are orderly and done as they should be done are always dull! My chief interest in life has come through contact with other people. There would be nothing very interesting in describing myself looking at a beautiful sunset, but were I looking at that same sunset with [Greta] Garbo at my side – that would be something to write about!

Most of the exciting impressions of my life are centred around a few of those fortunate beings for whom the world is run – women. Women have taught me tremendous things about life, and – more importantly to me as a worker – tremendous things about my job. Mother, with her terrific enthusiasms and her tenacious courage which never allowed her to be downed by anything, was my first heroine. When I was only six months old, she left me – the baby she adored – to whisk sixty girls off to the 1893 World's Fair at Chicago [USA], where she cleared the board of every prize she could possibly win, and brought such musical renown to Wales that she was commanded by Queen Victoria to Osborne [*to attend an audience*]. The Queen was living in great seclusion and retirement; and in those days Osborne was considered impenetrable; it was almost a national sensation when the doors were thrown open to a little Welsh woman and a choir of sixty girls.

Clara Novello Davies

When mother returned to Cardiff the whole town turned out to meet her. Accompanied by a torch-light procession, her carriage was dragged by singing men and women to our little house in Cowbridge Road. But amid all the excitement, the flowers and the cheering, Mother had but one thought – the baby she had not seen for six months.

She ran into the house and upstairs to my room, where she rushed at me; nearly frightening me to death! I screamed and howled at the top of my voice – even then I had strong lungs – the baby she had flown back from a royal palace wasn't having any of her; I wanted nurse.

My howls continued for at least five minutes; eventually they began to subside. I allowed myself to be held – I even allowed myself to be squeezed, and finally got off to sleep in Mother's arms. So terrified was she of breaking the spell that she sat in the same position for three hours – afraid that the lightest movement would wake me and set me off howling for nurse again! She needn't have worried – something that has remained ever since was at work inside me – her six months' absence had ceased to exist. From that moment to this my mother has been my first thought.

Don't, however, think this is a soppy mother-and-son love story. It isn't! We have fought like demons when our temperaments have clashed. What level-headed business sense I have is derived from my father; this level-headedness has always been a bone of contention between mother and me. Heaven only known I have enough drive; but not one tenth of her energy and go-aheadness. She needs even more discipline than I do!

And how terribly important discipline is to those elect beings who are blessed or cursed with the artistic temperament. I chafe against discipline, but I respect it. I have, with help, developed quite a lot of it. One of the people who has taught me self-discipline in my work [*Film & Theatre*] is a woman whose name is a household word – Gladys Cooper.

If I had to describe Gladys Cooper in one word – one quality – it would be simplicity. With Fay Compton the quality would be warmth; with Madge Titheradge, temperament; with Isabel Jeans, brilliance; with Lilian Braithwaite, concentration; with Lily Elsie, glamour. I have adored acting with these ladies; I should like to have them all in a play together – it is only the salary-list that makes it impossible. There would be no bickering and no backbiting for they are all too big.

Ivor Novello & Gladys Cooper in The Bohemian Girl (1922)

Gladys Cooper has changed tremendously. When I first knew her she was so dazzlingly beautiful that when she came into a room it seemed as if all the lights had suddenly been turned on. She is still beautiful; but now her beauty is spiritual. Her eyes have gained the loveliness of tolerance; she is less reserved; she is sadder, yet she is gayer [happier]. I have always told Gladys that the missionary spirit was too highly developed in her character – she took a straight line herself and expected everyone else to toe it! Underneath a proud, assured exterior there is a depth of shyness and reserve – crowds terrify her.

I can imagine nothing more painful to her than what happened when – years ago – we both went to Arran in Scotland to make a film of Bonnie Prince Charlie. Forced to go about the streets in full make-up and costume as Flora Macdonald, she was followed everywhere by an excited crowd of some five hundred Scots; to embarrass her still further she had as a companion a Bonny Prince Charlie who had no shame at all (nor have I now!) I wouldn't have cared had there been a thousands of people. I fancied myself in my kilt; I liked myself with fair hair so much that, given the slightest encouragement, I would have dyed my own black hair and dispensed with a wig. In fact, I loved all the fuss which was made of us. But it was agony for Gladys; I think she must have hated me at the time – she so retiring and I so forward. Gladys was all for sneaking out of side doors and trying to escape notice in the back streets, but for me the only exit from the hotel was through the front door and the crowd! This difference in our characters might have caused a serious breach in our friendship. But it didn't. Since those days Gladys Cooper has gained in tolerance and I, I hope, in modesty. We now meet on a common ground of understanding.

One of the most embarrassing things that has ever happened to me was when Miss Cooper visited America for the first time, while I was in New York filming in The White Rose for D.W. Griffiths. She had decided to give herself a much needed holiday. Never having been to America she wanted, very rightly, to see the New York theatres (then at their best), and planned a flying visit. She had hoped to arrive unannounced and unnoticed, to see a few plays, and then return to London in time for her new production [of the play] Magda. I am hardly likely to forget the day before she was due to arrive. I picked up a newspaper, and the first thing I saw on the front page was a large photograph of Miss Cooper; inset, a very small one of me (humiliating!) Underneath, to my intense horror, was the caption: 'Gladys Cooper crosses the ocean to marry Novello film actor.'

[*This situation had in fact been set up my D.W. Griffiths to deflect any rumours of Novello being gay – this to protect his considerable investment in Novello as a sex symbol and film star. Novello and Gladys Cooper were in on the publicity stunt from the start and happily agreed to go along with it to generate press.*]

As, at the time, Miss Cooper was still married to Captain Buckmaster [*although separated*], nothing could have been (or was) farther from our thoughts. I went down to meet the boat. Instead of being able to welcome Gladys in a natural and friendly manner, I had to shake hands with her very formally and, at all costs, prevent being photographed together. Strangers had to be dragged in to stand between us! The boat was swarming with reporters and press photographers; if we moved a few yards they followed us. Miss Cooper was bombarded with the most idiotic questions, and was repeatedly asked whether it was true that she was going to marry me. All this publicity and bother so acted on Glady's shyness-complex that she nearly bolted to her cabin intending to hide there and return to England in the same boat.

[*Had it been as Novello suggests in this hindsight account, and they were innocent of any collusion, it would have been much simpler to not meet Gladys off the boat...*]

One night she and I were of a party which went to the Ziegfeld Follies. Will Rogers – on the stage – suddenly noticed Gladys Cooper sitting in the front row of the stalls. He turned to the audience and shouted out: 'Ladies and gentlemen, the loveliest thing that has ever come into this theatre is sitting in the front row. I don't know who she is, but I'll trouble her to stand up and show herself.'

[*This seems suspiciously like another of D.W. Griffiths's publicity stunts to mask his star Novello being gay, getting them reported in the press attending theatres and such like together.*]

Gilbert Millar, who was with us, whispered to Gladys: 'It's no good, you'll have to do it.' Indeed there was such a clamour going on in the theatre that it seemed not only best but the only thing to do, if the show was to continue that evening. With a blush, the like of which has long since passed out of fashion, Gladys stood up in her simple dress of apple green, turned to the audience, and bowed. I am positive that everyone in the house agreed with Will Rogers – as she stood there with her head bent, she was, surely, the loveliest thing that had ever entered a theatre. It always arouses in me a violent desire to laugh sardonically when people say 'What a fine actress Gladys Cooper has become!' Why, in 1914 Gladys was acting magnificently in My Lady's Dress, having already taken London by storm in Diplomacy, so what is all this 'become'?

And one thing that does certainly annoy me is to hear Gladys described as 'hard'. She has only to be seen in her own theatre, where she is beloved by everybody from the actors and actresses to the scene-shifters and the call-boy; or in her own home, where she worships and is worshipped by her children, to realise that Gladys is the essence of softness and womanliness. Why, she is not even a good business-woman, despite her success in theatre business. She often laughs at herself.

Gladys Cooper

Director D. W. Griffiths

Fay Compton and I have literally grown up together, although it is true that Fay was married, had a child, and was famous in the theatre long before I thought of going on the stage. But that was because she was so early and I so late. Fay has a quality of modesty that is almost an inferiority-complex; this, strangely enough, only applies to the thing at which she is supreme – acting. Congratulate her on an exquisite performance, and she will reply: 'Oh, do you really think so? I thought I was so bad!' But ask her if, by any chance, she plays golf, and she will immediately say: 'Of course. I'm very good!'

Fay has everything an actress should have – temperament, voice, looks, heredity, complete disregard of convention, and warmth. Years hence she will be known as the Ellen Terry of our time.

Fay Compton

Ellen Terry

Fay reads widely and well. If she recommends a book to me, I read it; I know I shall love it. Incidentally I am now very fond of books – I don't mean only reading them, but the actual volumes, in their neat and coloured array of shelves; and if they are first editions or 'association copies' so much the better. But there was a time when a book was a thing to be read and done with; and it was then that like the poor Indian I cast a pearl away richer than all my tribe.

Mr. Lloyd George was a family friend, and to me a sort of fairy uncle; one day he gave me a set of Robert Louis Stevenson, with his name and mine on each of the fly leaves. Alas, I was possessed with a passion for drawing, and could never lay my hands on enough scribbling-paper; so the blank pages were irresistible. One by one I tore them out, and covered them with the profiles of imaginary beauties; and now Kidnapped is the only one that remains intact.

Fay is also an exceptionally fine musician. Our greatest joy is to listen for hours to such music as the Ring, 'Tristan,' Debussy and Ravel. If Fay had worked with her singing (this generation has almost forgotten that she started her theatrical career singing little songs in Pelissier's Follies) Maggie Teyte would have had to look to her laurels! There is such a tremendous feeling for music in Fay's voice.

She is all temperament. Some actresses can pretend to cry, and do it most realistically; Fay really does cry – always – even on the hottest matinee. Also, she is far and away the most unpractical woman I know. During the eighteen years I have known her she has lived in twelve different houses; always she has taken the new one while still living – apparently permanently – in the old one. Her sensitiveness is known to everybody, and everybody teases her about it.

Constance Collier tells a story of her which illustrates this super-sensitiveness. Fay was acting in The Little Minster [*play*] at the Queen's [*now Sondheim Theatre*], and Constance in Our Betters at the Globe [*now Gielgud on Shaftesbury Avenue*] (the two theatres are practically next door to each other).

One night Fay burst into Constance's dressing-room with a face as white as a sheet and great tears rolling down her cheeks. She flung herself at Constance's feet and sobbed and sobbed. Constance immediately feared the very worst.

She imagined one of three things had happened. Either Fay was bankrupt, or she had suddenly had the news that her husband and son had been killed in a dreadful accident; or a Harley Street specialist had given her a month to live. At last, punctuated by the sobs, the truth came out. Lifting her tear drenched face to Constance, she faltered out 'Darling, why are people so cruel? I went in at the stage door just now, said good afternoon to the call-boy, and oh! – he cut [*ignored*] me!'

Constance Collier is a mistress of exaggeration; but whether the story is true or not, it might well be, so aptly does it point to Fay's absolute lack of self-importance. She really cares and is troubled about the most absurd trifles.

Fay is the most versatile actress we have. I wonder who else but she could have been a brilliant principal boy in pantomime (Dick Whittington) in January, the loveliest Ophelia of our time in February, and a dowdy little schoolmistress (Autumn Crocus) in March? Her versatility calls to mind a story which Gladys Cooper delights to tell against herself. Once when she was acting at the Adelphi Theatre, her stage-manager overheard the following conversation between two men in the stalls bar.

First man: "It's remarkable. Magda – Mrs. Tanqueray – and now Peter Pan. There's been no-one like her since Sarah Bernhardt!"

The stage-manager – adoring Gladys – thought to himself: "How nice to hear these things said! These men must certainly have a drink." [*on him*]

Second man: "Well – I don't like her!"

(Exit stage-manager swiftly)

12

When Isabel Jeans sweeps on to the stage in a cloud of white fox furs and orchids, the instant impression is of the essence of sophistication – here is a woman who knows the world; the woman who might well have given the first cock-tail party and invented Chanel! Oh! How wrong! Her stage appearance is but a purely synthetic version of Isabel. To enable her to face an audience she has developed a manner, a walk, and a way of speaking, all tremendously effective so much so that to mention 'an Isabel Jeans part' is enough to call up a definite mental image. In reality, she is extremely domesticated; her delicious house in St John's Wood is efficiently and admirably run. This home-wrecker (on stage) is the most devoted of wives and (this in a whisper) she sows and embroiders beautifully.

I saw her give a lovely and sincere performance in The Captive, which was unfortunately seen by few; the play, because of its unusual subject, not being allowed by the Censor [*Lord Chamberlain's department that licensed plays up until the 1960s*] to be publicly acted. I am quite positive that if Isabel were given a suitable opportunity she would make a great name as an emotional actress; able, at will, to discard completely all her outer trappings of sophistication. I should like to act with her in every play, and would, if there were not two very formidable dangers. One is that we should never stop giggling! I can imitate her voice so exactly (and do at parties) that I can convince myself that my own voice is hers. Hence there is always the risk, when we are acting together and I hear her speak to me in the voice I can do so well myself, that I shall be reduced to helpless laughter and roll on the stage. The other danger is that I should fall violently in love with her!

[*This expression of falling in love was a way to again deflect any thoughts that Novello might be gay – it protected his career and at this time it was also illegal.*]

Talking of Isabel Jeans naturally leads to the other Jeans whose name is not Jeans – Jeans being the stage name of Ursula. Ursula Jean's first job in London was with me. It was her hair gave it her. I was rehearsing The Firebrand, but still had not been able to cast the all-important part of the model with whom I, as [*the character in the play*] Benvenuto Cellini, was desperately in love. I didn't want a dark [*haired*] girl; this would involve the wearing of a fair wig, and the naturally fair girls I had seen couldn't act the part (all right, you blondes, this was then!). One morning I was given a letter from Sir Gerald du Maurier introducing a Miss Ursula Jeans. Out of politeness to Sir Gerald, I saw her. At that time Ursula was quite unknown; I met a girl with a lovely face but, to my disappointment, she seemed dark [*haired*]. 'She's nor good,' I was thinking to myself, forming polite sentences to the effect that if she would be good enough to leave her address

Ursula Jeans

Constance Collier

something else might turn up, when I thought I noticed a glint – a gold hair – peeping from under her tight fitting hat. In my best actor-manager voice I commanded her to take it off. At one a cascade of sunshine flooded the stage. Without hesitation I said: 'All right, my dear. You're engaged.'

She was. She signed the contract that morning, made good [*had a great success*] in The Firebrand, and from that day to this has never looked back.

Jose Collins has just written a book about herself, in which she has been delightful about me. Thank you, Jose, you're a darling! What thrills you've given me! You were never the accepted musical comedy type – where were your blue eyes, you fair hair? – but what extra things you had; the thrilling bird-like voice soaring up to soft top C's; the real star quality. And how terribly undisciplined you were! After all, you had enough personality not to need all the limelight on you, leaving the rest of the cast in complete darkness. It wasn't your fault – but with one degree less concentration on yourself you would have said that 'the play's the thing.'

You've done wonderful things for my music [*Novello is referring to the many songs he wrote for revue shows in the 1920s and early 1930s*] You fought, insisted, screamed, when there was talk of one of my numbers being cut; moreover you justified your violent [*protestations*]. I wonder if you remember, when I was playing at Blackpool and you at the Gaiety, my teaching you your new song over the telephone? The day Jose Collins left the musical comedy stage was a death-blow to glamour – there has been nobody like her since.

Jose Collins

George Grossmith Comedian

Chapter Two

*"Noel Coward has told me that he has had hundreds
of abusive letters – not one of them signed."*

It was amusing (for me at least) to read in Sam Goldwyn's reminiscences that Mae Marsh was temperamental and difficult. I do not refute Mr. Goldwyn; after all, his experiences with Mae are of the time when she became a world sensation in The Birth of a Nation and Intolerance, and her salary, even in those days, was fantastic. I speak only of the Mae Marsh I knew (and know).

Mae, when I first met her, was a little, freckled, ginger-haired girl with a ridiculous sense of humour. Our meeting was strange and extraordinary. D.W. Griffiths had cabled for me to go to America and play Joseph the hero of The White Rose. I landed in New York one morning, to be met with a message that I was to rehearse the film that afternoon! So, with the ground still swaying under my feet [*the result of being at sea on a liner for several days*] (I had not had time to recover my 'land legs'), I made my way up to the top floor of Keen's Chop House on Sixth Avenue where rehearsals were in full swing.

Nervously I pushed open the door and stepped into the middle of a Griffiths's film. Surrounding me were all the people I had adored in the series of marvelous films which Griffiths had made. But I was introduced to no one. I heard Griffiths say: 'Novello, go over to Miss Marsh and look down on her.'

Mae Marsh & Ivor Novello in The White Rose (1923)

Mae was being supported in an upright chair by Neil Hamilton and Carol Dempster. The scene was apparently one of intense anguish – I went to her and did as I had been told. To my amazement, Mae looked up at me, with tears streaming down her face, and sobbed: 'Oh, Joseph, I do love you!'

These, of course, were the days of the silent screen; having until then only done a few English films, I didn't know about this Griffiths method of stark realism; my face must have shown how taken aback I was by Mae's words. She burst into fits of laughter, and then, and only then, I was introduced to the company.

My association with Mae nearly resulted in catastrophe. Anonymous letters were the trouble. I have never suffered from the attentions of anonymous letter-writers [*1933 version of today's internet and social media trolls*]; pests whose fate I considered should be connected with boiling oil. To me this is the most indefensible of crimes. Noel Coward has told me that he has had hundreds of abusive letters – not one of them signed. At first they caused him great unhappiness; then he devised a plan to deal with them – a vigilant secretary, who consigned them straight to the waste-paper-basket. On second thoughts, perhaps they *are* pushed into my letter-box; let me assure the senders that I, also, never see them. I have a vigilant secretary too!

Mae, as the world knows, is a devoted wife and mother. Before we went to Florida for the filming of The White Rose I dined several times with her and her husband, Louis Lee Adams – a most delightful man whose journalistic duties rarely allow him to get away from New York.

When we got to Florida the company – like all film companies – split up into various groups and cliques. Neil Hamilton had his wife with him; D.W. Griffiths was always preoccupied with the making of the film and hardly spoke to anyone unless it was Carol Dempster. Mae, her small daughter Mary, my secretary Lloyd Williams, and myself formed our own group. We bathed, we went to movies, we drank innumerable ice-cream sodas and – heavens, how we laughed!

The film was nearly finished, our stay was coming to an end, when one morning Mae said to me: 'I haven't heard from Louis fro over a week. I can't understand it.'

We arrived at New York at the Pennsylvania Station. Mae was met by her husband. I greeted him warmly, only to be cut [*ignored rudely*] direct! For a moment I thought he hadn't seen me: his face of thunder put me right!

That evening Mae rang me up. It didn't need much imagination on my part to know that she, at the other end of the line, was crying. Through her sobs I gathered that some dear creature in the company, possibly male, more probably female, had written a series of anonymous letters to Louis insinuating that Mae and I were madly in love with each other, and that Mae had even expressed a hope that she would be able to get a divorce and marry me!

[*This would be great publicity for the film and it would be unsurprising is D.W. Griffiths was behind this to boost the profile of his two stars!*]

The awful part of the business was that Mae and I had been inseparable in Florida; whatever Mae said, this incontrovertible fact could not be dislodged from Louis's mind. I knew there was only one thing to be done; I hung up the receiver and, at the risk of several black eyes, went straight along to see Louis and Mae.

I did the clever thing and the offensive. 'Look here, Louis,' I said, 'I don't mind a bit your thinking these things about me. Of course I'm in love with Mae – I've been in love with her ever since I saw her in The Birth of a Nation. But I'm in love with an actress called Mae Marsh; I shouldn't care a damn if I never saw Mrs. Louis Lee Adams again.'

Louis looked astonished. 'But,' I went on, 'what I do object to, is being bored for six weeks by Mae raving about you – and then finding there's nothing to rave about!'

Louis regarded me in silence, a silence which lasted for at least a minute (and how long a minute can be!).
The he started to laugh. So did Mae. And, finally, so did I.
That laughter saved the situation. From that time to this, Louis and I have been the best of friends.

[*No doubt Louis would also been made aware that Novello was gay*]

Two years after, when I cabled Mae asking her to come to London and play the lead with me in The Rat for Gainsborough Pictures it was Louis who insisted that she should accept. He said he knew she would be well cared for.

The only other famous American film star I have played with is Ruth Chatterton. Ruth prides herself on being the most unpopular woman in Hollywood. She is. But she is also the most loved. There is a reason for this paradox. When Ruth first arrived in Hollywood she was one of the greatest names of the New York stage, but this, in Hollywood, didn't mean a damned thing. The talkies had not started; only the baby-doll type or the screaming vamp were of any use at all to the Hollywood Moguls. Ruth was ignored – professionally and socially.

Naturally, her pride was hurt. Had she been a free agent she would have returned to New York. But she wasn't; her husband, Ralph Forbes, was doing too well in silent pictures. She stayed in Hollywood – but oh, how she hated it! What a very unpleasant instrument second fiddle is!

Ruth Chatterton

Then, like a bolt from the blue, came the talkies. They wanted people of intelligence; they wanted voices; they wanted an actress; they wanted Ruth. She was the first talkie star.

But Ruth had learnt a lesson. She had learnt to select, and the people she chose to be her friends were those who had chosen her in obscurity. Lois Wilson, Elsie Janis, Laura Hope Crews; these were her friends. They still are. Ruth had no use for wild whoopee and no time for insincerity. She likes folk either simple or complicated – the simple people are her old friends, the new ones are the complicated people she finds in the ever-growing Hollywood colony of French, German, English and Italian screen artistes.

I met Ruth Chatterton at a party at Clifton Webb's, the Jack Buchanan of New York. I was thrilled. Ruth looked at me her lovely cynical grey eyes; when she heard that I was about to go to Hollywood, all she said was: 'Really? I hope you like it!'

Some-one pushed me to the piano; I played Isolde's Liebstod. As I sounded the last few chords I happened to look where Ruth was sitting, and into her eyes. Grey – yes! Cynical – no! There were tears running down her face. She came over to the piano; putting her arm around my shoulder, she softly whispered: 'You poor little boy – you play the Liebstod like that, and you're going to Hollywood! Never mind, perhaps I can make life pleasant for you.'

When I got to Hollywood, she certainly did. Ruth's house – one of the loveliest there – was a second home to me. Her parties were wonderful, and so cosmopolitan that they might have been given in Paris, Rome, Berlin or London.

Ruth, besides being a charming and intelligent woman, is a little ruthless! She was going to do a picture – Once A Lady – and thought she saw a part in it for me. I read the script and knew it was not so. I hated the part. But one look into Ruth's eyes and, against my better judgment, I said I would do it. 'Don't take any notice of the script, darling,' said Ruth, 'We'll build that part up!' Heaven knows she tried, but it was no good, the part just didn't exist. My one flutter into celluloid in Hollywood was a complete failure; if I hadn't hurtled home when I did and acted in several plays and films in quick succession – doing the stuff I can do – Once A Lady might have settled my hash [ruined my career] for good and all.

In my life Lily Elsie is like King Charles's head – I can't keep her out of the picture. When, after years of retirement, she said 'yes' to my persuasions to act in one of my plays, I could hardly believe that I had heard rightly. Lily Elsie was really going to act in a play of mine! I thought of the days when, at the age of fourteen, I had waited, night after night, outside the stage door of Daly's [*Theatre, Leicester Square*] just to catch a glimpse of her – some nights she even said good night to me! She was then playing in The Merry Widow; there is something about this piece which I swear no musical play has ever had, before or since. That is why, I think, even when it is revived with the most unsuitable casts, it always succeeds. The story is right and the music is right. I saw one revival without Lily Elsie. Never again! I would rather keep my memories intact and lovely.

It is incredible that Lily Elsie was only twenty when she created the lead [*role*] in The Merry Widow, yet that is all she was. Four years later she retired from the stage – yet there is still no better known or better loved name in our profession. Of course, it's glamour. She inspires in men the spirit of chivalry; in women, the desire to be like her.

Joseph Coyne & Lily Elsie
The Merry Widow, Daly's Theatre, London 1907

Lily Elsie has one phobia – she hates to be called Lily. Her unfailing test of whether people know her well, or don't, is what they call her. If they address her as Lily, she never has known them and never will. Her name is Elsie. It always has been and always will.

[*As a child star in music halls she was billed as Little Elsie, she adopted Lily Elsie as a stage name as a natural progression of that when she was older.*]

Underneath her extreme femininity is an iron will. She has strength of character and a loyalty only to be expected from the captain of an English cricket team or a first-rate boxer. When I was in the throes of my troubles [*producing*] The Truth Game; my cast deserting me on all sides, my friends driving me frantic with their sympathy [*because they thought his play terrible*], Lily Elsie and Viola Tree alone stood firm.

They had the courage of their first impressions – they loved the play when they had read it, and they still loved it when, at rehearsals, everybody else was loathing it. If it hadn't been for Elsie's amazingly staunch quality, I almost believe I should have thrown up the sponge [*given up*].

No one, watching Elsie radiantly float on to the stage, would think she was quivering with fright. Every entrance she makes is an agony [*for her*]; this struggle with her nerves has been the one factor which has prevented her from following up her success in The Truth Game. She is always being inundated with splendid offers to return, once more, to the stage.

My [first] meeting with Lily Elsie was, surprisingly enough, at 10 Downing Street. I had always wanted to meet her; also I had written an operetta which I was terribly anxious she should play in – but I didn't know anyone who knew her. Finally I went to the Prime Minister's wife and daughter, Elizabeth Asquith, and asked her to invite Lily Elsie to tea. My heart was beating so violently when we were introduced that I loudly hiccupped! This started us both giggling, and we have giggled together ever since – Elsie has a glorious sense of humour.

My day-dream that she should play in the operetta came to nothing; I played her the music, but she didn't hear it. Outside, on Horse Guards Parade, the band was blaring away full tilt. That was bad enough. In addition, Mrs. Asquith insisted on performing impromptu solo dances to each tune. Much as I adore Lady Oxford, on that occasion I would have given my soul to see her carried off by a hawk! But that strange, bewildering afternoon founded a friendship between Elsie and myself which is stronger today than ever.

The person responsible for the turning point in my career is Constance Collier. I got to know her at a time when I needed the balm of encouragement and sympathy. It was during my disastrous appearance with Gladys Cooper in Enter Kiki. We had first encountered each other during the filming of The Bohemian Girl – but it was during the Kiki days that we became really friendly. I had heard that Constance Collier was a terrifying woman; I immediately realised that the haughty Roman Empress had an aptitude for fun equal to that of a star clown at a circus. Constance, Viola Tree and Beatrice Lillie have had more to do with whatever sense of humour I possess than any other three people in the world.

My friendship with Constance was instantaneous. I found myself talking to this older woman as I had never talked before. She has that magical quality of being interested in other people before she is interested in herself. Struggling with dreadful ill health, she yet contrived to be gay, witty and utterly courageous. I nearly lost Constance through the illness that threatened her life [*diabetes*]; it is a great tribute to her strength of will that she returned from the edge of the grave – or more literally from a Strasbourg hospital [*she underwent the first use of insulin there*] – better in health than she had ever been before, with her great comic powers and unfailing wit unimpaired.

During the run of Kiki we saw a lot of each other. She was then playing her famous Duchess in Our Betters. It was I who was directly responsible for her accepting this engagement. She came to me, almost in tears, and said: "How dare they offer me such a part? To think that my last appearance was in my beautiful Peter Ibbetson, and they suggest that I should play this horrible caricature!." I read the play. "Constance," I said very firmly, when next I saw her, "you will play this part, and you will also walk away with the play. For tho' [sic] first time you will show an audience that a Roman Empress can have a sense of humour!"

"All right," she replied. "I'll take your advice, but I won't sign a contract! So if I suddenly hate it too much, even in the middle of the run I can walk out of the theatre and no one can stop me."

She appeared in the play for eighteen months, and never missed one performance.

During the run of Kiki I felt that my career had been blasted suddenly in its infancy. Constance wouldn't allow this. "My dear boy," she said, "we've all got to have these failures. I've had dozens. Now is the time to make a big effort. What was that apache story you were telling me about?" I fished it out. She liked the title – excellent – why didn't I make The Rat into a play? "I'll help you if you like." She did. The Rat saved me. I shall always be deeply grateful to Constance. Even when she completely let me down over her part in The Truth Game – a part which I had written especially for her – I knew, underneath my disappointment and bitterness, that Constance and I had something deeper and more solid than could be hurt by broken promises and slidings away. We can laugh at that estrangement now – we do – but at the time it was painful.

One lesson I have learned in this strange enchanting profession of mine is that when it comes to work contracts, friendship does, and should, go by the board.

Constance Collier naturally leads me on to Lilian Braithwaite; had it not been for Constance's defection, Lilian and I would probably have never acted together, and never become the tremendous friends we are today. If I had to choose one woman of all our profession to be the sole adviser of a National Theatre it would be Lilian. There is nothing she doesn't know about the stage. When I am acting in a play in which, unhappily, she is not, my first anxiety is that she should see my performance. I shall then know exactly what is wrong and exactly what is right with it.

Her critical faculties are extremely highly developed. This makes some people afraid of her, but if everybody in the theatre world had as honest a point of view which, however, she sometimes carries almost too far, the stage would gain in simplicity and integrity.

I wish I could quote instances of the material good that Lilian does by stealth – one never hears it from her, one hears it from grateful sister-actresses, vowed to secrecy, who suddenly appear in new clothes, and looking prosperous (half the battle!), to hunt for engagements and frequently, with the help of the clothes, obtain them.

Lilian has created four of my favourite characters in my own plays; Mrs. Brandon, the ten-per-cent lady in The Truth Game; then Mrs. Plaintiff, the vague, match-making mother in Symphony In Two Flats; next (the greatest imaginable contrast) an exquisite study of a world famous actress in Party; and finally (needless to say I don't mean finally), the languishing, secretly amorous Lady Lilian Bedworth (a name which caused Lilian to raise her eyebrows) in Fresh Fields. I am deeply grateful to Lilian, and I hope to show my gratitude by providing her with parts as long as she graces the stage.

I suppose almost my most intimate friend is Viola Tree. We first met in 1913. It is now 1933 – if I don't see Viola for a whole year we pick up our contacts just where we left off! I don't know whether she is an actress or not – heaven knows she ought to be – to me she's just a glorious accident. I wish such accidents happened more often! Viola has never attempted to grow up. She has all the wide eyed adoration of beauty of a girl at her first party. She has read everything, heard everything, seen everything, and even if all these experiences have "gone in one ear and out of the other," they have left on her mind a definite pattern – a very beautiful one.

Viola's conquest of America was quite extraordinary. New York had never seen anything like her. She arrived totally devoid of make-up, her hair flying in the wind, with one extremely well cut costume full of holes, and a battered suitcase. She left as chic as the last number of Vogue, and smothered in gardenias.

But this wasn't the real Viola – not the one I like. I like the Viola whose clothes only fit her where they touch, riding a bicycle through the most congested London traffic, beating a man with a hat for ill-treating a horse, striding up Regent Street with the gait of a young goddess; in fact, the daughter of Sir Herbert and Lady Tree. People meeting Viola casually think "Oh, yes – vague and affected." Let them read her book Castles In The Air; that will show them the real Viola, and honest, a striving, defeated artist, rising above her defeat, putting it behind her and laughing through her tears.

Chapter Three

"The attendance I danced on the Widow was urged by the passion I had for Lily Elsie – a passion which has lasted until this day; in fact, the glamour she has for me increases every time I see her!"

I should have been a preacher – a methodist of the fiery revivalist type, such as were my great-grandfather, and my great-great-grandfather, who both assisted at my christening (five generations were present at this ceremony; surely a unique beginning to my life!) so, obviously, I ought to be exhorting souls to repentance, instead of enticing them into the pit! [*theatre*]

I am told that I could sing before I could talk – and why not? My mother was the foremost singing-teacher in Wales; all my earliest memories are associated with the sound of fresh Welsh voices. It has been said that no singer has come out of Wales in either this or the last generation, who has not, at some time or other, been taught by my mother.

The first few years of my existence, were passed in a whirl of pupils, male and female, both coming and going; of Eisteddfods; glorious singing by Welsh miners, and rigid attendance every Sunday morning at a nonconformist chapel where mother played the harmonium for over thirty years.

At the same time I was running wild, dependent to an unusual degree on my own company, and only seeing my glamorous mother for two days a week – but we had two days! Even then she coloured everything for me by the force of her radiant personality.

In those days Cardiff was a great centre for music; most of the famous musicians of the time went there to give concerts. Our home was a rendezvous of all these famous people. Such celebrities as Agnes Nicholls, Patti, Johannes Wolff, the cellist, Jean Gerardy, Clara Butt, and Kennerly Rumford were frequent visitors. Clara Butt and Kennerly Rumford became engaged when staying with us. I gave them valuable assistance, for I, at the age of five, acted as the go-between and liaison officer. Clara would call me into her room in the morning and say: "Ivor, run down to Uncle Bertie and say 'bah'!" Thereupon I would patter downstairs to Uncle Bertie's room and deliver this laconic message. Uncle Bertie would then say "Ivor, run up to Auntie Clara's room and say: 'boo'" But the official engagement was not announced until much later.

Clara Butt & Kennerley Rumford

It was as a Paige at their wedding in Bristol that I made my first noteworthy public appearance. Ten minutes before the ceremony was timed to begin I had eaten myself ill with strawberry ices. Not only had I spooned the ice into my mouth, but all over the front of my white satin frock. Mother, in an agony at my un-paige-like appearance, covered up the damage as well as she could with face powder.

Adelina Patti

Outside the church a woman exclaimed: "Look at that darling little angel!" If she had only known, the darling little angel was, actually, feeling like nothing on earth, and choking down a tremendous urge to be horribly sick!

Once I sang a duet with Patti. I hasten to explain that the occasion was unpremeditated and unrehearsed; my age but thirteen. The famous prima-donna, in Cardiff for one of her numerous farewell concerts, was, as usual, Mother's guest.

She took a great liking to me; I told her all my boyish enthusiasms and dislikes. In the artist's room on the night of her recital, she discovered that I adored musical comedy – but not any more than she did. Her greatest favourite was Our Miss Gibbs, the gem of the piece to her the duet made famous by George Grossmith and Gertie Millar – If You Were Just The Sort Of Fellow. I gurgled with excitement, because I also adored that duet, and before I quite realised what was happening we were singing the music lustily together, I trying to keep my end up against her glorious voice; this just a few minutes before she was due to walk on to the platform and begin her recital with a solemn operatic aria!

The Musical Comedy star of the Gaiety Theatre, Gertie Millar

One of the most tragic experiences of my life – thank heaven, there have not been many of these so far – was when, one morning, I woke up to find I could sing no more. This was a far more serious thing to me than the breaking of an ordinary boy's voice. It was my education that was disappearing. For five years, as solo boy at Magdalen College School, Oxford, I had sung for my supper. At that time I took everything for granted; naturally a career at the University would follow school. But this was not to be. At first I thought my new croak was nothing more than a sore throat, not to be taken seriously. But the croak persisting made me realise that my voice had broken. My boyish soprano had lasted until I was nearly sixteen.

Such a family myth in time did this voice become, that I regret that the gramophone in those days was like me – in its infancy; the time when exceptional choristers voices were recorded, not yet. I am afraid that no marvel of science will ever give me a record that will satisfy my curiosity as to whether my voice really was as good as I have been led to believe!

There is at least one person besides my mother who still has a vivid remembrance of that voice, or at least had when I last met her two years ago in the south of France. When I was seven, I went one morning, to a small provincial hotel carrying a bouquet of flowers fresh picked from our garden. They were from my mother to a lady who had come from London to recite at one of her concerts. At the hotel I was shown into a suite of rooms, to find, still in bed, marvellous Mrs. Brown-Potter, her glorious red hair in vivid contrast with the white of her pillow. Having presented her with the flowers, I was taken with a violent desire to show off; I asked if she would like to hear me sing, and immediately came out with Poor Wandering One in my bell-like voice. Strangely enough, Mrs. Brown-Potter had never forgotten that occasion.

Mrs. Brown-Potter

I was an only child; I might easily have been coddled and spoilt; I never was. My mother's strenuous activities – three days in the week she taught in London, three days in Cardiff and the remaining day in Bristol (she recently computed that she had given well over a million music lessons in her life!) – did not leave her much time to devote to me; the result was that I was left very much to my own devices. Father – the head of the Glamorgan Rates Department – always stayed with the rates in Cardiff, and I saw as little of him as of mother. My father and mother were happily married for fifty years; their characters and pursuits were almost as wide apart as the poles. This was possibly as well, for father's extreme steadiness and balance served to check mother's amazingly exuberant temperament; incidentally, it also acted as a leaven on my own impetuosity!

My other boyish passion was the theatre. I am often told I have an immense knowledge of the stage; if I have, it is because I have always been completely engrossed in the theatre, and everything connected with it. I started going to the play alone when I was barely eight! Perhaps owning but sixpence in the world, my enthusiasm would drive me to borrow half-a-crown from the cook, or, indeed, any likely victim; take the horse bus from Maida Vale to Oxford Circus, and spend a glorious afternoon perched high in one of the west-end galleries.

But before this, when I was living in Cardiff and could not have been more than four or five, mother being away in London, the maids, schemed to go to the local theatre. The one obstacle to their plan was master Ivor, who, obviously could not be left alone. So master Ivor was taken with them. The fare which served to initiate me into the glamour of the footlights was The Secrets Of The Harem, surely one of the most blood-curdling, appalling and horrifying melodramas ever produced. In one scene, the Sultan's favourite wife was strangled by the chief eunuch and thrown out of an open window into the Bosphorus, which conveniently flowed at the back of the stage. This was the scene which, with its terrifying death screeches and realistic splashing of water, fairly bit into my youthful imagination, and indeed still recurs to me in the form of nightmares!

Mother, having travelled by the midnight train from London, arrived home in the early hours of the morning to discover her son in screaming hysterics. No wonder! After that, melodrama was taboo for me; I was allowed no stronger fare than musical comedies and pantomimes.

But they are meat and drink. The theatre was more than an escape from real life to me. It was real life. As far as the theatre is concerned, I am the world's most easily-got person; in any audience I am the first to laugh and the first to grope stealthily for my handkerchief and pretend to blow my nose. Third-rate actors in the tawdriest of theatres can grip my imagination and wring my withers! I have not even yet lost the capacity to be frightened in the theatre.

My school holidays were mostly spent in Maida Vale, where mother had an academy of music. Most of her young ladies were on the stage – two were in The Merry Widow. This musical comedy I contrived to see right through on twenty-two occasions, not to calculate the more numerous times when I saw only the last act. The final curtain was at an unusually late hour; if I was at another theatre, as soon as the curtain came down I would dash along to Daly's Theatre, knowing that I could slip up the gallery stairs at that late hour without being called upon to pay, the guardian of the pay box having by this time departed; the management quite sensibly thinking that no one would be foolish enough to come along and pay a shilling at that late hour.

The attendance I danced on the Widow was urged by the passion I had for Lily Elsie – a passion which has lasted until this day; in fact, the glamour she has for me increases every time I see her! One of the biggest thrills the theatre has given me was when, in The Truth Game, I was instrumental in bringing Lily Elsie back to the stage after her long retirement following the great days of The Merry Widow and The Dollar Princess.

When my singing voice failed, there was much family argument about my future. The possibility of my education being continued at Oxford University was considered; the fact I had been a schoolboy at Magdalen College would have helped me to a further scholarship; but this idea was soon dismissed as being financially unsound.

Father wanted me to go into a shipping office, employment which he considered reasonably safe and secure, at all events not so hazardous and precarious as writing music, for which mother argues that I had a talent. At school I had developed a small flair for composing which had impressed her. Only recently I found, in some old papers, a highly complicated and florid waltz dating to those days (I at once made certain that no one else should find it!). Mother's intuition, or perhaps faith, having triumphed over father's cautiousness, I was dispatched to Dr. Brewer at Gloucester to unravel the mysteries of harmony, counterpoint and composition. Dr. Brewer was not long in remarking that I was the only really hopeless pupil he had ever had; and that I should never be able to master even the simplest rules.

But being convinced that the way to success was to write music that was almost unplayable and unsingable (a belief that now seems to pass current with some modern composers!), I managed to compose a waltz, that did its best to fulfill these conditions. Proudly I sent it to mother; through her influence – that and nothing else – it was accepted and published by Boosey & Co. This was exciting enough, but my head whirled when in an amazingly short space of time after this I was summoned to London to accompany Evangeline Florence at the Albert Hall in this identical song! This concert, which made the reputation of one of mother's then most promising pupils – Wilfred Douthitt, who sang one of her songs and fairly brought the house down – nearly destroyed mine for good and all. Despite the overweening confidence on my part, my song was a dead failure. There was hardly enough applause to get us off the platform.

Luckily I am endowed with a temperament not easily discouraged. It is certainly not downcast to failure. As Noel Coward would say – I rise above it! To ignore failure and to try again is a fundamental part of my philosophy of life. So, nothing daunted by my lack of success with this first song, I went on writing and writing, and eventually hit on a song that made a success – The Little Damozel.

The realisation that I could get songs published at the age of sixteen so enormously elated me that I cast off the dust of Brewer and his organ loft from my shoes, and descended on London, where I lived with mother and filled page after page of manuscript books with music.

It was always a great cry at home that "Ivor must never go on the stage; it would spoil him." Had it not been for this I should have started as an actor at least ten years before I did. I nearly did when I was seventeen. There was some bother with mother, and smarting with resentment, I rushed to Daly's Theatre and introduced myself to the manager – Merlin Morgan – as Clara Novello-Davies's son. This, when I told him I wanted to go on tour as a member of the chorus, made him think I had my mother's backing, and although he expressed surprise at my request, he promised that I should go out with [*cast of*] The Count of Luxembourg and he would let me know when rehearsals were to start. Brimming over with excitement I rushed home and broke the news. It was received with stony silence.

Week after week went by, and no word came from Daly's. I became anxious. One morning, as soon as I heard the postman's knock, I ran downstairs to the box. I found a postcard from Merlin Morgan with the message: "As you have not answered our previous correspondence, we have reluctantly been compelled to fill the place we were holding for you." Then I understood the mysterious silence in which Daly's had seemed to be wrapt; mother had got hold of the letters! Now I know she was right; I hardly thought so at the time.

Ivor with his Mother and Father

I went on composing music. Full of confidence, I offered to write the score of a pageant for a Festival of Empire to be held in Canada. Although the pageant was never produced, my expenses were paid to Canada; on these I managed to see quite a large bit of the world for nothing. I visited New York, where I had an unforgettable experience at a party given by Mrs. Benjamin Guinness. I mixed with a crowd which held such famous personalities as Melba and Caruso. But I had eyes only for one lovely Italian woman. Someone told me it was Lina Cavalieri, whose beauty was then matched with La Bell Otero's, and whose history was even more romantic. Many people think Sheldon and Cavalieri had her story in mind when he wrote the marvellous success Romance for Doris Keane. I had never seen a more beautiful woman, nor have I since. She wanted to dance, and asked the band to play a tango tune. But when the band struck up, no one took to the floor. I got up from my chair, and asked if she would dance with me (something inside of me regarded this amazing piece of daring with admiration). She did. The nearness of her face, which was absolutely flawless in its loveliness, the smell of a particular perfume she used, went to my head. That dance was breathless, intoxicating. It was one of my first glimpses of the wonder of beauty.

I came back to England by way of Montreal, where a small dog so caught my fancy that I bought her and called her after my first song success – Damozel. I booked a passage on the Empress of Ireland – mother had written that I must be back in London by a certain time, as she was giving a concert of my works, and the Empress of Ireland would get be back the day before. But the morning before I should have sailed, the landlady came to see me in great distress and said that Wudge (as she called Damozel) had gone. Wudge had crept into my heart; I was frantic with dismay. For hours I went all over the city making enquiries here, there and everywhere – but no Wudge. Nor was there any Wudge the following day. Hearing that another boat was sailing the next morning which, by way of scramble and Glasgow, would land me in London a few hours before the concert, I cancelled my passage on the Empress of Ireland and booked instead on the Pretorian. Having done that, the search for Wudge was resumed. But it was all to no purpose; I went on board without her.

Two days later two cabled came to the ship. One announced that the Empress of Ireland had been rammed in a fog and gone down in ten minutes. Of the 1367 people on board, 934 were drowned, including poor Laurence Irving and Mable Hackney. The other was from my Montreal landlady briefly announcing that Wudge had turned up the day after I left. Whether Wudge had genuinely got lost or had merely been engaged on some amorous adventure will never be known, she certainly did me a good turn [and saved my life].

Back in London, I still busied myself with writing little songs. In my trunk was the complete music (libretto and lyrics) of a dreadful comic opera which, so far, and thank heaven, has never seen the light of day or theatre. But as lately as two years ago I was utilising, for other purposes, its tunes and songs.

Happily, or unhappily, before I could prevail upon anybody to produce this, war broke out; mother urged me to write a patriotic song, threatening to do it herself if I did not. This threat was sufficient; the song was composed, refused by my own publishers, but accepted by another. Neither mother nor I thought much of it, except that we considered the tune good. But it was a song that one way or another I made a great deal of money by; it was called Keep The Home Fires Burning. It was first sung in public by a small pupil of my mother's –

Sybil Vane – at a Sunday League Concert at the Alhambra [*Theatre, Leicester Square*] in 1914. At the last moment I was desolated because mother couldn't come; but father anxiously filled one of the stalls seats. I played the accompaniment for Sybil, and I remember how intimidated I was when I walked on to the stage and found the band of the Grenadier Guards grouped on a platform at the back.

Sybil Vane – Keep The Home Fires Burning

Sybil sang the first verse and refrain. Then, as she began to repeat the refrain, to my utter astonishment, I heard the audience joining in. When the refrain came after the second verse, they came in with us. After that they sang it as if they had known it all their lives. Eventually we had to sing it nine times before the audience would let us go.

When I got off the stage I knew I had got something extra good! I literally rushed home to Aldwych [*The Flat at 11*] to tell mother the good news. She, loving soul, nearly wept, and was bitterly distressed that she had not been at the theatre to share in my good fortune. Some people considered it was the words which made this song. This may or may not be so, but the fact remains that all the words (including the title), were written by me, with the small exception of the last two lines. The authoress of these was poor Lina Gilbert Ford, an American woman living in England. The sad thing was that she had sold her share of the words outright, thinking she would do better this way than on the basis of a small royalty. Of course, I had insisted on my usual royalty; the best advice I can give any writer or composer is always to retain some interest in their work. Never sell anything outright.

Lina Gilbert Ford

To celebrate the success of the song I gave Lina a grand piano. Alas, soon after, during an air raid, Lina's house was wrecked by a shell and the grand piano – no longer very grand – was left suspended between one floor and another. But the really dreadful thing was that the shell killed Lina and her small crippled son whom she had lived for and idolised.

At his invitation, I went to see John McCormack, on one of his visits to England. He greeted me with: "I want to give you the most expensive dinner the hotel can provide; don't hesitate to order the best of everything." I asked why. McCormack with his charming and beguiling Irish accent, replied: "Haven't you been the means of my earning twenty thousand good English pounds – by means of gramophone records of your song." McCormack has never forgotten what recording Keep The Home Fires Burning brought him. When I was in Hollywood he showed me the most lavish hospitality at his lovely house there.

John McCormack

I joined the Air Force, but on my numerous wangled leaves still contrived to write comic operas and songs. But the success of Home Fires almost became a tragedy. The royalties steadily rolled in, and I began to develop into the laziest of human beings. "Why work," I asked myself, "when all one has to do is to write one song and it brings you everything you want or desire?" And so it seemed at the time.

It was during my R.A.F. days that I first met Winston Churchill. Eddie Marsh took me, in my uniform, to lunch with Lady Randolph, and there was her formidable son. He seemed very easy to get on with, and when he was told I had written Home Fires, he introduced the topic of popular songs. He had a surprising memory for the music-hall choruses of his Sandhurst time (just before I was born), some of which had survived into my generation, while others had not; and we were both getting quite worked up over the exchange of reminiscences across the table, when suddenly, after one of

Eddie Marsh & Winston Churchill

my contributions he burst out laughing, and said in a tone which I could only look upon as ribald: "Do you know, you ought to be in a home."

A slight shock passed through the company, and as for me, I was flabbergasted. What had I done to provoke this shattering diagnosis? The, from time long past, the memory came back to me that once there had been a song called You Ought To Be In A Home and all was well.

Soon after the Armistice I went to America on a pleasure trip, still imbued with the feeling that to laze through life was the finest thing one could do – I was actually beginning to make a fine art of it. But in New York – perhaps it was the celebrated air – something revolutionary happened inside me. Whatever it was, I arrived back in England with a superabundance of energy. I can't account for this new feeling. Perhaps it was because the war was over, and in those days we all imagined that a new era was beginning. I had a feeling that it was now up to me to make use of every bit of time; actually I have never stopped work since – but I am still at a loss to understand the change in me that then occurred, and have never succeeded in probing the actual psychological reason. However…

I got back to my mother's flat in London to find a telegram from the Daniel Mayer Company summoning me to Paris. I gathered that Mercanton, the film producer (he died last year), particularly wanted to see me with a view to my appearing in a film. I was more than surprised; I was astounded – I had never had any association with film studios, was not an actor, and had never appeared on the stage. I afterwards learnt that

Mercanton had been in London looking for somebody to play in The Call Of The Blood (the film adaptation of Hichen's Bella Donna) and had been shown a picture of me I had given to Rudolf Mayer. Mercanton immediately made up his mind that only I would fit in with the type he had in mind – that of a young Englishman with a Sicillian grandmother – and shouted: "That's the man I am looking for!" Mayer quietly said: "That's Ivor Novello; he's a composer." Mercanton said: "If he is at all receptive, we'll soon make him forget that!" So off to Paris I went. Mercanton, to his relief, found that I was not so dumb as he had feared; three weeks afterwards, I was in Sicily, playing opposite Phyllis Neilson-Terry in my first film.

It has always happened that even from its beginnings my career has been pursued in the full glare of the limelights. What progress I have achieved – what mistakes or money I have made – have right from the start, been always under these ruthless lights. Most actors have had the definite advantage of obscure beginnings, and of being able to find themselves in the provinces, thus gaining confidence before being called upon to take the centre of the stage in London. I have always felt that the initial stages of my professional life were marked with two immense disadvantages – the disapproval of the elect and the adulation of the mob!

Happily they balanced. I remember that at a time when I was nightly packing a London theatre to overflowing for a year, one of the more vulgar paragraphists [journalist] (who has since lapsed into obscurity) solemnly advised me to give up trying to act or, alternatively, to go and learn my job in a provincial repertory company. Consequently there has always been a great feeling of surprise if I have been any good in any part I have undertaken. It wasn't until I appeared in New York – much to the surprise of my London friends – received undiluted praise and quite unprejudiced criticism, that I learnt to disregard confirmed crabbers [*critics*] and to have confidence in my own judgment and in what pleased me.

Louis Mercanton – Swiss Film Director

Desdemona Mazza & Ivor Novello in Call of the Blood (1920)

Ivor Novello & Phylis Neilson-Terry in Call of the Blood (1920)

Chapter Four

"I have already mentioned the prejudice my family had against my going on the stage. My film appearances did much to dispel this..."

As it happened, in Call Of The Blood, I proved to be photogenic – also I learnt a great deal from Mercanton. The film was one of extreme beauty, and captured the imagination of audiences, what was more, it set me on the road to being that apparently unforgivable thing, a popular favourite. A series of films followed, the immediate successor to The Call Of The Blood being Miarka in which I played with that incomparable actress Rejane. It was her last appearance in public. The beautiful, commanding, glittering and typically French comedienne had by then shrunk to a little old lady with great burning eyes and a devastating and all embracing smile. She was so frail and small that it seemed the faintest puff of air would blow her away. In the film she had a death scene; she acted it marvellously; perhaps some presentiment had come to her, for she said to me: "This is just the dress rehearsal." She knew. Two weeks after the final shot of the film had been taken, Rejan died.

There has been one quite alarming episode in the filming of Miarka. The scene of the story was partly laid at Les Saintes Maries, in the Rhone Delta, where according to legend the

Three Maries and their gypsy handmaid Sara landed from their voyage across the Mediterranean after the Crucifixion, and where for centuries the gypsies of all Europe have congregated on an annual pilgrimage in June. Rejane, as the gypsy grandmother, was to die in the crypt of the rugged little old black pilgrimage church, and there we all went from the chateau which Mercanton had taken near Avignon – Mercanton himself, Jean Richpin, the picturesque, grey haired, altogether delightful author of the novel on which the film was based, and the whole company of actors and actresses.

Gabrielle Rejan – French actress

The morning was spent in shooting [filming] the extraordinary crowds of pilgrims on the beach, and in the afternoon we went down from the church, which was all begarlanded and ablaze with candles, into the dark crypt for the death scene. The camera was clicking [*turning*] like mad, Rejane acting like an angel, I dissolved in tears by her bedside, when suddenly a menacing crowd of [*actual*] gypsies broke in upon us. In their eyes the cinema was an invention of the Devil, and our proceedings a sacrilege (perhaps they were?). It was an anxious moment. The men of our party made a circle round Rejane, who showed no sign of fear, and carried her up the steps, through the church, and at last, to our great relief, safe into the open. Meanwhile Mercanton was reasoning with the invaders. In vain he showed them his Government permit; their spokesman answered with spirit, "Le Government, c'est nous"; and so for the nonce it was. Of course the last thing that Mercanton or any of us wished was to offend the religious feelings of the gypsies, and as soon it appeared that there was no hope of moving them, we retreated with what grace we could and went back to the chateau, where with much ingenuity Mercanton rigged up a crypt in the great barn.

My next film was Carnival. Including as it did Matheson Lang, Hilda Bailey and myself, it can safely be said that this was the first super-production to be made in England; it certainly opened the eyes of the British film industry to the fact that spectacular films, involving an enormous financial outlay, could yet be made to pay. Carnival was followed by The Bohemian Girl, with a cast that makes Grand Hotel pale – Gladys Cooper, Ellen Terry, Constance Collier, Aubrey Smith and Henry Vibert. It was this film that secured me my one and only contract with D.W. Griffiths, then the only film director who could sell a film on his own name. Griffiths may have lost his magic now, but I cannot think of any greater thrills than the first showings of Birth Of A Nation, Intolerance, Way Down East, The Orphans Of The Storm, and finally the picture in which I appeared with Mae Marsh – The White Rose. Incidentally this was the last Griffiths film to make big money. I had a very stupid part – that of a sanctimonious clergyman utterly devoid of humour; I think it was the inevitable reaction from this film that made me conceive and act that bold bad boy, The Rat – a character without one redeeming feature in his make-up excepting a capacity to laugh at himself, yet who managed to capture the popular imagination to such an extent that I played him 600 times on the stage, and also made three entirely different films dealing with his adventures. Still the fans clamour for the original to be made into a talking picture.

I have already mentioned the prejudice my family had against my going on the stage. My film appearances did much to dispel this, and no one was more delighted than father and mother when I received and accepted an offer to appear as Armand Duval in Sasha Guitry's play Deburau, at the Ambassadors Theatre. My salary for this was exactly one tenth of the film salary I was receiving.

Oh the difference between film acting and stage acting!! I had acquired complete confidence in myself when facing a battery of cameras in a studio, but when it came to the first rehearsal of Deburau I was paralysed with nerves and overwhelmed with self-consciousness, and couldn't manage to speak above a whisper. Before each rehearsal, I went through agonies, determining to open my mouth, but all to no purpose; a rehearsal had no sooner started than once again I could do nothing but mumble hoarsely. It was not until the dress rehearsal that I was able to speak out – as I have been doing ever since! I have learnt the lesson that the boy at the back of the gallery has paid his entrance money like every one else, and has the same right to hear every word as the befurred and bejewelled millionaires in the front row of the stalls.

In Deburau I found myself in very exalted company – that may have accounted for the nerves; for in the cast were Madge Titheradge, Robert Loraine, Leslie Banks and Jean de Casalis; all greatly experienced artistes. It was only their friendliness and encouragement that kept me going.

Jean de Casalis

Madge Titheradge & Novello

The play didn't succeed – but I had tasted blood. From that moment until this – although I have naturally continued my interesting and also extremely lucrative film career – the stage has always been, and always will be, my first consideration.

I next acted at the Kingsway [*Theatre*] in two plays – The Yellow Jacket, a Chinese drama in which I was a complete failure (lack of experience) and in Spanish Lovers, in which I made a success (I was ideally suited). It was during the short run of Spanish Lovers that I first began to notice people standing outside the stage door. As I had done this myself for years, I was not greatly surprised – but I was when I discovered that it was me they were waiting for. Mostly at the beginning it was older women who, as I came out of the stage door, pressed chest-comforters on me, believing that the hacking cough which I had put on for my part really belonged to me permanently. I was also the recipient of six rosaries, all with crosses attached. I have never been able to explain these particular gifts – I am not a Catholic – unless it was because of the Spanish atmosphere of the play.

People began to open autograph books for me. They would say: "Are you the Mr. Novello who also writes music?" and when I shamefacedly admitted that it was so, [they would] ask me for my signature. And so it has gone on until now I sometimes find as many as forty or fifty fans waiting for me.

Perhaps I developed late in life; but I still find life – people – anything I do – frightfully exciting. I can honestly say that I never feel bored. It may be that I know instinctively how to avoid anything that would not interest me; but I really do get enormous pleasure and a great kick out of everyday life. For instance, I have never got over the thrill and novelty of being a success. Every time the final curtain falls on a first night, and the audience calls for me, it is as wonderful as the first time it happened. In much the same way I never feel embarrassed to find a crowd waiting at the stage door, nor do I get bored with it as my friends seem to think I shall. On the contrary, I adore it!

After all, it is the adulation of these fans that has put me where I am. There are some people who rebel and chafe against herd popularity, imagining that what the mob likes can't be right. I sometimes think that these are only people who have never had the luck to achieve popularity. I have had that luck, and I value it. Perhaps it is something to do with warmth – something that one is able to give out on the stage and communicate to the audience. Perhaps it is because I want to be liked, and feel a real affection for the people sitting on the other side of the footlights. I do believe that what you give them comes back a hundredfold.

There is also another aspect of the fan question that I do not overlook. Multiply the crowd at the stage door by the number of days in the year on which I appear at the theatre, and it comes to a rather considerable figure. Sooner or later every one of those waiting people will pay money to see me in some new play – and that means to me my Rolls Royce, my house in the country, my swimming pool – all the other material things I value and that make life pleasant for me. Is it any wonder I like that crowd?

Some fans are faithful indeed. There are many who still stand at the stage door, whom I have known for years. Nothing is sweeter to me that the loyalty of these very dear friends.

It was during the run of Spanish Lovers that the magic word 'actor-manager' occurred to me. I loved the play and adored the part. At the end of three weeks, when the piece had failed to attract [big enough audiences], I decided that I would 'try out' my popularity in the provinces – where I had never acted – and go on tour.

I was getting something like 2,000 letters every week from film fans, and I wanted to test if they would roll up to see me personally. I think I was the first British film actor to do this –

and roll up they did. Instead of making £20 a week [£900 in 2022], as I had been doing in London, I returned after a fortnight in the provinces, with £300 [£13,500 in 2022] in my pocket – and that was after I had paid the entire expenses of the venture, including full London salaries to all the company.

My luck in the provinces should have taught me a lesson. Obviously I should have followed this up with another play and toured it all over England – but no, I did not. Instead I chose to do something which proved to be the biggest set back I have ever had – and I hope I shall never have another like it. What I did was to appear with Gladys Cooper in an entirely unsuitable part and in an entirely unsuitable play: Enter Kiki. At the age of 24, looking, as all my photographs of that period rightly show, like a boy of 19, I essayed to play to play the character of a masterful actor-manager of 45. I was practically laughed off the stage; the critics had a field day. It was my first bitter lesson of learning one's job in the limelight. Unfortunately it also reflected badly on poor Miss Cooper, usually sound in her risks and judgments.

I felt inclined to flee the footlights forever – to nurse my hurt. But there was a small restless animal nibbling at my brain – it was The Rat. I had originally conceived of this film scenario; then, with the help of my dear friend Constance Collier, it was turned into a play and put on the stage at a cost of £120. Before the first act was on paper, a tour of nine weeks had been booked, and the project, patronised by even our dearest friends and laughed at by our dearest enemies, emerged triumphantly at Brighton with 39 curtain calls to its credit – and with the actor-manager £70 overdrawn at the bank!

The original tour of The Rat was extended from nine to twenty weeks. We packed every theatre in which it was played, and finally came to London to a rapturous first night – this time ten more calls than at Brighton; all this exactly six months after my disaster in Enter Kiki.

Ivor Novello & Gladys Cooper in Enter Kiki (1923)

In The Rat I was well suited in the part, and beautifully produced by Constance Collier; I consider that these two circumstances, added to the contrast with my recent failure and the surprise that was felt at my progress, that made The Rat the sensation it undoubtedly was. But although my name had now acquired a certain monetary value from the box-office point of view, I had yet to face tremendous setbacks in the next few productions for which I was responsible. My next play was Old Heidelberg; I played my favourite part. Perhaps the play was revived too soon after the war, perhaps people had forgotten there could be a loveable German – anyhow the play failed.

The came one of the most exciting thrills of my life. Gladys Cooper had put on Iris at the Adelphi Theatre with herself and Henry Ainley, but whether or not the play had dated (it had first been produced at the Garrick in 1901) it was doing poor business. After three or four weeks it became a question whether losses should be cut and the play withdrawn. Meanwhile, I had taken off Old Heidelberg (I can now safely relate what followed because Miss Cooper has already given her version of the story) and I had no other play ready for production. Naturally Miss Cooper wanted Iris to continue; she suggested that I join the cast in place of an excellent actor who was unfortunately ill-suited to his part. On a Wednesday night I saw the play; on Thursday morning I refused the part; on Friday I accepted it; on the following Monday I played Lawrence Trenwith for the first time. Believe it or not, at the end of my first week the receipts had gone from £900 to £2,400. I tell this story in no boasting spirit – indeed, far from it. I am convinced the real reason was the public, who adore romance, wanted to see Miss Cooper and me playing together. There is a phrase beloved of the less exalted playgoer: "She so fair and he so dark" – and that's what they got!

Iris ran for over five months; after that my second play Down Hill was produced. It was an early experiment (a little too early as I found) in the application of film technique to a stage play [*structure*]. It was written in twelve scenes; this was quite undreamt of in those days, except in Drury Lane or Lyceum melodramas. Unfortunately (for me) it was also produced at a time when the critics had vehement prejudice against the cinema encroaching on the stage.

Here, then, was a grand opportunity for them to wreak their vengeance! And they did. I was treated as a filmstar bitten with an absurd desire to act upon the legitimate stage and, absurder still, to carry a film studio [*technique*] into west end theatre.

My Part in Down Hill required me to run the gamut of the emotions; in some scenes my friends thought I was very odd, and my enemies, very bad. I regarded the play as a technical exercise – the various stages of the hero's career were so contrasted that at the end of the run I felt as if I had been playing in six different plays, instead of only one. But the experience was invaluable; I began to have some conception of what I was up against in embarking on a career as an actor.

Although London was distinctly sniffy about Down Hill, I am willing to take a bet that if I were to write and produce it now, the public, who have since learned what film technique is, would turn up in droves. But the time was not then ripe. Yet the provinces – bless their hearts – adored it. I took the original company on tour, creating a precedent which I have since adhered to – believe me it pays. Although prices are cheaper in the provinces, the theatres are larger and hold as much and often more money than the west end theatres.

I cannot understand the attitude of those who think that what is good enough for London is too good for the provinces. Human nature is much the same everywhere; audiences in Manchester and Brighton will laugh and cry at the same points in a play as do those in London. Indeed, they are often quicker to seize the finer points of a play. Acting in the provinces has taught me more about handling an audience than anything I've done.

Frances Doble

Phylis Monkman

Phyllis Monkman, snatched from the Co-optimists, played her first straight part in Down Hill. Not only did she prove herself a delightful comedienne but, particularly on one memorable night, showed she also had great dramatic gifts. In one scene where a laugh would have been fatal, she caught her foot in a telephone wire and was thrown to the ground. The wire then turned itself into a mad octopus, forcing her to play a three minute scene while lying flat on the stage. So sublimely did she do this that the audience never realised that anything untoward had happened, and there wasn't even a titter – except from me! For the rest of the performance Phyllis and I dared not meet each other's eyes.

Frances Doble, who is to star in Ballerina, also made her London debut in this play, and was so appealing and so lovely in a small part, that I altered the ending of the play and made her the heroine.

Shortly after this, following a thrilling tour of The Rat, I got bitten ,quite wrongly, by the high-brow bug. The bite was almost fatal. I am not a high-brow – I am an entertainer. My object is to fill the plush [theatre seats] Empty seats and good opinions mean nothing to me; I am perfectly satisfied if I can invent or produce a play which primarily attracts audiences and only secondly wins critical approval. But the fever excited by my touch of 'high-browitis' led me to appear in a series of plays which, had I looked into my heart, I should have found I had no belief in at all. The Firebrand and Liliom (on the first night of which something happened to the Russian producer's [director] novel smoke effect; the smoke drifted into the auditorium and nearly drove the gasping and coughing audience onto the street) both made serious inroads into my capitol. [*Liliom would be turned into the hit musical Carousel some years later by Rogers & Hammerstien*]. They were quickly followed by Sirocco which had, so I should imagine, one of the most sensational first nights in the history of the theatre, nearly ending in a free fight!

This play, underwritten by Noel Coward and over-produced by Basil Dean, was received with screams, hisses, boos, cat-calls, and every other possible mark of disapproval.

The final curtain descended on a scene of indescribable din and chaos. Noel behaved superbly – he insisted on taking a call, to "face the music" as he called it (music! It was like the first scene of the Tempest) instead of turning his back on it. Meanwhile I stood in the wings, as near hysterics as I am ever likely to be – I viaulaised my career blighted; my connection with the theatre ended for ever. "Why," I thought, as I left the stage door, "had this tornado - this sirocco – descended on me?" A gallery girl plucked me by the sleeve and said "We expected better!"

"So did I," I replied with bitterness.

Noel Coward

Yet there are some people who, despite that heart-melting Bitter Sweet and the epic of Cavalcade, describe Sirocco, as "dear Noel's best play!" May God forgive them their taste or their lying tongues.

Sirocco kept me off the stage and away from the theatre for several months. I felt disheartened, mortified, galled. What had I done to deserve that first night's hostility? "All right," I thought, "Films – films –films! No more personal contact." In fact I was quite determined never again to face an audience. It was a bad time for me; momentarily I had lost my courage. But my temporary withdrawal had its definite advantages. I considered the causes of my recent failures, and resolved in future to believe in myself and my own judgment not those of other people.

Three months after Sirocco, I was in the throes of writing a light comedy; three months later the play was in rehearsal – it was The Truth Game, my first real step to establish myself as a writer of plays which conform to my idea of pleasing the public without antagonising the critics. I had a superb cast. It included my adored Lily Elsie – I could hardly believe that she was acting with me in a play of mine; Lilian Braithwaite, who was able to make the comedy success of her marvellous career – an entirely new line for her; and Viola Tree, who brought, as Mrs. Patrick Campbell remarked, "outdoors indoors," and gloriously upheld, as the great and good humoured comedienne, the traditions of her illustrious father. [*Sir Herbert Beerbohm Tree*].

It was in the truth game that I discovered I could make people laugh – not only by the lines in my play, but also by my own acting. Any actor will tell you that of all the things that this gives him the most satisfaction. Let another member of the company kill and actor's 'laugh', by an unnecessary move, or by speaking too quickly, and the actor will wish him dead at his feet!

Lilian Braithwaite, in this play, rendered me an unforgettable service; not only by playing a good comedy part superbly, but by accepting the part at all – at the time there was every reason why she should have refused. The production of The Truth Game brought more complications than have been my experience in any other theatrical venture. I think, perhaps, they were started by my inferiority complex, a complex I never suspected I had, but which was undoubtedly brought to the surface by the failure of Sirocco, and so very much in the ascendant at the opening rehearsals that I completely lost all confidence in the play, At the end of the first week, Constance Collier, who had always in the past given me tremendous encouragement, and for whom the part of Mrs. Brandon had been written, left me flat! Sir Gerald du Maurier, who had promised to produce [*direct*], pronounced the play hopeless (without, he later confessed to me, having read it!).

Lilian Braithwaite

Mrs. Patrick Campbell

Ellis Jeffreys, stepping into Miss Collier's place, was soon downed by the general depression and also threw up her part! Only Viola Tree and Lily Elsie stood as firm as rocks.

Ellis Jeffreys

We were now within ten days of the date announced for the first night. I had already sunk £4,000, and the rent of the theatre was eating a further £450 weekly; I was in despair. Ten days to go and no producer [*director*], and the all important part of Mrs. Brandon not filled. Suddenly I had an inspiration – Lilian Braithwaite. She was appearing in a play, but fortunately (for me) the last weeks had been announced. I rushed to the Garrick Theatre, fell into her dressing room, and almost collapsed. As I did so I could not help reflecting that I was going through absolute hell, and my days were being made miserable, merely because I was trying to present, at a theatre, a gay little comedy.

Lilian pushed some port down my throat, and from a distance of a million miles away I heard a voice saying; "darling, I'll play that part if it's the worst in the world." And this from an eminent actress who hadn't read the play, but had watched two of her eminent sister actresses walk out of it.

I still lacked a producer [*director*]. Willie Graham Browne – encouraged by his dear and brilliant wife, Marie Tempest, who has always been sweetness itself to me, and utterly belied her quite undeserved reputation for terrorising the younger generation – came to my rescue and took charge. He did wonders for the play. At the first rehearsal, in the middle of Act 1, he burst out with "Why, this is a divine play!" – the first cheering words I had heard for days; and during the final week of the most anxious time I have ever lived through, hope began to spring up in me again – perhaps we should pull it off after all!

Lily Elsie & Ivor Novello star in The Truth Game

Chapter Five

"But where was my lovely Lily Elsie? The play hardly seemed the same without her..."

On the first night of The Truth Game the audience, doubtless softened and sympathetic because of my troubles, which had become public property, were amazingly generous, and – thank heaven – the belief some of my friends had in the play were more than justified. The poor, despised Truth Game was acted in England over 400 times. I played it myself in America, as you will hear in a moment, for upwards of six months with Viola Tree, and we took New York by storm. Finally it was made into a picture by Metro-Goldwyn Company; in fact it was this play which induced Metro-Goldwyn to give me a nine months' contract.

Success is a strange and fickle thing. I followed up The Truth Game with Symphony In Two Flats, played by practically the same cast. After a very successful run in London the Schuberts took the play, lock, stock and barrel, including the entire London company to New York. We opened in a heat wave and closed in a heat wave. Unfortunately it was the same heat wave, and it hadn't lasted very long.

I had always heard that the moment after a production in New York, six picture companies (at least) would be battering at one's doors, armed with contracts and tempting suggestions. But so far as I was concerned, the picture companies might have gone out of business. For there was only a ghastly silence. What was I to do? What I didn't want to do was go back to England with my tail between my legs. The Schuberts luckily solved my problem; they still queerly believed in me, and suggested a production of The Truth Game. Viola Tree was cabled for, and a fortnight later arrived in New York with an enormous brown paper parcel, a toy balloon and one dollar – all typical of darling Viola!

Billie Burke (Mrs. Florenz Ziegfeld) played Lilian's part exquisitely and quite differently. The star sytem (which still flourished in New York) demanded that the part of Mrs. Brandon should be of paramount interest in the play. By a few judicious alterations and without much real damage, I managed to make it so.

Billie Burke starred with Novello in The Truth Game on Broadway

Billie was given the curtains of the second and last acts, and a song was introduced. But where was my lovely Lily Elsie? The play hardly seemed the same without her; every night I wished it were possible for her to be in the cast again. And I should liked to have heard Lilian's 'bitter-sweet' comments on those New York performances.

But New York did a great deal for me; it took away ninety per cent of my fear, and dispelled a certain tentativeness which had been a much fought-against drawback in my make-up for years. The New Yorkers didn't care a dime that I had been first a composer, then a film actor, then an actor plunged into leading parts without experience – they saw the finished article (let me hasten to explain that I mean finished in the best sense of the word, not the worst!) and they seemed to like it.

After The Truth Game first night the film companies were far from silent. Before noon of the next morning five companies had telephoned asking me for film tests. Eventually I accepted the apparently handsome proposition put forward by Metro-Goldwyn – but exciting as this appeared at first it was not quite so handsome on closer examination; indeed this contract proved to be the most prolonged disappointment of my career.

Somebody had told me that Hollywood would break my heart in six months; anyhow I'd have the hell of a time. In the train I wondered and the nearer it got to Los Angeles the more utterly miserable and friendless I felt. I'd given a party in New York; Joan Crawford and Douglas Fairbanks had come. I told them I was going to Hollywood and they'd asked me to let them know when I was arriving. I cables to them.

When the train puffed and clanked into the station, I looked out of the window, and there, on the platform, was Joan waiting for me. It was such a friendly gesture that my spirits went up at once. I climbed into her car (and what a car it was!) and in a minute we were speeding towards the house I had rented in Santa Monica. That night I dined with her and Douglas, and the next morning she called for me and insisted on taking me to the studios and introducing me to everyone. She could not have done more to make my entry into Hollywood easy and delightful.

My immediate job at the studio was to prepare a screen version of The Truth Game. I was given an office, and met Bernie Hyman, one of the supervisors whose job it is to see that eight or more pictures are turned out every year. Bernie handed me a manuscript; a script writer's idea of what the film version of my play should be. "Take it home and read it" said Bernie. I did. It was my second night in Hollywood; when I went over that script it gave me the first taste of the hell Hollywood can be to an author. It was awful; anything but my play! I began to feel bad.

Aubrey Smith

Clark Gable

Garbo	Douglas Fairbanks & Joan Crawford

The adaptor had tried to make the screen story just as the play was done on the stage – a plan which I think is usually utterly hopeless when translating a stage play into terms of the cinema. And the really appalling jokes which had been introduced, to liven up the action, made me shudder.

When I walked into the studio the next morning my face must have looked as long as the proverbial fiddle, for Bernie at once said; "I see you read it!" I nodded. "Terrible, isn't it?" he added. Then I knew that I should be all right. Bernie was obviously a kindred spirit and a man after my own heart.

We had a conference at which I made everybody roar with laughter by remarking: "Let's face this play. I don't know why you bought it, but I'm very glad you did. Now let's alter the whole thing." When we had recovered from this, Bernie said: "You are the first author who has come into this room and suggested altering his own play."

Honesty goes in Hollywood. Say what you think and you're all right. After the pow-wow I started on the script myself.

During the nine months I was at Hollywood I made eight different versions of The Truth Game. About all that remained of the play when I had finished with it was the name of the characters and the title – and that was altered on the first day of production!

One morning, two days after my arrival, the telephone bell tinkled. At the other end of the line was a very old friend – Lilyan Tashman. She told me she was just starting out for her bungalow on Mailbu beach, and was going to call in on me on the way.

Half an hour later we were hugging each other and talking as hard as we could go. Then she suddenly remembered. Outside, she said, were Paul Lukas, Kay Francis and Greta Garbo. I had never met Garbo. It was thrilling that she was actually waiting outside my house!

She was dressed in trousers, a striped sweater, a sailor's reefer coat, and a beret pulled tight over her lovely hair. She was also wearing the blue glasses which she imagines disguise her out of recognition.

We talked – the others drove away; we hardly noticed their departure – and continued to talk. We must have talked for over an hour and a half – time seemed to stand still. I say we talked, but it was I who prattled away, Greta merely throwing in an occasional question. I told her about London, Berlin, Sweden (how delighted she was when she discovered I knew a few words of Swedish!) the people I met; what I did and what I hoped to do.

There was nothing of the great star about Greta. She was simple, unassuming, unaffected. Her face fascinated me. Even the old clothes, the beret and the glasses could not hide her loveliness. And her eyelashes! Marvellous eyelashes that curled above her eyes like peacock's plumes; the longest and most wonderful eyelashes I have ever seen.

She had to go. We stared at each other, then "Auf wiedersehen," she said.

"Really auf wiedeershen?" I wanted to see her again.

"Really auf wiedsershen,"…and she was gone.
Gone for good. I never saw her again while I was working and playing in Hollywood.

I met Pola Negri. She was Different. She really was the film star of fiction and the stage. She took it for granted that you were interested in nobody but her. Pola was trying to come back, but alas her day had gone – the day of the temperamental movie star was over; posterity will judge her by the silent pictures she made

Pola Negri

Lilyan Tashman

Pola with immense pride, told me that she was the first woman to dance barefoot in the Russian ballet – this in her queer accent and a great rolling of r's. She said that her mother was aristocratic but that her father was all gypsy.

She must have told that story to a lot of people; it was quite a gag in the studios for a star, when she made some foolish mistake, to exclaim: "It's the gypsy in me!".

What absolutely amazed me in Hollywood was the ignorance of the film people of names which are household words everywhere else. I was sitting in my office one morning discussing The Truth Game with Bernie Hyman, when one of the caged authors, who had a room next to mine, burst in and excitedly displayed a programme of a play of mine which had been done years before in London. He found it in a pile of papers and thought it would interest me. On the cover was a picture of a very lovely and astonishingly beautiful woman.

"What a picture!" said Bernie. "Who is she?"

I quietly told him not to be a fool; it was Gladys Cooper.

"Never heard of her – is she on the pictures?"

When I had patiently explained to Bernie exactly who and what Gladys Cooper was, he wanted to cable her right away with an offer of a handsome contract!

It was typical of Hollywood. They know nothing of names that are famous throughout Europe. But if anybody has appeared in a tuppeny-ha'penny film – they know them.

I had a very odd experience one night. Richard Barthelemess and I went with a party to see a revival of Griffith's Way Down East – the silent film that made Richard famous. In the cinema I sat next to him. Suddenly, on the screen, appeared a face as near physical perfection as I should imagine any masculine face can get. I gasped – for it was Richard; but not tubby Richard of the fleshy cheeks sitting by my side. One had to look at the face on the film, it was so fine. This, thoughtful, well modelled, almost ascetic; I noted the instant effect it had on the women in the audience. They gasped like me, but not my gasp of astonishment. Their was one of undiluted admoration!

Richard Barthelmess

After the film we had supper at Hollywood's most famous restaurant: The Brown Derby. Richard was very silent. I asked him what the trouble was (but I knew). It was the picture. Been a bit of a shock to him. "If you hadn't known who it was, would you have recognised me?" he queried, in a somewhat miserable voice.

I tried to cheer him up. I said I should have, but I could not help adding that it was like looking at someone through a distorting glass. "You've got complacent, Dick," I said. "You are one of the best actors on the screen, you're certainly one of the biggest favourites. But you've forgotten what you were. You've let yourself go."
It was two months before I saw him again.

Once more the scene was The Brown Derby. Richard walked in one night with his delightful wife. But it was a different Richard from the man of two months before. It was the Richard Barthelmess of Way Down East – the fat all gone; the sensitiveness and fineness of the face restored.

It made me think that Hollywood doctors should advise their patients to go and see the films they made in the hey-day of their youth and beginnings.

The longer I stayed in Hollywood the more disappointed and disgruntled I became. I longed to pack my trunks and get back to England. One explanation of my unhappiness was that I went to Hollywood to do one thing and stayed to do another. My contract was a double one. Primarily I was to act and only secondarily to write, and that, presumably for myself. It was not until I had been in Hollywood some time that it began to dawn on me that Metro-Goldwyn didn't want me to act – they had got their actors. What chance had I with Ramon Navarro, Robert Montgomery and Clark Gable all clamouring for stories.

All the time I was in Hollywood I longed to act – everybody knew this. Someone said I was too English. This quite staggered me – it seemed such an absurd remark to make until it was explained. I was told there were at least 5,000 picture houses in America whose audiences had never heard an Englishman speak. English was like a foreign language to them!

Now I look back at my regrets at not being allowed to act with something more than a chuckle. If I had been, these last two years – the most exciting and certainly the most successful of my theatrical career – would not have happened. It may sound a bit Pollyanna (America's slighting name for an optimist), but I do believe that everything turns out for the best.

But if Metro-Goldwyn had got their ready-made stars they had not got their ready-made writers. I was only wanted to write – and write I did. I have never written such rubbish in my life.

My total output during my stay was my own screen version of The Truth Game – after twelve other writers had tried and failed – otherwise I merely tinkered about to little purpose with the work of some fifty other authors. Net accomplishment – very little!

The Hollywood method of writing film plays convinced me that until one individual thought is applied to film writing, no film will ever have the slightest artistic merit, still less the permanent value which of course only artistic merit can give. Some say that the film, being only a step-child of the theatre, cannot aspire either to art or to permanence – this I deny absolutely. But it is true that so long as the hotch-potch system is in force, lat week's film will be as difficult to see as yesterday's newspaper to read, and just as stale and unimportant.

Apart from this feeling of futility and some personal dissatisfaction, I had a glorious time in Hollywood. The powers that be were kindness itself – the stars threw open the front doors of their homes to me – and as a film fan I had a real busman's holiday! But as a person with some individuality (I hope) – it was hell!
All these glamorous 'wicked' film stars are actually dear little things. They lead a narrow but perfectly-formed existence. Practically their only topic of conversation is 'shop' – work – work – and more work. Ask them what they are working for, what they are going to do when financial security is attained, and a silence descends upon them. There was one exception. One well-known star actually replied thus: "When I retire, aw, I don't know. Guess I'll live in Paris, or Rome, or some such crazy place!"

But, heavens! Some of them are nice!

But the scandalous stories – the parties – the divorces – the queer happenings that are woven around the lives of these quite suburban people are, in my opinion, absolutely non-existent, and only the deliberately concocted propaganda of fevered publicity agents – nothing but a lot of ballyhoo intended to put (and putting) Hollywood on the map. True, there has been a crop of divorces lately in the great film village; but these divorces would have happened if the protagonists had been the Swiss Family Robinson Jones &

Brown, instead of names which have been made familiar to all and sundry by way of the screen. If film stars marry with all the spotlights of their own particular studio focused on them, then they are divorced under the blaze of every spotlight in Hollywood. Admitted that their affections are as variable as ordinary people's, they do work! They put in more hard graft than any other human beings I know. There are breaks between pictures, usually lasting a fortnight; even this time they spend getting fit for the coming picture! Is this living? Is it even existing? I found not.

And – in vulgar parlance – I beat it.

Ramon Novarro - The Film Star & Novello's friend in Hollywood

On my way back from California to New York I had a sinister experience. Three days before I left Santa Monica I gave a party. All the people who had been so charming to me in Hollywood were there – Joan and Douglas, Ruth Chatterton, Lilyan Tashman, Ramon Navarro, Billie Burke and a host of others. In the morning Edgar Wallace rang me up: he said he had a slight cold, and was afraid he wouldn't be able to get along and say goodbye. I left California three days later. Travelling with me was a dog who had walked into my house at Hollywood and made himself at home. He is lovely but ridiculous; ridiculous perhaps because he doesn't quite know what he is – Airedale of Alsatian! He has the beauty of one and the sweetness of the other.

His quarters were in the guard's van [on the train]; three times a day, on that long, hot journey, I took him his meals. At Chicago I changed trains; as soon as we were off again I took along Jim's midday feed. In the van was a porter sitting on an enormous packing-case, making out his list of passengers. I asked him if he would be nice to Jim (which he was) and jocularly added "What an enormous case: I hope there's no one inside!" "Sure there is," he very casually replied. "It's a film-writer who died in Hollywood." At that he lifted up the label and showed it me. I glanced at the name. It was a terrible shock to me; but completely refuted the general belief that animals can sense the presence of a dead body. My Jim was completely happy in the company of a great sportsman travelling on his journey – the name I had read on the label was Edgar Wallace.

Fed up with inactivity and the futility of my Hollywood adventure, I made up my mind to resume actor-management – the thing of all things in the world I like doing best. I love responsibility. So I cabled London, took the Prince of Wales's theatre on a rental, and produced I Lived With You – my first really wholly congenial part since The Rat. I had awful tremors on the first night. After all, it was two years since I had appeared in London; I wondered if I had been forgotten. But when the queue for the pit and gallery began to form forty-eight hours before the doors opened, my nerves calmed down.

I Lived With You was a strange phenomenon. Never had I acted in a play which went so well – not even The Rat – and yet in its five months' run we never once played to really terrific business. Once in the theatre the audience laughed themselves silly but the great majority of the public did not come. This revived the old argument as to whether the public are as much interested in lower middle-class life as they undoubtedly are in what is called high society.

I can quite understand and sympathise with people who live drab lives liking to see something more cheerful on stage – but I cannot see why people with everything in the world they desire should dislike being reminded of the other side of the medal. A friend of mine once heard the Victorian great lady of great wit, Lady Dorothy Nevill, say that she didn't care to read about her own world, which she knew backwards – give her a novel about a kitchen maid or a shop walker! Surely this was good sense; but I wish more of the present day 'stalls' agreed with her!

Included in the cast were Ursula Jeans and Minnie Rayner. Ursula, to my mind, is one of the most brilliant of the younger actresses on the London stage; I look forward enormously to her forthcoming season at the Old Vic, where Shakespeare will give her an added beauty and depth of expression. Minne have a grand, genial, rollicking performance like the great comedian that she is.

It is disappointing, when one seizes the Bull by the Forelock, or Time by the Horns, and they come off in one's hand; or when one Takes a Tide in one's Affairs at the Flood; and it dashes one upon the rocks; and this was my lot on my meeting with Bernard Shaw. It was at a time when I fancied myself as Christian in The Pilgrim's Progress; and was not Mr. Shaw always writing about the dramatic quality of Bunyan's dialogue? What a triumph if I could get him to make it into a play for me! But I didn't know him, and couldn't pluck up courage to write to him.

One evening I went with Eddie Marsh to see Yvette Guilbert at the Arts Theatre, and there was the great man, sitting just behind us. Eddie introduced me. Here was my opportunity – perhaps a turning point in both our careers – Shaw's best play, and my best part! I put my suggestion to him, and he beamed upon me.

"Excellent," he said, "excellent! But you are a dramatist – why not do it yourself?"

So that was that.

Playwright George Bernard Shaw

Sarah Bernhardt

Chapter Six

'I've often thought to myself "were they better, those others, who have passed on and left a legend?"'

I have written these impressions in my flat over the Strand Theatre [*now the Novello Theatre*], where I have lived since 1913. Mother had the flat first. When, during the war [*WW1*], she went to America, I took it over.

I shall never live anywhere else. It has an entrance that would bring shame to a tenement building. It has a lift the size of a sardine-tin, which Viola Tree described as "a small cardboard box suspended on a piece of string." Yet every crisis of my career, every heart-ache I've experienced, every thrill of every first night, has had this flat for a background.

There is an old cliché, "if these walls could only speak." If they could, I think they would say some very nice things! They would whisper to each other: "What about those parties during the war – Ivor rushing home on leave, ringing up all his friends; supper ordered from the Savoy?" This tiny flat has nearly burst its walls with every stage celebrity in London. They weren't all celebrities when they first came here! I look at my party book from 1918 to 1928, and I see the names of Fay Compton, Leslie Henson, Phyllis Monckman, Lily Esie, Gerald du Maurier, Seymour Hicks, Ralph Lynn, Beatrice Lillie, Maise Gay, Teddie Gerrard, Lauretta Taylor, Noel Coward, Jack Buchannan, Violet Lorraine, Phyllis Dare, Nelson Keys, Elsie Janis…I could go on and on.

Phylis Neilson-Terry

Jack Buchanan

It is lovely to think that in my party book of today most of these dear friends and gifted people still scrawl their names. This flat seems to have been made for parties – all the rooms open one into the other. There are never any separate groups, those dampers of any party, and, I can't explain why, people lose their shyness here and don't mind doing their stunts with nothing to gain except the pleasure to be given to friends.

Once, in a burst of extravagance, I engaged an orchestra of 25 to play to an audience of 12. Not for swank, but simply because I was thirsty for music; the 12 were equally thirsty and appreciative. It was a wonderful evening.

Beatrice Lillie

Paul Robeson

Heifetz has played here, Maggie Teyte has sung, once Paul Robeson sat on the floor and sang spirituals, the Dolly Sisters have danced and Mrs. Patrick Campbell has recited. Burlesque dramas have been improvised and enacted with a cast comprising Fay Compton, Beatrice Lillie, Nelson Keys, Leslie Henson, Noel Coward, and Constance Collier, with myself playing horrifying incidental music on the piano.

Anyone will tell you that the actor's time is from midnight until 2am. These are the hours of relaxation. Everything during the day has insensibly led up to the night's performance; once that is over you can sit back and laugh and cry and argue and listen to music. And that was the time of my parties.

Nowadays I don't give so many; perhaps I'm working harder. But it's nice to look back on the many friendships and the many exciting romances which have started in this small flat.

Ivor's Flat – Above the Strand Theatre
[now the Novello Theatre]

The Music Room

I have elsewhere described the many lovely leading ladies I have acted with - but oh! - how did I come to omit the adorable Ellen Terry? I feel proud that I can say I acted with Ellen Terry. I don't think the darling lady knew she was acting with me - or that she was acting at all! She played the nurse in my third film The Bohemian Girl, the part was not an exacting one; it required tenderness and bewilderment because she was bewildered by the studio, the camera and all the paraphernalia of filming.

Vivien Leigh

There had been some slight muddle about her contract; one morning she was sitting in her chair looking absolutely angelic. There was silence, the camera about to turn, her daughter, Edith Craig, was anxiously hovering in the background. Suddenly, in the midst of this tenseness, Ellen Terry said, "Edie, Edie – which film am I in?"

But if ever a human being had magic, instinctive magic, Ellen Terry had it. It was there, like a halo round her beautiful head. Some years later I had the privilege of entertaining her – not once, but four times – in a box at The Rat. On the first occasion she was obviously enjoying the play so very much that I asked her brother Charles (my business manager) to take me to see her after the second act. She talked most interestingly about the play, and said she would like to come to every matinee. As I left the box I heard her say to Charles "What a nice, kind boy that is! Who is he?"

Actress Ellen Terry's brother, Charles, was
Ivor Novello's Business Manager

I am proud that I can claim to have acted with her, and I am proud that I was an usher at her memorial service. She had desired that no mourning should be work at her funeral; it was quite extraordinary the feeling that this created; it seemed as if the people present had put away all thought of depression or grief that she had passed away. The impression was as if a group of very dear and close friends had assembled to say au revoir to their most beloved, on the occasion of her departing on a long happy journey.

I have just finished reading the new Ellen Terry memoirs. I cannot imagine anything more beautiful and poignant than that last phase of her life, 'Ariel Imprisoned.'

Contact with most of the famous actresses of our present day stage has taught me one thing. It is my experience that the higher the accomplishment of the actress, the more renowned her position in the profession, the more unassuming and sweet is the woman. Their success has only been obtained by unceasing effort and tireless work, and what is more, the longer they ornament the stage, the harder they work!

It is the people who are not sure of themselves, and those to whom success has come too quickly and too easily, who give me – as an actor-manager – the most trouble.

I have always had a slight resentment against a famous name that has been dinned in my ears, the owner of which I have never seen. I have a great admiration for the things which are now, and an intolerance of the adulation, at the expense of the present, of the names that are gone and belong to history. I have seen wonderful acting by my contemporaries, and I've often thought to myself "were they better, those others, who have passed on and left a legend?"

When it was announced that Eleanora Duse was to appear, under Mr. Cochran's Management, at the New Oxford Theatre, I was tremendously excited. Friends of mine, who had seen her, spoke in hushed voices of the magic of her art. I could hardly believe that I was to see La Duse. The play was Ibsen's Ghosts; the house was packed to overflowing. I sat in a box, doubts in my mind; could she be as great as her legend? I was determined not to be overwhelmed by what had been.

I didn't know Italian, but of course I knew the story of the play. The curtain went up; there were a few minutes of conversation which might have been Greek to me, then – a door opened on the left hand side of the stage and a little old woman in black entered, not falteringly but swiftly.

Eleonora Duce

Her hands fluttered – she spoke. It was as if a flame had run through the theatre. She was utterly real, utterly wonderful. The legend was true.

I went to every play she gave that season and for once had to admit that far from too much, not half enough had been said. How I resented her years of retirement! Surely with so much to give, private sorrows and troubles should not have been allowed to interfere? I shall always think that an artist's first duty is towards the public. I have played with a famous film star on the English stage who was acting under the stress of all anxieties, aches and pains of a coming baby.

Ten years ago I saw Isadora Duncan dance at the Prince of Wales's Theatre. I had never seen her before, but her genius had been shouted into my ears for years – with inevitable results that when she first appeared I was instantly disappointed, and only saw a fat woman with a rather lovely face. Absurd! I thought – she shouldn't dance. She should remain a legend. But ten minutes afterwards I was at her feet.

The next day I was lunching with a companion at the Savoy Grillroom, and suddenly saw Isadora sitting among a group at a neighbouring table. I dashed to the florist's just outside and bought every rose in the shop – about six dozen! With my arms full of flowers I went across to the Savoy and laid them on the table in front of her. Like every one else Isadora loved homage; we started talking; my friend had to finish his luncheon by himself: hers melted away. She told me she was going to Russia in four days time. During those four days I don't think we were apart for more than four hours! I never saw her again.

But, to get back to my narrative. I am a glutton for work. After the run of I Lived With You there should have been a break in my activities until the provincial tour, which I had booked for the Autumn, was due to start. I thought: "think of it! The whole of August free; I shall live in the country, sun-bathe and laze, and get really fit for the big tour!" Not at all. Sebastian Shaw, playing in my other play Party at the Strand Theatre, asked for leave of absence. Partly as a gesture, partly because I couldn't bear not to act when there was a chance, I offered to take his place for four weeks. I was certainly much happier playing all through the terrific heat of that particularly gasping August than I should have been dangling my legs in a pool, day after day, for a month!

Last year I began to be accused of being too prolific. True, during the last eighteen months I have had five plays presented in London – but actually these five plays are all the result of three and a half years of hard work. Only one of them is what I might describe as a 'quickie.' It is safe to confess this now, because Fresh Fields is already in the eighth month of its run and there are still no signs of its appeal waning. I began Fresh Fields on a Friday morning in a Manchester hotel, and had it completely finished by the Saturday morning of the following week in a Birmingham hotel. I didn't have to rewrite one word. Heaven knows, I don't hold this up as an example or even as an encouragement to write quickly. It was just good luck. I had got hold of an idea, and – having well in mind for whom I was writing the play – could not get my thoughts on paper fast enough.

To write a play in eight days will probably never happen to me again – but it was once! Noel Coward once said to me: "Don't take any notice of the people who tell you that playwriting is a slow and laborious business. If you can't write a first draft of a play in three weeks – throw what you have done on the fire!"

Lately, some amusing comparisons have been made between Noel's work and mine. It was suggested there was a great spirit of rivalry between us. This is nonsense. Noel and I are the closest of friends; he has always been of tremendous help and encouragement to me. I have too much admiration for his genius to imagine that my plays can be compared to his.

Party is a real love child among my plays; I wrote it solely to please myself! I never intended it for a run; I visualised it as a Sunday show, played to a special audience who would laugh good-humouredly at the jokes against themselves. But I did want it produced; it contained many things which I had long wanted to say. In it I attacked lots of people I always wanted to attack, and upheld lots of people I had always wanted to uphold; this would be pointless if the play could not be publicly performed. So I approached Bronson Albery and discussed with him the possibilities of the play being produced at the Arts Theatre Club; but certainly with no thought of eventually transferring it to another west end theatre.

After we had rehearsed a few times we all looked at each other – Athol Stewart (who produced [*directed*] so brilliantly), Lilian Braithwaite (surely she has never played so exquisitely as in Party), Benita Hume (who literally leapt into stardom and threw it away to roast under the Klieg lights of Hollywood studios) and myself. This play, we all agreed, was better than we had thought; in fact, it was pretty good! The story of Party – the underlying drama – which, in reading, seemed of minor importance, had, in the acting, come very much alive.

One morning, one of my greatest friends in the world, a wise, witty and quite ridiculous person – Mrs. Leslie Henson – strolled into the theatre, sat down, and watched us rehearsing. After about half an hour she shot out of her seat and rushed to the telephone. Ten minutes later Leslie Henson and Firth Shephard were sitting in the stalls. Half an hour later, Leslie and Firth made me a proposition for an immediate production at the Strand Theatre.

The play was – if I remember rightly – more praised than any play I have done, and became a real vogue for six months. The film rights were sold to Metro-Goldwyn for eight thousand pounds (it's all right: I've paid the income tax!) and this was a play I had never intended for public presentation. How little we know!

During the run of this piece Mrs. Patrick Campbell, after seeing the play, went behind to see Lilian. I had never admitted the identity of Mrs. Mac but dear Mrs. Campbell, embracing Lilian, cried in her lovely London-Italian voice; "Oh, Leelean – you make me so much nicer than I really am!"

As I write this, Mrs. Campbell is on her way to New York to create herself on Broadway. Before she went I had a characteristic telegram from her: "Sailing Saturday on Aquitania to make your fortune!"

After Party came Flies In The Sun – my desperate attempt to be wicked. Don't worry, it shan't occur again! I've been rapped over the knuckles.

I cannot write about people I dislike. Flies In The Sun was a play about a group of idle decadents basking in the sun on the edge of the sea somewhere between Marseille and Capri. I had one great happiness in this play – I was acting with Gladys Cooper. Miss Cooper gave a magnificent performance of a character entirely opposite to her own sympathetic fresh-air personality – but, like the rest of the play, it remained a performance. All the wrong people liked the play, all the right people loathed it. I have a theory, a belief that there are so many more right people in the world than wrong; that is why, if my theory is true, the play failed. On its last night – usually a very sentimental occasion – I breathed a sigh of relief and turned instantly to a play about people I know, love and respect – Proscenium.

Before Proscenium was produced I was told that the time had not come for sentiment, and that true love and devotion were still pre-war jokes. I thank my guardian angel who is (let's face it) seldom off duty, that I trusted my own judgment.

I was also warned that no play about stage people had succeeded in London since Trelawny Of The Wells. One of my most treasured possessions is an anonymous telegram: "You've written another Trelawny!"

I did expect, with Proscenium, to attract the older, more mature playgoer; I am agreeably surprised and intensely pleased at the constant presence in the theatre of the really young generation – the 'debs' of next year who, what is more, are not above being moved to shouts of laughter and unashamed tears. Another thing that surprised me about Proscenium was the praise I received for portraying a man of fifty odd years, and that my disguise in the prologue was so good that I was unrecognisable! But the praise, I think, was misplaced. I find it just as difficult to play a youth of 26 (the part I usually play!) as a man of 50, my age being neither one nor the other.

In proscenium the appearance and manner of the Colonel is based on my dear father, who died two years ago when I was 4,000 miles away [*in Hollywood*].

People who don't know me imagine that because I act the hero in plays and because I have had a certain amount of success in the work I have attempted to do, I am spoilt, vain and intolerably conceited. This always amuses me. Quite obviously I have little to be conceited about; if my features have given any pleasure to people, that is a pure accident of flesh and gristle; if my work has won approval, I can only ascribe it to the fact that well knowing my limitations I have honestly tried to overcome them. Above all I have done my best to be sincere both on the stage and in my plays.

I am constantly being asked: "What of the future? – what would you like to become?" My mother, for example, cares little for the theatrical success which has come my way. She has a dream which I fear will never be fulfilled; that of seeing me conduct my own opera at Covent Garden. She has always believed in my music. A great many other people seem to share that queer belief.

Hardly a day passes but someone asks me in a voice choked with sentiment: "What has become of your music?" Nothing has become of it – it's still there! Let me try and tell you the truth about it. The days have long since gone when I had to think "I've got to turn out some tunes this week or the rent won't get paid." My conviction is that unless a talent can be regarded as being the real big thing in one's life so that it blots out everything else, then that talent is best left alone. That's what happened to my music. I get more enjoyment now when I sit at the piano and improvise with no thought of publication, than I ever get when I was under the necessity to write tinkling tunes for money. Also – financially speaking – a thing like The Home Fires only happens once.

As a composer of at least several successful musical plays [*revues in the 1920s*] I can (with heartfelt feeling) assure those people who think that a composer of light opera in England must surely become a millionaire that they haven't 'read the programme.'

During the year 1921 I had The Golden Moth (for which I had written all the music) running in London at the Adelphi Theatre, and A to Z, a revue (to which I contributed seventy five percent of the music), play at the Prince of Wales's. Yet my weekly income cheque from these two productions was less than half what I get one day's filming!

When I was writing music my next quarter's rent was an ever present anxiety; now, than k heavens, I can face it with equanimity! There was a time when music meant everything to me. I can remember when I was two-and-twenty standing at the back of the Gaiety Theatre pit on the first night of Tonight's The Night and thinking to myself: "If only one of my numbers could be sung in this theatre…!

As it happened the very next production there proved to me a piece with music entirely mine. It was Theodore & Co.

The score cost me three month's hard work, and included a first act finale which was 40 pages long. Two days before rehearsals started I took the manuscript to play to George Grossmith. I came out of the theatre, got into a taxi, and got out – leaving the only copy of the score behind. It did not turn up at that time, nor has it ever turned up since. It's loss meant that I had to do three months' work again in something less than three days. But it was done! I didn't go to bed, and just managed to finish the score in time, keeping myself awake with cup after cup of black coffee. Today I should have done it on cigarettes!

But I never smoked a cigarette until the production of The Rat – that was eight years after Theodore & Co. The part of the Apache which I played in The Rat required an excessive amount of smoking, which naturally had to be done with some air of realism. So, at the first rehearsal, I went armed with a tin of recommended Turkish cigarettes. I am still faithful to that particular brand; now it is rarely that I have not got one between my lips.

I have wandered a long way from what I should really like to do – my dream. It is not my mother's. My dream is to own a great theatre in London where, to quote Proscenium: "Only the highest standards – nothing but the best will appear." I should like to have a stock company of fine artistes, playing from four to six plays a year. My theatre would be something of a National Theatre, without the dreariness implied by the term. And to quote Proscenium again: "I believe in theatre; I believe in beauty in the theatre, I believe that in the theatre lies one of the roads back to sanity. I want to give the people the chance to dream again."

Ivor Novello – 1933

[Novello's dream would come true in some way eventually. The flat he lived in above the Strand Theatre is still there in London's West End, the theatre was renamed to the Novello Theatre by Sir Cameron Mackintosh when he took over ownership of the theatre and the flat in 2010. No more fitting tribute for a man who created so much and gave so much pleasure to countless audiences in the first half of the 20th century.]

[Novello's mother's wish also came true. After writing his autobiography My Life that covered his life between his birth in 1893 and 1933 he little realised aged 40 he was on the cusp of saving the fortunes of the Theatre Royal, Drury Lane with his music. A few months later the first of his spectacular musicals Glamorous Night opened in May 1935 at Drury Lane, followed by Careless Rapture (1936), Crest of the Wave (1937/8), The Dancing Years (1939). Then: Arch de Triomphe (1943), Perchance to Dream (1945), King's Rhapsody (1948) and Gay's The Word! (1951) produced at other prestigious London theatres. Novello composed the music and wrote the libretto's for all of them with lyrics by Christopher Hassall, Allan Melville and Novello.]

What Came Next...

1935

1936

1937/8

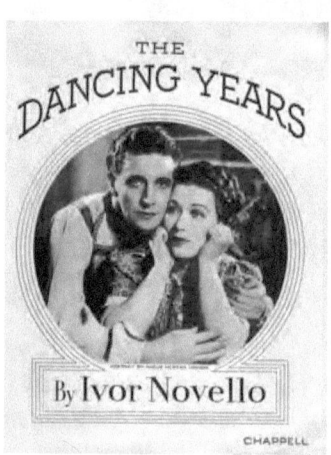

1939

These images courtesy of Nick Gaze and
the Ivor Novello Appreciation Bureau

Index:

A
Adams, Louis Lee. 21,22,23,
Adelphi Theatre. 66,110,
Albery, Bronson. 106,
Ambassadors Theatre. 60,
Alhambra Theatre. 48,
Arts Theatre. 106
Asquith, Elizabeth (Lady Oxford). 29,
A to Z (musical revue) 110,

B
Bailey, Hilda. 59,
Ballerina (play) 69,
Banks, Leslie. 61,
Barthelmess, Richard. 85,86,
Bernhardt, Sarah. 12,93,
Birth of a Nation (film) 22,60,
Bitter Sweet (operetta) 70,
Bohemian Girl, The (film) 5,29,59,99,
Bonnie Prince Charlie (film) 6,
Boosey & Co. (music publisher) 43,
Braithwaite, Lilian. 3, 4,5, 31, 32,72,73,74,106,107,
Brewer. Dr. 43,
Brown Derby, The (restaurant) 86,
Brown-Potter, Mrs. 39,40,
Buchana, Jack. 96,
Buckmaster, Captain. 7,
Burke, Billie. 78,79,80,90,97,
Butt, Clara. 36,37

C
Call of the Blood, The (film) 53,57,
Carnival (film) 59,
Capture, The (play). 13,
Caruso, Enrique. 46,
Castles In The Air (book) 33,
Cavalcade (musical play) 70,
King Charles. 25,
Chatterton, Ruth. 23, 24,25,90,
Churchill, Winston. 51,52,
Collier, Constance. 11,12,14,29,30,31,59,64,66,72,97,
Collins, Jose. 15,16,
Compton, Fay. 5,9,10,11,12,96,97,108,
Cooper, Gladys. 5,6,7,8,9,12,29,59,64,65,66,84,107,108,
Count of Luxembourg, The. 45,
Covent Garden (opera) 110,
Coward, Noel. 19,21,44,69,70,96,97,105,106,
Coyne, Joseph. 26,
Craig, Edith. 99,100,
Crawford, Joan. 79,80,81,90,

D
Daly's Theatre. 26,42,44,45,
Daniel Mayer Comp. (film) 52,
Dare, Phyllis. 96,
Davies, Clara Novello. 3,4,35,36,37,39,41,42,44,45,49,112,
Davies, David (Novello's father) 45,
Dean Basil. 69,70,
De Casalis, Jean. 61,
Deburau (play) 60,61,
Debussy. 11,
Dempster, Carol. 20,
Doble, Frances. 68,69,
Dorothy Nevill, Lady. 91,
Douthitt, Wilfred. 44,
Down Hill (play) 66,67,68,69,
Drury Lane, Theatre Royal. 67,
Duce, Eleonora. 102,103,
Du Maurier, Gerald. 14,72,96,
Duncan, Isadora. 103,104,

E
Elsie, Lily. 5,25,26,27,28,29,35,42,43,71,73,74,77,96,
Empress of Ireland (liner) 46,47,
Enter Kiki (play) 29,30,65

F
Fairbanks, Douglas Jr. 79,80,81,90,
Firebrand, The (play). 14,69,
Flies In The Sun (play) 107,
Florence, Evangeline. 44,
Frances, Kay. 82,
Fresh Fields (play) 32,105,

G
Gable, Clark. 86,
Gaiety Theatre. 38,111,
Gainsborough Pictures. 23,
Garrick Theatre. 66,73,
Garbo, Greta. 2,81,82,83,
Gay, Maise. 96,
Gerard, Teddy. 96,
Gerardy, Jean. 36,
Ghosts (play) 102
Gilbert Ford, Lina. 49,50,
Golden Moth, The (musical revue) 110,
Goldwin, Samuel. 19,
Graham Brown, William. 74,
Grand Hotel (film) 59,
Griffiths, D.W. 7,8,9,19,20,21,22,59,60,85
Grossmith, George. 16,38,111,
Guilbert, Yvette. 92,
Guitry, Sasha. 60,
Guinness, Mrs. Benjamin. 46,

H
Hackney, Mabel. 47,
Hamilton, Neil. 20,21
Herbert Beerbohm Tree. 33,71,
Henson, Leslie. 96,97,107,
Hicks, Seymour. 96,
Hope Crews, Laura. 24,
Hume, Benita. 106,
Hyman, Berie. 80,81,84,

I
I Lived With You (play) 91,
Ibsen. 102
Ibbetson, Peter (play) 30,
Intolerance (film) 60,
Iris (play) 66,67
Irving, Laurence. 47,

J
Janis, Elsie. 24,96,
Jeans, Isabel. 5,13,14
Jeans, Ursula. 14,15,91,92,
Jeffreys, Ellis. 73,

K
Keane, Doris. 46
Keen's Chop House. 19,
Keep The Home Fires Burning. 47,48,49,50,51,110,
Keys, Nelson. 96,97,
Kingsway Theatre. 61,

L
Lady Randolph Churchill. 51,
Lang, Matheson. 59,
Lillie, Beatrice. 29,96,
Liliom (play) 69,
Little Damozel, The (song) 44,46,
Little Minster, The (play) 11,
Lloyds George, Mr. 10,
Lorraine, Robert. 61,
Lorraine, Violet. 96,
Lucas, Paul. 82,
Lyceum Theatre 67,
Lynn, Ralph. 96,

M
Magdalen College School, Oxford. 39,43,
Marsh, Eddie. 51,
Marsh, Mae. 19,20,21,22,23,60,92,
Mayer, Rudolf. 52,53,
Mazza, Desdemona. 55,
McCormack, John. 50,
Melba, Dame Nellie. 46,
Mercanton, Louis. 53,54,57,58,59,60
Merry Widow, The (operetta) 26,42,77,78,86,87,107,
Metro-Goldwyn (film company) 77,78,86,87,107,
Miller, Gertie. 38,
Miller, Gilbert. 8,
Morgan, Merlin. 44,45,
Monckman, Phylis. 68,96,
Montgomery, Robert. 86,
My Ladies Dress (play) 8,

N
National Theatre. 31,112,
Navaro, Ramon. 86,89,90,
Negri, Pola. 83,84,
Neilson-Terry, Phyllis. 53,54,55,96,
Nicholls, Agnes. 36,

115

O
Old Heidelberg (play) 66,
Old Vic (theatre) 92,
Once A Lady (film) 25,
Our Betters (play) 11,
Our Miss Gibbs (musical comedy) 38,
Orphans of the Storm, The (film) 60,
P
Party (play) 32,105,106,107,
Patrick Campbell, Mrs. 71,72,97,107,
Patti, Adelina. 36,37,
Prince of Wales's Theatre. 91,
Proscenium. 108,109,112,
R
Rat, The (play) 23,60,64,66,69,91,111,
Ravel. 11,
Rayner, Minnie. 91,92,
Rejane, Gabriella. 57,58,59,
Richpin, Jean. 57,58,
Robeson, Paul. 97,
Rogers, Roy. 8,
Romance (play) 46,
Rumford, Kennerly. 36,37,
S
Savoy (hotel) 103,
Savoy Grill. 103,
Secrets of the Harem, The (melodrama) 41,
Shaw, Bernard. 92,93,
Sheldon. 46,
Sheepard, Firth. 107,
Sirocco (play) 69,70,71,72
Smith, Aubrey. 59,
Spanish Lovers. 61,62,63,
Strand Theatre (now Novello Theatre) 95,105,
Stewart, Athol. 106,
Symphony In Two Flats (play) 32,77,

T
Tashman, Lilyan. 82,83,90,
Taylor, Loretta. 96,
Tempest, Marie. 74,
Terry, Charles. 100
Terry, Ellen. 10,59,99,100,101
Teyte, Maggie. 11,97,
Theodore & Co. (music revue) 111
Titheridge, Madge. 5,61,
Tree, Lady. 33,
Tree, Viola. 28,29,32,33,71,73,77,78,95,
Trelawney of the Wells (play) 109,
Truth Game, The (play) 28,31,32,43,71,72,77,78,79,80,82,84,97,
V
Vane, Sybil. 48,
Vibert, Henry. 59,
Vivien Leigh. 99,
Queen Victoria. 3,
W
Way Down East (film) 60,85,
Wallace, Edgar. 90,
Webb, Clifton. 24,
White Rose, The (film) 19,20,21,60
Williams, Lloyd. 21,
Wilson, Lois. 24,
Wolff, Johannes. 36,
Y
Yellow Jacket (play) 61,

Part Two

In Search of Ruritania...

LAVENDER & LILACS

"God knows what magic it was, but, whatever it was, he had it!"

Phyllis Monkman - Actress & friend.

This is not a sentimental journey, but an attempt to discover what truly occurred "once upon a time." I always remember somebody once saying to me: "The past is like another planet - they do things differently there." For reasons I will never truly understand, a hugely successful man from that past has influenced my life and career. There have been great times, and times that were not so great. But in spite of this it has never been dull and always, always intriguing. The name of the man was Ivor Novello. And yes, I will agree, they certainly did "do things differently there." My determination to go *In Search of Ruritania*, to unravel the mysteries surrounding Novello, and attempt to make sense of him and his work, and those who worked with him, has been nigh impossible. Looking back, knowing what I know now, I doubt I would have ever started. But, as you will discover, at the age of five when the seeds were sown in my mind, the mind and imagination are a sponge which soaks up everything in order to make sense of the relatively new world which surrounds it.

Neither is this an attempt to create just another biography about Novello; although you will discover much about him by the time you have turned the last page. Besides, many biographies have been penned, all in their own way informative and have laid down for posterity a detailed, if not somewhat over sentimentalised, chronology of his career and personality. Those written in the years immediately following his death in 1951, aged 58, seem to joyously wallow in the tragedy of his early demise, and sanitise him to the point of banality. For me Novello deserves more honest and open analysis. He deserves to be appreciated as a person with faults and failings like us all and as a remarkable creative artist. I feel confident in stating that he would have been the last person to consider himself "perfect." It is so easy with Novello to inadvertently sink into the sentimental, as so many did when watching his musicals and plays, and I am determined that will not happen within this story. Maybe others have slipped into this trap because of what Novello stood for in terms of his creative vision and the romantic characters he created within that. In a sense they all had a hint of the Edwardian standards which inspired him as a young man, ones which are alien to us a hundred years on, but not so to his audiences because they reflected a more stable society which was smashed apart and destroyed as a result of the First World War.

The attempt to sanctify his memory, however good intentioned, has in fact caused more harm than good. It has made Novello seem a bit boring and uninteresting. The loyalty of his friends and colleagues was admirable, and to them he was certainly worthy of being Saint Ivor. After all, he was the goose that laid the golden eggs for all of them by keeping them in work. Good intentions do not always bear positive results, and it would seem this approach did much to ensure Novello and his legacy disappeared beneath the waves of public recognition as swiftly as the Titanic sank beneath the waves of the North Atlantic. None of these early books even hinted at Novello's homosexuality, not surprising as it was unacceptable socially and more importantly illegal. At the time of his death in 1951 it could have also resulted in profound embarrassment, not to mention possible legal action, for his lover and long-time partner Robert Andrews, who survived him by another twenty years. However, to eradicate Novello's homosexuality from any study is to leave out a vital ingredient in understanding him and his work. In the more enlightened times in which we live, it is no big deal to be gay. That said, there are still male celebrities who conceal their sexuality for fear of ruining their careers. When you rely on thousands and thousands (if not millions and millions) of admiring female fans to keep your star burning brightly, the last thing you want them to know is that you prefer men! So it was for Novello, and so it is still today for some. Novello's early biographers understandably glossed over these elements of his life and intimated mysteriously that he had secret "women friends." Indeed he did, but not in any way were they sexual relationships, just ones of friendship and adoration on his part. Thankfully it is now possible to examine and fully understand Novello's personality, sexuality and creativity. I believe his homosexuality was a vital ingredient, and a hidden essence that made him such a successful artist.

I have had many a fraught conversation with old Novellians and those today who are captivated by him; I'll add that I obviously consider myself among them but perhaps devoid of the rose-coloured spectacles and hence any cloying sentiment. They dislike discussing or even acknowledging his sexuality, prison sentence, or indeed anything which might deviate from his supposed perfection. Novello had human weaknesses like us all and was a complex and enigmatic character even to those close to him - futile then not to add these elements into any serious discussion or consideration of his life and work. Without them maybe he would never have achieved so much, or brought so much pleasure to countless thousands in the dark days that were the first half of the 20th century; after all, what was happening around him in the world was as much an influence on his creativity as his own imagination and drive. One could even argue that without the political and social climate within which he lived the opportunities would not have been there for him to use as golden opportunities. Fate was kind to Novello, very kind indeed.

As you will discover as my story unfolds, I have myself quite by chance been drawn into the world of Novello in spite of the fact he died eight years before I was born. My journey began when I was a child, and I never made a conscious decision to explore or involve myself in anything to do with Novello, his life or work. It just happened. Yet the more I was pulled into his world, the more I learned, the more fascinated I became. On several occasions in recent years it has been suggested I consider writing a biography. I always hesitated, mainly because I felt I had to have something new to say - or approach the subject in a different way. Since my involvement with Bob Altman's movie *Gosford Park*, I receive letters and emails from people all over the world who want more information on Novello. This alone made me realize there is an audience out there who crave information.

It also occurred to me that my own experiences and encounters along the way have been fascinating, ludicrous, sad and at times funny. *In Search of Ruritania* is about my own journey and the journey Novello experienced in his lifetime. You could say that while Novello was the centre of attention at a ball in a glittering world, through a strange quirk of fate I have been able to peek through a crack in a doorway leading to that world and not only glimpse what lay within, but also to experience its unique atmosphere. My hope is it will do justice to us both, enlighten you along the way, and give you a more honest perspective of Novello and his world.

Oxford Beginnings

My journey to discover Novello began in Oxford, the City of my birth, and the home of my fascinating and eccentric aunt. On occasions my aunt would look after me for the day to allow my mother to embark on some mission or task that would be impossible to conduct with a five-year-old hanging on the end of her arm. I would be scrubbed and dressed in my best clothes and issued with instructions on how to behave. My cowlick would be wetted and brushed again and again to make it stay down - all to no avail! Try as my mother might, the offending hair would pop back up defiantly. The said cowlick was as a result of my young hands grabbing a pair of scissors during one of my mother's dress making sessions. She let her eye wander for two seconds from her errant child, and I snipped off a clump of hair. As it grew, it would only grow up! No doubt my mother wished the same for me.

So prepared, I would cling on to my mother's hand as we made our journey through Oxford, up the High, through to the Broad in the shadow of Wren's Sheldonian Theatre, past the Randolph Hotel, Martyrs Memorial and onto St Giles towards North Oxford's Victorian gothic mansions; all suitable abodes for the Munsters or the Adams family. As we turned into my aunt's driveway, my feet would sink into the gravel making it harder for me to keep up with my mother's unaltered stride. The crunch of the gravel would fill me with a slight foreboding. Pulling the big brass knob attached

to a wire, which activated the bell attached to a coiled spring inside the house. On letting go the knob was snatched back with a thud, at which my mother would exclaim: "It's ringing." The huge and highly polished front door would swing open with enough drama and flourish to take your breath away. One could imagine a glamorous stage star was about to make their dramatic entrance in the first scene of a play. With the breath taken away from a wide-eyed and slightly scared five-year-old, the breath would be sucked back. With it, the musty smell of vintage lavender scent would invade my nostrils, and leave me feeling like I would never smell anything else ever again. It lingered for a long time; indeed I can still smell it today after the passing of my aunt and over forty years. I remember being fixated with the highly polished brass letter box and the squeaky hinges - with hindsight it could have been a hint that dear aunt Mabel was indeed herself slightly unhinged! My fixation was more likely by way of steeling myself for the inevitable onslaught of her huge bosoms as she clenched me in a hug by way of greeting. My five-year-old body would be swamped by huge dollops of warm, lavender scented flesh with the hard coldness of her pearls pressing into my cheek like a deluge of hail stones. Grabbing my hand she would hold it tightly as we stood together and waved to my mother as she walked away down the gravel drive. The crunch of her footsteps growing quieter, my heart beat getting faster and louder. With trepidation I was led by my aunt into her big, gloomy Victorian house. I would watch the huge front door swing closed and wonder if I would ever see it open, or my mother, again.

The swish of silk and the rattle of pearls would accompany us as I struggled to keep up as aunt Mabel glided down the hall, my hand sweaty in her iron grip, my little legs moving like wobbly pistons desperately trying to keep up, until we reached the parlour. The room was full of heavy furniture, ornaments and a colossal parlour palm in one corner. Its deep green leaves looming over me menacingly, as if its huge hand shaped leaves would pounce on me the moment I took my wary eye off it. The sweep of the drapes at the huge bay window punctuated the oppression of the room and seemed to glory in their slightly faded silk fashion. Silver picture frames adorned the mantle above the crackling fire, for it was always alight come summer or winter as I remember. The hiss and spit of the logs added to my trepidation and would always make me jump. The burns on the rug in front of the fireplace testament to the capability of those spitting logs and what they would, if opportunity arose, do to me.

In the far corner stood a grand piano shrouded in a huge fringed shawl with yet more silver photograph frames displayed fan like on its lid. In most of these frames were pictures of a man. His appearance was posed, formal and intriguing. There was nothing casual in his demeanour, not like normal family photographs I had seen and been part of. Mostly they were black and white or sepia in tone. My aunt would talk about the man in the silver frames with animated enthusiasm. The tone of her voice would change and convey a gentleness and melancholy that was reserved for when she spoke of him. In my mind it seemed logical he must have been her long departed lover or husband, the loss of which had been clouded by time and grief to a point where only the very best memories of their relationship had become distorted or embellished to a point where they no longer resembled the actual truth of their life together. How at such an age I could think such a thought is beyond me, but I am convinced I did! She would speak fervently of his musical gifts and with a rattle and swish would glide over to the piano, sit on the stool slightly inelegantly, which would surprise me as she seemed normally quite elegant in her movements, but maybe it was the clear liquid poured from the green bottle which caused this anomaly?

Slowly and with relish she would lift the lid and stare intently at the keys, as if she were willing them to play themselves. But maybe she was trying her hardest to focus her eyes so she could actually see them with some clarity. Most times she would suddenly look across at me as if she had forgotten I was there. In truth she probably had, her mind wandered off to goodness knows where. Her eyes would, inevitably, mist over with tears and she would grapple like an inept magician for a tatty lace handkerchief neatly placed in the sleeve of her dress. Dabbing her eyes and laughing at her own embarrassment, and mine, she would blow me a kiss and wink at me, then point to the Egyptian box on the table at the side of the chair in which I was sitting, legs dangling over the edge. I always disliked sitting in that huge chair because my feet didn't touch the floor and thus I was unable to make a hasty escape if the looming hands of the parlour palm, the spitting logs or my aunt's bosom and pearls lunged toward me for yet another bone crushing hug. However the Egyptian box, which was thus named due to the pharaoic emblems painted upon it, was my favourite as it was always full of chocolates! "Munch away darling," she would twitter, "I want to play you this divine piece of music. He could have written it especially for me - he was such a handsome and wonderful man." She would play the first few bars of *We'll Gather Lilacs* with a passion and feeling which was on the verge of scary.

By this time my fears had been slightly diminished and my full attention taken with munching chocolates. I would munch away and watch her as she became enveloped in the music and her thoughts of the past. Her fingers pounded away like erratic Daddy-long-legs, her rings flashing as they caught the light and sending reflections dancing across the ceiling and walls with all the colours of the rainbow.

Presently she would glide across the room with a sprightliness that belied her advancing years and reverently remove a 78 record from its stiff cardboard sleeve. Placing it on the brass horned gramophone she would slowly turn the winding mechanism. The record would begin to spin which would accentuate the warp and make me feel slightly sick as I gazed at it hypnotically. She would then gingerly lift the arm and place the needle on the record. It would almost screech in protestation and make the most hideous hissss and crackle, hissss and crackle - like a witch screeching as she burnt at the stake, I thought. The needle would suddenly find the groove and the witch was silenced to be replaced by the sound of a ghostly orchestra striking up, as if they were at the end of a very long tunnel far, far away. The melody from *Glamorous Night* would play out full blast and, even allowing for the poor quality of sound, it stirred something inside me which at the time I couldn't really explain. The voice of a woman singing would glide from the great horn and soothe my ears, momentarily I would abandon munching the chocolate in my mouth and listen transfixed. To me she sounded like Snow White in the Disney film I had recently been to see with my parents. Aunt Mabel would swirl around the room caught up in the melody in waltz time. Her movements those of someone much younger as she danced with an unseen partner. The sun, just to add to the surreal sight, broke from behind a cloud and sent its rays piercing through the windows into the gloom of the room. Dust particles danced frantically around my aunt in an almost frenzied fashion until they looked like little stars orbiting her private universe. I could not begin to imagine or understand what thoughts must have been in her mind, but I can honestly say it was only a handful of rare occasions when she looked truly happy. Ultimately the music and the woman with the Snow White voice would come to an end. The needle would hit the end of the groove and would hissss, click, hissss, click as my aunt collapsed dramatically across the chaise longue exhausted by her activities. Listening to her panting breath, my nostrils would twitch in recognition of the stale lavender smell which seemed to intensify. The sun, as if on queue, would skulk back behind its cloud and the gloom would descend once again upon the parlour. I would munch quietly on my chocolate and watch my aunt as she laid there, eyes closed, her bosoms and the dreaded pearls would heave up and down, up and down, up and down, until her breathing became normal. Invariably she would doze off for a few minutes. The hissss, click, hissss, click of the gramophone needle at the end of its groove seemed to echo in the room.

It was many years later that I realized the picture of the man in the silver frames was Ivor Novello. The woman singing like Snow White was Mary Ellis, one of the eminent musical theatre stars of the 1920s and 30s. Little did I know I would one day meet her and discuss *Glamorous Night*, Novello's first Drury Lane musical in 1935, in which she starred. What was it about Novello that had captivated the likes of aunt Mabel and made them so emotionally attached and obsessive? Phyllis Monckman, an actress and contemporary of Novello's, on hearing the news of his death said: "I just lay there and looked at the wall. I couldn't take it in. God knows what magic it was, but, whatever it was, he had it!"

But more of that later. We are in Oxford and Novello too had connections with the City. Indeed, it was where he developed his talents as a musician and found independence from his mother, Clara Novello Davies, and his father, David Davies, the council tax inspector from Cardiff, Wales.

The very atmosphere created by Oxford has inspired generations. The City is beautifully pickled in history, which has given it a unique flavour and texture. By very nature it is a City with a transient population that provides under graduates for its colleges, colleges which are collectively known as

Oxford University. It nurtures young minds and then sends them out into the world to do their worst. The roll-call is endless and not one I wish to detail here - others have done that for those who are interested. But Prime Ministers and future Kings as well as world leaders in medicine, engineering, politics, music and the arts have passed through its system.

The University buildings seem to emanate a sepia glow, which punctuates its status haughtily. Viewing its spires from a distance does give them a dream like quality, but on closer inspection they lose some of their glamour amid the hustle and bustle of the never-ending conflict that is town and gown. This is aided by the intensity of the pot-pouri of architectural styles from ancient to modern that reflect its historical development and longevity. Time and the vagaries of the English weather have taken their toll and shrouded these remarkable buildings in a faded elegance, in latter years this has been aided by car pollution and acid rain. Oxford is capable of ensuring a loyalty from its inhabitants; whatever the duration of the tenure. It inevitably draws one back to its uniqueness and fills even the most cynical with a nostalgia. For me the City looks modestly on the achievements of its past occupants, tolerates the present, and rejoices in the possibility of what the future may bring. It has elements of all this in its day-to-day existence.

St Giles and the High are to me the most beautiful. The timelessness of the covered market with its bustly atmosphere still has one foot in the past. The Butchers still hang Venison, Pheasants, Turkeys, lifeless but fully feathered and furred, outside their shops. Disconcerting for some, but still reminiscent of old faded photographs of shops that adorned every high street or village a couple of generations ago. They can do this because the shops are enclosed within a larger building, thus any hygiene or health laws are not breached. The Randolph Hotel still retains some of its Victorian grandeur and stands haughtily on the corner of Beaumont Street, gazing along St Giles to North Oxford and the Banbury Road. The New Theatre still welcomes touring musical and opera productions, and the Oxford Playhouse presents more modest and high-brow plays along with the yearly Oxford University Dramatic Society presentations. OUDS is as famous as the University and I was once fortunate to be a member. Our first production was Checkov's *A Month In The Country*. It was politely received by eager parents and friends, but alas the critics were less impressed. Their headline was "A month in the Playhouse!", which said it all! But we soldiered on, as those involved in theatre do, with dwindling audience and determination not to let this setback dint our confidence unduly. The second production was Shaffer's *Amadeus*. This was received with a much more positive critique, and with hindsight it was probably because it required a manic enthusiasm to bring it to life on the stage. We all possessed the manic enthusiasm of youth, so thankfully it spilled over into the production. Even then we were aware of the hallowed footsteps of the great and good who had strode across that stage with varying degrees of success. The likes of Sir Laurence Olivier, Vivien Leigh, John Gielgud, Ivor Novello and Oscar Wilde to name but a few. Perhaps we all hoped their essence or spirit remained and would somehow imbue us with their talent and success. Optimism was our everything. We would spill out of the stage door after each performance and take the three strides into the Playhouse public house. Never have so few footsteps been so convenient for a clutch of thespians - as it had been for all those who had performed at the Playhouse. The pub walls covered in their autographed photographs. One could sit and read the inscriptions for hours and gaze at the famous faces staring down, whilst sipping half a pint of warm beer.

The University's Sheldonian Theatre, designed and built by Sir Christopher Wren, has witnessed performances and music recitals for generations. It rarely recognizes the more modern taste in music but instead bathes itself in the classical and timeless. The choral concerts are electrifying and one instantly forgets the hardness of the bench seating, or the feeling of vertigo should you be seated in what feels like perilously steep upper galleries. The building seems to have the ability to embrace and protect you to the point where any thoughts are erased from your mind once the concert begins. The seats themselves are a testament to the longevity and history of the hall - even the very floorboards. There are curves where more than likely several thousand previous bottoms have perched before you, the steps also similarly shaped by countless thousands of feet as they arrive for an event. The acoustics are excellent and it is difficult to imagine a better venue for a choir, solo performer or to appreciate the skill of a concert pianist or organ recital. The Christmas carol service is definitely something not to be missed, or at least experienced once. It captures the magic and old fashioned ideal of Christmas - one where the vulgarities of blatant commercialization count for nothing and influence nothing. Magdalen College Choir School educates and trains young choristers who present an annual concert at the Sheldonian at Christmas and other events throughout the year. They join the school at a young age and receive a thorough education in music and other academic subjects. It is a unique education and available on merit to the very few.

The year 1903 saw two new arrivals at Oxford. One would be transient, the other permanent. At a house on the Banbury Road, Joseph and Emily Phipps arrived home with their new baby daughter. They had discussed possible names, and eventually decided on Mabel. The air was crisp and autumnal so Emily didn't linger as she stepped out of the carriage gently cradling her daughter, pulling up the blanket to make sure the cold didn't penetrate the child's warm cocoon. Her husband, Joseph, helped her and led her towards the door. The maid, Millie, waited on the step to greet them and gave a little bob curtsey as they passed. The fire was roaring in the parlour. Millie closed the big front door, glad to be shutting out the cold lest it should make the whole house chilly.

Not too far away at Magdalen College, the ten-year-old David Ivor Davies was escorted by his Mother, Clara Novello Davies, into the Presidents office. Sir Thomas Herbert Warren was a formidable but kindly character who had seen it all and was the living embodiment of a Victorian academic. He had a passion for poetry and music and dominated the very atmosphere of Magdalen. He was again captivated momentarily by Clara's sparkling diamond brooch, which puzzled him as such jewelry was possibly not suited to day-wear and struck him as rather ostentatious. His first impression of Clara had been less than positive. She had seemed a rather overbearing person with delusions of grandeur above her station in life. That said, her determination for him to a least audition her son for a chorister school scholarship had eventually worn him down with the hope she would give up and stop pestering him. He agreed to the audition and was quite convinced her son's abilities would not match her colourful and glowing descriptions. The boy had staggered him with his "raw and natural musical talent, and his soprano voice was remarkable and full of possibilities with the right training." For once he was wrong and accepted it with good grace. The scholarship had been immediately offered and accepted.

His attention then turned to the young David. He was a handsome child with a mop of dark hair and large, brown expressive eyes. His smile seemed to light up the room as he sat a little nervously by his mother's side. He was also remarkably confident for a ten-year-old, with a self-assurance that some twice his age did not possess. He decided there and then the boy had a quality that was hard to describe or define adequately; although he detected shrewdly there was an air of melancholy about him that could manifest itself into laziness if not managed promptly. Gossip about his abilities preceded him amongst the choristers.

"I remember the day that he arrived and we discovered he already had a remarkable musical talent," recalled a fellow pupil at Magdalen, Felix Aylmer, "we put him on a table and made him sing to us. I don't know whether I had similar vocal chords or what, but we always used to get our diseases at the same time of year. So we were constantly in the sickroom together, and when convalescing we used to make for the music-room and play duets. I remember him producing the first copy of *The Merry Widow*." This hugely popular Edwardian Operetta would inevitably have a huge influence on the young David in years to come.

Clara's dogged determination and a lifelong principle of never taking "no" for an answer was in part responsible for her young son's acceptance into the prestigious Magdalen College Choir School. Her husband had, for once in their marriage, put his foot down and adamantly refused to even consider David being sent to such an expensive fee paying establishment. This was not for reasons of denying his son a once in a lifetime opportunity, or as an act of stubbornness towards his wife, it was for purely practical reasons of a fiscal nature. His salary, and his wife's extravagance where money was concerned, had stretched his ability to keep them afloat. His occupation as a tax collector for the local council in Cardiff had status and a reasonable salary, but struggled to keep abreast of Clara's grand schemes and dreams. However, he didn't take into account his wife's obsession when it came to the musical education of their son. She stormed and screamed and pleaded he reconsider, as she believed it would be money well spent. But all to no avail. She then made enquiries and discovered a scholarship was available. She would get David a place by the only means possible - he would win that scholarship. And so it was, much to the consternation of her husband. She set about her mission and pestered Sir Thomas Herbert Warren mercilessly.

Who could blame her or any mother? After all music and singing was her life - and her occupation. She taught singing to anyone who wanted to learn regardless of their ability to pay. As a result she had a flat in London's Maida Vale, rooms in Gloucester, and of course their family home in Cardiff. With abounding energy she traveled between these three residences and taught all comers with her zest, enthusiasm and determination. Her client list included aristocrats, coal miners and there was never any distinction made between rich and poor. If anyone had a passion to sing or play the piano, Clara had equal passion to teach them - even if they paid her not a penny. This disregard for any kind of financial responsibility was a trait she had all her life. There is no record of what on earth her husband thought of these exploits, and the costs involved in terms of rent and servants. It must have been exhausting just to be with Clara, not to mention extremely frustrating having to struggle to support these exploits financially.

Her greatest personal success, and the one she rode on the glory of for most of her life, was the success she had achieved at the Chicago World's Fair in 1893. Leading the Welsh Ladies Choir at the prestigious event they had swept the board and won every prize and acclaim. This created such hysterical news coverage around the globe that it came to the attention of Queen Victoria. Clara was summoned along with the choir to perform for the old Queen at Windsor Castle. This was heaven to Clara and as far as she was concerned established her as a prominent person in the eyes of the monarch and the country as a whole. She had achieved fame and relished its possibilities. To add to the honour, Queen Victoria presented Clara with a diamond brooch as a token of gratitude for her hard work and the success she had brought to the nation. Clara would wear that brooch every day for the rest of her life, regardless of the outfit she was wearing, and worried not at all of its suitability as an appropriate adornment. Her fame was capitalized upon and savoured, but it didn't make the slightest difference to her eccentricities or lack of financial management skills.

The young David Davies must have felt more than a little nervous and intimidated by the atmosphere he encountered in Oxford during those early days. One must consider his age and the fact he was separated from his mother and father to live as a boarder at the school. For a ten-year-old it must have been an unsettling and daunting experience. He did settle down and he did work hard and make a name for himself as a boy soprano with a remarkable and clear voice. This won him many solo performance opportunities as Head Chorister and gave him a taste of the fame he would achieve in later years. His achievements are also noted for the more academic side of his studies and his grades were high for English and grammar. David's own account of his time at Oxford were in later years a little over sentimentalised and shrouded in the hype of celebrity speak. That said, they were the accounts of a normal young boy who embraced the atmosphere and the exceptional training it offered. He predictably sang solo the likes of *Oh For The Wings Of A Dove* at the Sheldonian Theatre, and also performed at the May Day ceremony atop the Magdalen Tower. These traditions still continue much the same as they did in David's time. His letters to his mother beseech her to send more food parcels, especially cakes and biscuits. They reflect the normal desires of juveniles separated from hearth and home and express a wish for "decent grub" as David put it succinctly. No matter what the food was like in halls, anything from home tasted delicious by way of association. As is usual with boys of his age he managed to get into trouble and was duly punished for his misdemeanors. Not so unusual; indeed had he not been the subject of such disciplinary admonishments it would have been more surprising.

Another contemporary was Brian GL Hickey, whose son Col. Michael Hickey remembered many stories his father passed on to him about the young David Davies and the overall experience at Magdalen. Many of the boys were "vile in their behaviour" he recalled, and were often in trouble for pranks or misdemeanors. The homosexual behaviour of some boys was rife and they were a prime target for many of the Dons who were predatory in their desire to seduce the young choristers. Indeed, some of the Dons were barred from entering the chapel and associating with the choristers as a result. Such was the threat from older Dons that choristers were encouraged to go everywhere in pairs. It would seem that the young David was himself embroiled in numerous sexual liaisons, and was on one occasion caught in the chapel behaving inappropriately with a fellow chorister. This was reported to Sir Thomas and, David and the other boy concerned, Webb, were duly punished and told in no uncertain terms that such an "abuse of the chapel" would not be tolerated. A letter focusing on the abuse of the chapel for "inappropriate behaviour" was duly sent to their parents and filed in the college records.

It was indeed at Magdalen under the watchful eye of Sir Thomas Herbert Warren and the Choir Master, John Varley Roberts, that the young David acquired his skills in musical composition, harmonic structure, and boy soprano abilities. There is no recorded evidence to the quality of David's voice, so much of its praise needs to be taken on the trust and objectivity of those who have recorded it for posterity. W McQueen Pope waxes lyrical about this early talent in his book *Ivor: The Story Of An Achievement*; but then he was a personal friend and PR guru to Novello the celebrity. However, there must be a great deal of truth in the claims as David would never have gained admittance to Magdalen Choir School without a fairly exceptional ability vocally; and he did become Head Chorister. The musical composition skills he would acquire would go on the serve him well in later life, but his career as a singer would not be enduring.

Varley Roberts was a force to be reckoned with at Magdalen and many claimed that he enhanced the reputation of the school during his time there. He was an eccentric Yorkshire man, who spoke with an equally broad Yorkshire accent. He ruled the boys with a rod of iron and could be vicious in his use of physical punishment. Many a chorister had been thwacked across the head with a heavy prayer book or music score for real and supposed misdemeanours. As Head Chorister, David would have been very much the focus of his attentions, and would have benefited from his considerable experience and skills. Varley Roberts was, beneath his frightening exterior, which often manifested itself in terrifying rages, a kind and gentle soul. He would often, for no apparent reason burst into tears, leaving the boys bemused and confused as to what brought on this overt show of emotion. Underneath, recalled Col. Hickey's father, he loved the boys and wanted the best for them.

His eccentricities were also evident in his renditions on the chapel organ. He loved to play Bach and would get so swept along in his enthusiasm, that he was known to forget what he was supposed to be playing and make up for it by sweeping into florid improvisations to cover his forgetfulness. During services in the chapel he forbade any of the congregation to join in singing the psalms with the choristers. On one occasion he heard a male voice from the congregation joining in, and abruptly stopped playing the organ. The choristers struggled on unaccompanied, as Varley Roberts dramatically swished back the curtain concealing the organ, and promptly glared furious and red faced at the errant congregation member. David and his fellow choristers struggled to keep their composure and not erupt into the laughter they could feel welling up inside them. The poor man in the congregation was of a certain age and oblivious to Varley Roberts' fury, his face so red it seemed it would pop, accompanied by the steam coming from his ears. At the conclusion of the service David, Hickey, Webb and others were convulsed with laughter whilst changing. A few minutes later Varley Roberts swept in, gown flapping with the coordination of an inebriated bat, and announced happily that the errant member of the congregation was in fact an "old boy" and was so overcome with emotion had felt he had to join in with the choristers, as he had in his youth. So he could be forgiven and Varley Roberts happy again. In this almost surreal and eccentric environment, David would enjoy every opportunity that presented itself; be that of a physical nature or of the more intellectual or musical educational aspects of Magdalen life.

Another ludicrous situation arose during a Christmas Eve gathering of the Oxford Fellowes. The Fellowes were lavishly entertained at this annual event in the Great Hall at Magdalen. The choristers duly sang the first part of Handle's *Messiah* and then a banquet would be served to the Fellowes. After the meal, the choristers then had to perform the second part of the *Messiah*. As the Fellowes were indulging themselves some of the choristers managed to sneak away some wine and sherry and began to drink heartily. During the final part of the Messiah, one boy had drunk so much he was turning green with inebriation. During a somber section of the concert he vomited violently into the Grand Piano. Varley Roberts, accompanying on the piano, was furious and, with his face popping with rage, just glared at the poor boy and dared him to falter with his solo. He duly carried on to the end and was finally carried away by his fellow choristers amid much hilarity. No doubt the holidays were eagerly anticipated, if only to allow Varley Roberts time to calm down.

David would go on home visits and stay with his mother at her flat initially in Maida Vale, but during his time at Oxford she moved to more central and spacious accommodations in Hanover Square. No doubt to the horror of her husband who would have fretted about the costs as usual. It was during these home visits that the young David started to visit the West End's theatres and became obsessed with the famous Edwardian actress Lily Elsie. In 1907 she was playing the lead in Lehar's operetta *The Merry Widow* at Daly's Theatre. In today's parlance it would have been termed a "smash hit." All London flocked to see the production and, more unusual at the time, it appealed to rich and poor alike. Not too far away the Gaiety Girls captivated audiences at the Gaiety Theatre. The charms and talent of Gertie Millar, George Grossmith, Edmund Payne and Connie Ediss held court nightly. Personalities that are now forgotten, but in their day household names. David watched them all from the gods of the theatre and never forgot what he saw.

The Gaiety Theatre and Daly's Theatre are long gone but both were the most eminent and famous West End establishments of the time. Daly's Theatre was situated in Leicester Square and was built in 1893. Designed by Spencer Chadwick and Charles John Phipps under commission of the theatre director John Augustin Daly. It was demolished in 1937 to make way for the Warner Cinema. The Gaiety gazed elegantly down the Strand from Aldwych. It first opened its doors in 1864 as the Strand Musick Hall (sic), rebuilt by Charles John Phipps in 1896, to be replaced by a brand new building in 1903 when it reopened its doors as the Gaiety Theatre. After laying empty for many years after being bombed in WWII it became almost derelict and was demolished completely in 1957 to be replaced by offices.

During her time at Daly's Theatre, Lily Elsie was regarded as a poised, elegant and very charismatic star with huge popular appeal. Her image was reproduced in the hundreds of thousands in magazines, periodicals and on post cards. The young David would pester his mother's servants to give him pennies so he could purchase a ticket to watch Lily Elsie's performance from the gods of the theatre. He admitted to going time and time again just to study her and for the "thrill of hearing her sing the Widow." As the show was quite long, he even managed to see other plays and still manage to get to the Daly's for the last act; often sneaking in unnoticed by the theatre staff. Much of what he experienced during these visits to the West End of the Edwardian age, in terms of production values and quality and talent, he absorbed into his own artistic aspirations.

The years prior to 1914 was a time of great wealth and prosperity with the heart of the British Empire still beating and controlling. Income tax thresholds were set at such a high level that only a small percentage of the population were liable, and other taxation was also at a minimum. Indeed it was also a very imbalanced society which almost encouraged the accumulation of wealth for the few while the vast majority of the population were quite poor and struggled to make ends meet. Theatres and Music Halls were the forms of mass entertainment at the time as there were no other competitors. Cinema had yet to be developed and refined into a story-telling art form and there was no radio or television. The theatre also offered a window to a world of excitement and glamour which many, like David, could only dream of.

This lost Edwardian world of elegant poverty was the world that the young David absorbed into his very being. Its values in terms of the quality of productions in the theatre which he witnessed he never forgot and when opportunity arose he emulated those standards in a time when they had been all but forgotten. Indeed they were the very standards which set him apart from the rest and made his shows shine and "fill the plush" like no others. Usually to the bewilderment and consternation of those with more high-brow aspirations.

At the time of his frequent visits to see Lily Elsie as *The Merry Widow*, he announced to his mother he didn't want to be a musician, instead he wanted to go on the stage as an actor. Clara was horrified. She had fought so hard and struggled so much to give David the best of opportunities to develop into a fine musician and composer and, as far as she was concerned, that is what he would do. It must be remembered that the profession of acting was looked down on quite severely by polite society at the time. Voicing a desire or decision to work in the theatre as an actor or performer was tantamount to declaring an intention to set up as a prostitute. The reverence and respect shown to actors today did not exist in the pre war era of Edwardian society. Clara listened and smiled and made a mental note to make sure this ridiculous desire never came to fruition for her son. She would put a stop to it whatever the cost or action required. But in spite of his dream, life went on and David continued at Magdalen until his personal bubble burst spectacularly, which resulted in the first real traumatic experience of his young life. The year was 1909, he was sixteen years-old.

Legend has it that David had sung a solo in The Sheldonian Theatre one night to great success and was showered with compliments. The next morning he awoke with a sore throat and rushed to see the school doctor. He was informed his voice had broken and his boy soprano days were over. David left an account of this day and described how shocked and distraught he "ran to Angel Meadow crying bitter tears" whence he flung himself down on the grass and "cried for hours at this injustice."

With the breaking of his voice it was alleged his association with Magdalen and Oxford also came to an end. He could no longer be a chorister without a voice and, brutal as it seemed, brought to an end this period of his young life. At least that was the official version of his sudden departure. The truth was in fact a little less dramatic, tragic or sentimental in flavour. Col. Hickey recalls his father saying on several occasions that Novello was in fact "asked to leave" under a cloud. He had become so active and obvious in his homosexual behaviour with choristers and Dons that it could no longer be tolerated or swept under the carpet. This also resulted in him not being eligible for a bursary that would have enabled him to continue his education at Magdalen after his voice broke. The choristers were never discarded when they could no longer sing. All Novello's contemporaries, including Hickey, received such a bursary and completed their education. David didn't because he had been asked to leave due to his overt homosexual behaviour. Understandable then why he should want to reinvent the reasons for his sudden departure years later when he enjoyed international celebrity status.

Col. Hickey's father did keep in touch with David, and years later would attend a performance of *The Truth Game* which starred Novello and Lily Elsie. The occasion was Col. Hickeys parent's marriage in 1928. Novello asked them back stage and gave them a signed personal photograph. Col.

Hickey recalled that "my mother was so overcome at meeting him she couldn't quite believe it" and she treasured the memory of that occasion.

David's life after Magdalen was bitter, and he soon discovered that, as happens to some boy sopranos, his voice had gone for good and henceforth he struggled to hold a tune vocally and there was no hope of retraining to improve it. Clara comforted him and welcomed him at her residence in Hanover Square. David's father decided and promptly suggested he should make applications to Cardiff council for a good but safe desk job. Clara stamped on this immediately, much to her son's relief. Finally defeated, her husband gave up and resigned himself to fading into the background of his eccentric and strong willed wife and equally errant son. Instead the young David would offer piano lessons to paying pupils and work on his own compositions, alongside his mother who continued to impart her exuberant style of training to those willing to pay for the art of singing and piano. David began trying to compose songs and sent off many efforts to London's music publishers. All were returned with rejection slips but he carried on in spite of these early disappointments. It was at this time he made the decision to change his name to Ivor Novello. It sounded a bit more exotic and romantic than David Davies, and it was hoped it would encourage a music publisher to accept his work. Ivor was his middle name, and Novello had been the name of his mother's maternal grandmother, so it seemed the perfect, if not slightly grandiose, solution.

The year 1914 would change everything for Ivor Novello and the rest of the World. Little did he realize that history was preparing the ground for his first commercial success, albeit a success that was borne out of the greater horrors that would unfold, and instigate some intriguing meetings. He would find himself involved with the descendent of the only British Prime Minister to be murdered, be offered artistic support using "murder money", narrowly escape death in a plane crash, meet Winston Churchill and a young actor called Robert Andrews.

In Search of Ruritania

SPRING OF THE CAREER

"I have never had any ambitions. I have been content to enjoy their success."

David Davies - Novello's father.

Sir Thomas Herbert Warren had been right about Novello's melancholy and his innate ability to be lazy. Novello did recognise both of these traits in himself which went a long way to help him control them. That said he would at times relinquish himself to the joy of being completely lazy and equally allow himself to be engulfed by melancholy. He also managed to turn them to his advantage and subsume these elements into his creative drives - but only eventually.

Exposed to the harsh realities of life made Novello grow up fairly quickly once he had departed the charmed existence he enjoyed at Magdalen College and Oxford. After a brief, and wholly unsuccessful sojourn at a music school in Gloucester, where the principal declared Novello to be "too lazy to achieve anything", he returned to Hanover Square. For the first time he experienced the need to work and generate an income on which to survive. During the first couple of years his mother had to bully him into doing something productive. He reluctantly, for the most part, began to teach piano to usually inept pupils, mostly young girls from well-to-do families. He was earnest in his desire to help his pupils but found it infuriating that few of them had any real ability or talent to progress satisfactorily - at least to his demanding standards. Perhaps much of his frustration was as a result of feeling lost and aimless and being in a position financially where he had to earn a living and contribute to the household expenses. All this forced responsibility managed to achieve was to propel him into the depths of melancholia. In fairness to his equally earnest pupils, Novello was probably just not cut out to be a teacher in that monotonous kind of routine. One thing he hated was repetition, it created boredom which he also detested. He openly admitted his absolute hate of having to physically carry anything; this loathing remained with him for the rest of his life. He did manage to salve his creative aspirations by frequenting the West End's theatres and especially the melodramas and pantomimes at the Theatre Royal, Drury Lane. He loved the spectacle and excitement of the earthquakes, erupting volcanoes, train crashes and other such effects created realistically on the stage of that respected theatre. These were events he would never forget and create them in his own way at that very theatre in years to come. But at the moment he was almost penniless and feeling pretty fed up about his lot in life.

Another contention for Novello at this time was his sexuality. During his time at Oxford, as we have discovered, he did indeed have sexual encounters with other boys and Dons and a recollection of those exploits has been passed on by one of his contemporaries. As unpalatable as it might seem to some, most young boys have some kind of homosexual dalliance; borne out of curiosity and sexual awakening generally. The percentage who are actually homosexual by true nature is miniscule. More often than not those who were willing to participate in such experimentation would then ridicule the object of their tryst as a way to deflect any suspicion on themselves. This kind of behaviour would further confuse those whose nature it was into thinking they were the only person in the world to crave same sex experiences. It is all part of the psychological trauma one suffers when "coming out" as we say today, but in Novello's time there was just personal acceptance of one's sexuality and no "coming out" except to those nearest and dearest who were deemed as trustworthy. It is now widely accepted that homosexuality is something one is born with and not, as was widely believed at that time, an illness that was to be despised and cured by whatever means possible. In the first part of the 20th Century it was certainly something that was never discussed or admitted, as being a practicing homosexual was also a criminal offence; resulting in a fairly hefty jail sentence for those caught, not to mention the ever present threat of blackmail should anyone discover the fact. Thus it became something hidden and secretive to all but those who participated in such activities.

One such example of the secrecy was the formation of the "Yellow Sock Club" for homosexual men in London. Its primary function was a secret form of communication to those like-minded in their sexual desires. There were of course certain clubs and bars that were frequented by homosexuals who naturally mixed with heterosexuals. Should you see a chap wearing yellow socks, it was a silent form of communication to let other like-minded men know he wanted to meet someone for sex. Intriguing and probably quite exciting in an illicit kind of way. There is comedy though to be found in all situations, and I can't help wondering how many chaps innocently wore yellow socks and found themselves bewildered at the knowing looks and winks from other men whenever they wore them.

Most people find it difficult to understand the agonies and trauma of coming to terms with homosexual feelings. These feelings can trigger an emotional vortex which leaves the bearer exhausted, but eventually wiser and more content. Some never come to terms with their nature and others fight it to the last. Many men have married some poor unsuspecting woman in the belief that once married the curse of being attracted to other men will leave them; and also to save constantly being asked why they never married and thus not confirming to societies expectations. Of course it doesn't and, seeing it from a logical and emotionally unattached perspective, never could. Novello did experiment with his sexuality and these wilderness years were where he fought his demons and finally came to accept his sexuality as something with which he could do nothing about but embrace. This kind of emotional development and struggle, as Novello discovered, can actually make for a much stronger person and also allows a heightened understanding of people's emotional needs and sensibilities. Vitally for Novello, it helped him find a way of connecting with people's emotions far more easily that most. Paradoxically, it can also serve to make women far more attracted to you. Novello always loved women for their elegance, beauty and wisdom. Women found him quite irresistible and it has to be said that he was a very handsome and charismatic character with an abundance of charm. All of which he would utilise and take full advantage of to progress his career.

In spite of being a handsome looking young man, he was also quite feminine in his demeanour. Today we would call this quality "camp", although not in an over the top Kenneth William's way, but he also possessed a wicked sense of humour and quick wit. This can be evidenced today when analysing his performance in the film of his original stage play *I Lived With You*. It gives an indication of his charisma and also his ability to write comedy; indeed his ability to deliver comic dialogue with near perfect timing and panache. It is then no surprise that he had admirers and willing lovers aplenty. Shrewdly he subsumed all these elements and his natural melancholia into his later characterisations as an actor which made him appealing to both men and women as a celebrity. His music in later years would also have an undertone of melancholy which would make it unique and unforgettable.

Novello decided to broaden his horizons, and having been bitten by the acting bug he was determined to do something about it. After a trip to Daly's Theatre he made the decision he would definitely become an actor. He once again announced this intention to Clara who promptly bit her lip and said nothing. Inside she was seething with anger and was determined this would not happen under any circumstances. She knew it would be pointless arguing with her son as she recognised her own stubbornness in him. Instead she smiled and bided her time. Novello went along to Daly's for an open audition for the chorus of a new show that would initially go on tour. He figured that although it was only chorus work he would get some valuable stage experience and learn some technique, but most importantly he would be on a stage! He auditioned rather well and was offered a contract. Informed by the management the rehearsals would begin shortly, and that a letter would be sent to him with the date and time he should report to the theatre. Novello was ecstatic and promptly rushed home to tell his mother the exciting news. She listened and smiled. As the days went on Novello threw himself into teaching his pupils and enjoyed the fact that it wouldn't be for much longer. After a couple of weeks had passed he thought it odd he hadn't heard from the management of the theatre. After three weeks he was truly puzzled and said so to his mother. She placated him by saying that one really couldn't trust theatre people, they were all unreliable. Better then if he concentrate on his music and compositions. After all, he had finally had a piece published. *Spring Of The Year* was indeed published in 1911 and sold a few copies, but they never set the world afire and made him no money apart from his small retainer fee from the publisher; which they promptly cancelled at the end of his initial twelve-month contract. The song was performed during a recital at The Royal Albert Hall by Miss Evangeline Florence, and described by the *Daily Telegraph* reviewer on 1st July, 1911, as "a gay and fanciful song," performed "in such a persuasive fashion with its light-hearted phrases that she easily achieved success." In fact the performance had been a disaster and resulted in a slow clapping of hands which embarrassed Novello and Miss Florence. She promptly admonished Novello for a less than satisfactory job of accompanying her. He was understandably wounded by this experience. Clara was quick to voice her opinion on the matter:

"So it was through the public that Ivor was given his first lesson in failure, and had his early ideas of easy success rudely shaken. And I was glad to have it so…"

The arrogance of youth was firmly put in its place and thus learned from. It does give an interesting insight into the petulance in his character at this time, and how his mother could quite happily slap him down a peg or two when she felt it was needed.

Clara promptly spurred him on to keep composing by informing him that Chappell Music Publishers were holding a competition for new composers to submit a score for a show. He set about working on what turned into his first operetta *The Fickle Jade*. He was filled with enthusiasm and became blinkered to the world as he worked on the book and the score of the show. It would be the first time he had attempted such a feat and not only enjoyed the experience but utilised much about the knowledge he had slowly acquired whilst watching all those plays and operettas in the past. It allowed him to put into practice his understanding of structure and form that is vital to anyone attempting to craft a theatre production. It requires an ability to not only create plot, storyline and characters but also embellish the whole with original music and songs. He surprised even himself. He was awarded second prize for *The Fickle Jade*. Hopes ran high that a production of the operetta would follow but it came to nothing. Another blow to his career aspirations that caused frustration and bouts of depression. In fact *The Fickle Jade* was never produced; although he did use some musical compositions from it in later shows.

To make matters worse Novello never heard from the Daly's management. By chance he happened to open a drawer in his mother's side table and there, to his horror, he found several post cards from Daly's. One read:

" Dear Mr Novello,

As you have failed to attend rehearsals, or to contact us by way of reply to our various communications, I have no choice but to inform you we have replaced you and thus no longer have need of your services."

Novello was furious at this terrible betrayal. He had taken more rejections and knocks to his confidence than he could stand and this discovery was the last straw. His own mother had deliberately sabotaged this opportunity by deception. He angrily rounded on her and accused her of trying to destroy his career. How she would do such a thing was beyond him and he swore never to speak to her again. She countered his anger by shedding floods of tears and pleading with him to understand she had done it only for his own good. She recognised his ability as a musician and she didn't want him to waste his time as an actor on the stage. She was convinced he would be successful and begged for his forgiveness. At his refusal to speak to her she took to her bed and announced she would not go on living in a world where her son could treat her so callously. Clara cleverly turned the situation around and made herself the injured party. It was the first of many more dramatic "death bed scenes", as Novello described them, she would play out in the coming years when she didn't get her own way over something. Gloria Swanson, or *Sunset Boulevard's* Norma Desmond, couldn't hold a candle to Clara when it came to dramatic scenes. Naturally after a couple of days of silence, apart from sobs of unhappiness emitting from her bedroom, and her refusal to eat anything, Novello gave in and pleaded forgiveness and begged her to get up and carry on. After obligatory tears and kisses of joy she leapt out of bed with her usual energy, as if nothing untoward had happened, and all was well once more. Their daily routine would continue once more underpinned by Clara's untiring zeal!

The outbreak of First World War in 1914 was the beginning of the end of the old order and, as it turned out, the seeds of the British Empire's demise were also sown. Not that it was apparent in those first weeks and months of the conflict. It would be the last time that young men would blindly march into war with joyous hearts, willing to sacrifice themselves for King and Country. It is hard for us to imagine today the social structures that were in place up to 1914. British subjects knew their place in the social scheme and never thought it was possible, indeed would never have conceived such a notion, to be dissatisfied with their place in society. The Royal family were revered and all demonstrated a deference to them. The aristocracy were dominant in politics and those running the country kept the old orders and traditions in place. Due to the incredible transformation initiated by shrewd Victorians the country was prosperous and had led the world in innovation and industrialisation. Many had feared the death of Queen Victoria in 1901 would see her errant son Edward VII dismantle and destroy his mother's legacy and plunge the country into crisis. This widely held belief was due in part to his irresponsible and, for the time, highly scandalous and immoral lifestyle as the Prince of Wales. The fears however were to be unfounded. As King many felt he embellished and heightened the standing of Great Britain around the world. It is true he loosened the over-tight propriety corset his mother had insisted on since the death of his father, Prince Albert, but by loosening the stays he enabled the whole country to breathe deeply and thus function with renewed vigour. The Edwardian era had been a great success and it was no longer frowned upon to enjoy the fruits on one's labour. It was okay to enjoy life and prosper if possible. It was cut short by his death in 1910 when he was succeeded by his son George V and his Queen Consort, Mary. Echoes of the Edwardian principles continued. Some say this Golden age died with the sinking of the Titanic in 1912, others at the outbreak of First World War in 1914.

During the first few months of the war Novello continued much as he had done. His mother kept up the pressure on him to keep composing music and songs with an eye to their possible publication. Clara was in some ways very shrewd and knew her son extremely well indeed. She knew he could be lazy and was always concerned that this trait would be his downfall. She knew better than most that to be successful in this world you have to make people listen to you, work hard and never give up. Never taking "no" for an answer is harder work than it might first appear, but it can bring results as she knew too well. All her life she had fought for any success or recognition she had received, and she was determined her son would do the same. His bouts of depression and "sad eyed melancholy" when things went against him made her outwardly furious with him, but inwardly she worried that these demons would suffocate the talent she knew he possessed. It is not clear why he was not called up for war service at the outset, but it was probably as a result of a heart murmur he suffered from around this time. It did cause some concern initially and he was eventually given a clean bill of health toward the end of 1915.

Towards the end of 1914 Clara had declared mischievously, with the intention of rallying her son out of his lethargy, that she would compose a song appropriate for the war - something to cheer up the troops. She composed a song and promptly sat Novello down to play and sing it to him. He was horrified at the result and demanded she never let anyone hear it. Sadly there is no evidence of this effort so we could judge for ourselves, but it certainly rallied Novello into action when Clara declared she would only agree to his request if he composed a song that was better. This had been her intention all along. He set to work and produced a song that would change his fortunes and his life. The song was called *Keep The Home Fires Burning* and was sentimental in flavour thus perfect for capitalising on the public mood at the time. The other significant event of 1915 was Clara's decision to move to more affordable accommodations, the Hanover Square apartments had become too expensive to maintain, and she also gave up the accommodations she rented in Gloucester. Clara had taken a new lease on a flat which sat on top of the West End's Strand Theatre, number 11 Aldwych. *Keep The Home Fires Burning* was the first thing Novello composed on moving into their new home. He decided it was a lucky address and lived there until he died in his bedroom in "the flat", as it was to be famously called, in 1951.

He had collaborated with an American woman called Lena Gilbert Ford on the lyrics of the song, and she is thus credited on the sheet music. The tragedy for Miss Ford is that she was only able to enjoy her contribution for but a short time. She was killed, along with her young son, when a German Zeppelin dropped a bomb on her Maida Vale house. It was one of the last air raid attacks on London where civilians were killed. Novello was to say some years later that he had in fact written most of the lyrics and that Miss Ford had only contributed a couple of lines. Whether this were the case or not, Miss Ford was unable to enjoy any of the royalties which would eventually flood in. Novello performed his song at a Sunday League concert at The Alambra Theatre, Leicester Square, for the first time and had been amazed how, by the repeat of the chorus, the audience had picked up the melody and were singing along. The song was instantly published and began to sell well. Most households at this time had a piano in the parlour and would enjoy singing at gatherings and family events. There was little else in the way of domestic entertainment.

During this period Novello had become friendly with the actress Viola Tree, the daughter of Sir Herbert Tree. They attended a performance by Lily Elsie, at His Majesty's Theatre, when Viola spotted Edward Marsh. Marsh was a family friend and worked for the government - he was Winston Churchill's private secretary. Viola introduced Novello and explained he was the composer of the new popular song *Keep The Home Fires Burning*. Marsh had never heard of it and was a little baffled and exclaimed "keep the what?" Novello took this on the chin and saw the funny side, indeed it became a long standing joke between them for many years. Viola promptly began to hum the melody and Marsh said he had indeed heard it but didn't know the title. Marsh and Novello became firm friends from this point and he even offered Novello artistic support if he needed it from his "murder money" fund. As it turned out it wasn't necessary because the royalties for the song began to arrive, Novello earned over fifteen thousand pounds, a huge amount of money at that time, along with lots of offers from theatrical managements who needed songs for their revue shows. Nevertheless Novello was naturally intrigued by the "murder money" offer and asked Marsh to explain.

By a quirk of fate, death and birth Marsh had become eligible to receive an annuity granted to his family, on his mother's side, after the assassination of one of his ancestors at the Houses Of Parliament. The ancestor was Spencer Percival, who at the time of his murder was the Prime Minister; indeed the only Prime Minister of this country to be murdered. He was shot by a timber merchant known as Bellingham who was impoverished by the government's refusal to pay him compensation for cargo lost at sea. Bellingham had been advised to make representations of his case to a member of the Cabinet; but all to no avail. He blamed his misfortune on what he considered to be the incompetence of the Prime Minister's government.

Thus on Monday, May 11th, 1812, Spencer Percival, the Prime Minister, accompanied by Lord Osborne, entered the lobby of the House of Commons. It was a quarter-past five in the afternoon. Lord Osbourne stood aside to allow the Prime Minister to enter first. The shot was fired by Bellingham who was standing in the lobby, and the Prime Minister slumped to the floor. He was heard to utter "Oh, I am murdered." Bellingham was jostled to the ground whilst the Prime Minister was carried to a sofa in the smoking room, where he died a few minutes later. A surgeon arrived from Great George Street and upon examination of the victim announced that a ball of "unusually large size had penetrated the very centre of the heart."

The Commons and the Lords were united in providing for the welfare of the late Prime Minster's family. A loyal address was sent to the Prince Regent with their proposal. The widow should receive one thousand pounds a year for life, and that a sum of fifty thousand pounds be held in trust for the twelve surviving children and their descendents. The Prince Regent gave the Royal assent to the grant. This enabled the Prime Minister's eldest son, Spencer, Edward Marsh's grandfather, to continue his studies at Harrow.

As for Bellingham, he was duly tried and found guilty of murder and sentenced to death by hanging. At his trial he had this to say:

"A merchant ship owned by myself and my partner had been lost in the White Sea, and although I had taken the precaution of having it insured at Lloyd's Coffee House I received no compensation. On getting no sympathy from the British in Russia I admit I became violent and abusive in my protests, and was thrown into prison without trial. On my return to England I consulted one authority after another, beginning with the Marquis Wellesley, and at last was advised to petition Parliament. This I set about doing after my third appeal to the Prince Regent had elicited no reply. I then called on my own M.P., General Gascoyne, the Member for Liverpool, who advised me to get sanction of a Cabinet minister. This led to an interview with the Prime Minister, Spencer Percival, who saw no good reason to support my claims."

On the death of an uncle nearly a century later, Edward Marsh became an heir to one sixth of the grant. Marsh always referred to it as his "murder money" and he decided to put this unexpected windfall to good use. Marsh was a homosexual and keen poet and supporter of the arts generally. He had formed the Georgian Poets Society, and became the self-proclaimed editor of the publication of the same name. Marsh also had a particular liking for young, handsome and talented men. Novello became one of the select few that Marsh considered worthy of his support. They included Robert Graves, Wilfred Own, Sassoon and Rupert Brooke. Rupert Brooke was his particular favourite but most benefited from the "murder money", along with the devotion of their benefactor, to ease their financial burdens. It is in large part due to Marsh that Brooke was able to develop his talent, devoid of any financial worries, and become one of the most famous of the war poets.

Marsh had contracted an illness as a child that had left him physically undeveloped sexually and thus impotent. He compensated by admiring the bodies of beautiful young men and enjoyed looking at their naked bodies as they slept. Brooke would often stay with Marsh and had a special fold away camp bed he would use on such visits. For many years after Brooke's death, Marsh would gaze at the permanently displayed camp bed and shed floods of tears as he recalled how handsome Brooke had been. The camp bed was always referred to reverently as "Rupert's bed." There were others who benefited from Marsh's benevolence, but Novello and Brooke were his favourites.

Once the success of *Keep The Home Fires Burning* had established Novello and, more importantly, brought him to the attention of West End theatre managements, his output as a composer was prolific. Revue shows were the staple diet of popular entertainment and the war had created a huge demand for satirical and comedy shows which offered escapism to the grim realities of events in the trenches on the western front. Most of these early songs are very much of their time and their meaning and significance are lost out of context. They were inevitably war orientated and the titles speak for themselves *Laddie In Khaki* , *When The Great Day Comes*, *Just A Jack Or A Tommy* and *Radiance Of Your Eyes* were all published in 1915. Novello was also commissioned, along with Jerome Kern to write songs and music for a new Gaiety Theatre show called *Theodore & Co* in 1916. He also provided songs and music for Andre Charlot's revue *See-Saw* at the Comedy Theatre in 1916.

Novello's friendship with Edward Marsh had become established by this time. After being given a clean bill of health the matter of war service now came to the fore. In 1916 Novello was 23 years old and could not avoid active duty any longer. Marsh suggested he enlist with the Royal Naval Air Service, as the initial training was undertaken in England and would thus prevent Novello being shipped off to France and the trenches. He duly enlisted and was stationed at Crystal Palace for his basic training.

The basic training shocked Novello in its brutality. Early mornings and physical exercise were his idea of hell on earth; playing sports even more so. Marching around a parade ground, and cross country runs, in the freezing cold with Officers screaming in his ear, he found almost unbearable. But he persevered and completed this initial stage of his initiation. Then his flying lessons started in earnest. From the out-set it didn't go at all well. After several hours of tuition Novello was obliged to take his first solo flight, which terrified him. He managed to take off fairly well and then envisaged flying around the sky until the fuel ran out as he had no idea how to land the plane. All the patient demonstrations carried out by his instructors had been in vain. He managed to get the aircraft within feet of the earth in an attempt to land when it flipped over and crashed. It burst into flames and the ground crew rushed to the wreckage fearing the worst, but miraculously Novello walked away without a scratch.

In spite of this he carried on to fly another day. Among the other airmen he was very popular, and enjoyed playing the piano and generally entertaining them in the mess. He continued to compose songs and music for shows in the West End, even though strictly speaking it wasn't allowed as he was in service. After several more close shaves, and the destruction of two more aircraft, the powers that be decided that Novello was not cut out to be an airman. Edward Marsh came to his aid once again and, by using his influence in government circles, managed to secure Novello a safe desk job at the Air Ministry. He was given an office in the Hotel Cecil, near Whitehall, which the War Office had requisitioned for the duration. Novello was relieved and managed to endure the boredom involved because he was able to live at "the flat", and continue to be part of the theatre world that surrounded it. Marsh had his reasons for protecting his new friend. He had suffered from the death of his adored Rupert Brooke in 1915, the same year he became enamoured by Novello. In many ways Novello filled the emotional void left by Brooke's death, no surprise then that he would do everything he could to protect him.

Marsh encouraged Novello to broaden his mind by encouraging him to read widely and also to practice writing poetry and prose. To further his education Marsh gave him Brooke's *Letters from America* to study and also encouraged him to set established poems to music. Marsh, on his daily visits to "the flat", 11 Aldwych, was bewildered by Novello's parents and declared that his Father "seldom did anything but amiably stare into space" and added he was "the laziest man I have ever met." Clara he found overbearing at times and so caught up in teaching singing she had "little time for anything but her own exploits." From this he concluded "there was something of a parental vacuum at 11 Aldwych, which I unobtrusively took upon my self to fill."

As the war progressed Novello composed songs and music for a musical comedy *Arlette* at the Shaftsbury Theatre, 1917, Charlot's Revue *Tabs* at the Vaudeville Theatre, 1918, and began working on music for the musical comedy *Who's Hooper* eventually presented at the Adelphi Theatre, 1919. This last show included a song with both words and music by Novello titled *There's An Angel Watching Over Me*. That song could certainly have been dedicated to Edward Marsh who had indeed been watching over him. There is little doubt that Novello would have been packed off to the trenches without the influence, intervention and support of his influential friend.

Marsh also introduced Novello to Winston Churchill and his wife Clementine at this time. Lady Randolph Churchill, Winston's mother, invited Marsh to bring Novello to dinner. She was intrigued to meet his latest protégé and admired *Keep The Home Fires Burning* (Novello had started to call it 'Keep The What?' by this time to tease Marsh). The friendship between Marsh and Lady Randolph was based on their mutual interest in the arts generally. Indeed Lady Randolph was the first to champion a National Theatre for Britain and had raised funds to the tune of one hundred thousand pounds. This money would eventually be used for the National Theatre, but many years hence. Winston was fascinated by Novello and they ended up singing risqué music hall songs as the evening progressed; much to the delight of those present. At some point in the evening Churchill bellowed at Novello "you'd be much better off in a home!," which caused an uneasy silence in the room for a couple of seconds. Novello, Marsh and Lady Randolph exchanged nervous glances, to which Churchill began laughing heartily. It transpired *You'd Be Much Better Off In A Home* was the title of a music hall song he liked. The meeting was a great success and started a life-long friendship.

Marsh's influence also allowed Novello to illicit an invitation to 10 Downing Street. The Prime Minister's wife, Margo Asquith, was a friend of Lily Elsie, and had arranged for her to be there to meet Novello. Afternoon tea was served in the drawing room and Novello attempted to play Elsie, as she was known to her friends, music he'd composed for a new operetta he had in mind for her. Every time he began to play the piano, a regimental band struck up on Horse Guards Parade, much to his annoyance, but Elise's amusement. The final straw, Novello recalled, was when "Mrs. Asquith made her entrance in time to the music and waltzed around the furniture." Not the most successful meeting with the woman he so admired from *The Merry Widow*, but it began a friendship that would result in a future collaboration between Elsie and Novello.

During 1917 Novello was attending the first night of a play called *Under Cover* at the Strand Theatre. He was accompanied by Edward Marsh. During the interval Marsh introduced Novello to a young flying officer. His name was Robert Andrews. Andrews had been a child actor and had carried on in the profession until he was called up for active service. He was also a homosexual and became Novello's lover and partner for the rest of his life;

although it has to be said that their relationship was far from monogamous! The title of the play was rather appropriate as their relationship remained publicly *Under Cover*, except to a chosen few of Novello's inner circle. It is perhaps wholly appropriate that the West End theatre in which they met, lived in "the flat" above, and produced several of Novello's plays, is the theatre which has now been re-named the Novello Theatre by Sir Cameron Mackintosh.

But at this time Marsh noted that he thought " Novello was a mercurial being of whim and impulse, unorganised, as indolent as his father, gentle in his ways, absolutely lacking in affectation." He also concluded that Novello "had received little guidance or understanding at home where there was seldom much domestic harmony beyond what came out of the piano. It's time like these when one wishes he had a family life in the usual sense of the word - to have been properly taken care of." Marsh was also concerned for Novello's health due to being "feverish with over excitement he had [already] been obliged to see a doctor for treatment of the heart."

Marsh was determined to educate Novello's mind, and to take on a paternal role in his life. He saw possibilities in his young protégé to develop into an artist capable of writing and composing music that was of a much higher standard than the "rag time music hall" efforts he'd produced for revue shows various to date.

By the end of the war Novello was enjoying the financial fruits of his labours. He was receiving royalties for the music and songs he contributed to successful West End productions, and the money was still rolling in from *Keep The Home Fires Burning*. He had also taken over the lease on "the flat" from Clara, allowing some privacy for Bobbie and himself at last. He was also demobbed, much to his relief, and could finally concentrate on his future. Not wanting to be too far away, Clara had moved into a similar flat, along with her husband, situated on top of the Aldwych Theatre.

As the 1920s approached Novello had every reason to be pleased with his achievements so far. However, the winter of 1918/19 had a shock in store for a world not yet recovered from the carnage of the trenches. It would kill more people than had lost their lives in the war; and worse, make no distinction between children, the young or the old, male or female, rich or poor. It was the worst flu pandemic ever recorded, and it killed an estimated 40 million around the world. The unique structure of the virus meant the majority of the victims were aged between 20 and 40-years-old.

The tragic events of the war and the subsequent flu pandemic resulted in an even greater shortage of young men in society. These events played a part in ensuring the handsome, romantic image and personality of Novello would fill a void in many lives - an emotional one. Fate and history would once again pave the way for Novello's future success.

ROARING THROUGH THE 1920s

*"There are only two perfect things in this world.
My wit, and Ivor's profile!"*

Noel Coward.

Battered and weary from the war and in shock from the viciousness of the flu pandemic, the world slowly began to recover some sense of normality. The age of the spinster and widow had also arrived. So many young men had been killed in the war that women outnumbered men greatly even before the flu pandemic cut another huge swathe through the male population of England. All those women needed someone or something to admire and love, or at least fill the emotional void that had opened up in their lives. There was little sympathy or solace for those who wallowed in their loss or lack of emotional support. Everyone had suffered terribly and the general consensus was to appreciate the fact that life had spared you. Stoicism was the order of the day, so upper lips were stiffened and that was that.

Relieved the war was over, and as a result of his new found wealth, Novello decided to take a holiday to New York. His publisher's had surprised him by sending a royalty cheque worth several hundred pounds. On enquiry he was told it was the royalties from USA sales of *Keep The Home Fires Burning* accrued during the war. After that he needed little prompting and arranged Atlantic crossing passages for Bobbie, himself and Clara. This trip is worth mentioning because he encountered a couple of people who would become his friends in the future.

Noel Coward was in New York on holiday when Novello arrived. Coward was not yet famous and was still networking with anyone and everyone he thought would be useful to his future successful career - he was convinced even then he would have one! At this time Coward would remark how he "aspired to be as famous as Ivor Novello." Interestingly, Novello had been writing successfully, and would continue to do so for a few more years, the kind of satirical and humorous songs that Coward later became famous for. Ironically, Novello's huge contribution in this area is all but forgotten. The song for Jack Buchanan titled *And Her Mother Came Too!*, a massive hit for Novello and Buchanan, which even today is at times wrongly credited to Coward, is evidence that Novello was creating this kind of witty genre long before Coward picked up the mantle. Even more strange is the way *Keep The Home Fires Burning* was eventually distanced from its association with First World War, in spite of it being sung and played by just about everyone in the United Kingdom and the USA. It outsold *It's A Long Way To Tipperary* by tens of thousands, yet that is the song now most associated with that war. However, Coward and Novello started a friendship they would pick up back in England. They had met and liked each other, and for now that was enough.

During this trip Novello indulged himself with theatre productions of every kind. Writing to Marsh he declared he had thus far seen " 26 plays, 6 Operas and been to 18 parties." One of his visits to the Metropolitan Opera House was due to his admiration for a particular composer, Puccini, whose Soeur Angelica was being performed. The young soprano made an impression on Novello, the quality of her voice and the grace and elegance with which she briefly commanded the stage impressed him. He thought no more about it. The young soprano was called Mary Elsas, who had to change her name to Ellis as a result of the war. Elsas sounded too German, and would not help her career, her employers at the Metropolitan Opera informed her; the result of anti German feeling due to the war. It would be several more years before Novello and Mary Ellis would meet again and become great friends. They would also take London by storm.

Clara too was networking in New York with her usual zeal and panache. She no doubt continued to cut an eccentric figure among the socialites of the City. Attending premieres and parties in her own right, and capitalising on her Chicago World's Fair success, and presumably that of her son. Never one to walk in anyone's shadow, and certainly not her famous son, she always captivated those she met with her passion and eccentricities. Before long she was again making lists of names of those who had expressed an interest in learning piano or singing. Clara couldn't resist such temptations, in spite of the fact she was several thousand miles from home. Unbeknown to Novello she made arrangements to renegotiate the terms of the lease on her apartment in Manhattan. She had decided to take up residence in New York during a trip there during the latter part of the war. She hired an attorney to negotiate new terms on the apartment, and at this point decided not to mention her plans to anyone. She would sail home with her son and then, once everything had been finalised, she would return to New York.

It is possible that Clara was in fact determined to compete with her son and match his success. Up to this point in their lives she had been the one who had been, to a greater degree, the prominent member of the family. No doubt it would have been almost impossible for her to accede that position to anyone, even her son! So with her usual boundless enthusiasm she hatched yet another grand scheme that would, she was convinced, catapult her once again to prominence. If she had given as much thought to the financial implications and feasibility of her plans, as she did to the artistic elements, maybe things would have been different for her. But she never did, as in her mind it was "only money" and sat way down on her list of priorities. Her husband had by this point given up his job with Cardiff Council and became content to fade into the shadows created by his wife and son. Their collective eccentricities and successes were a mystery to him - but he was proud of their achievements. Novello had signed over to him the retainer allowance Achsberg, Hopwood and Crew, his music publishers, paid him annually. It amounted to two hundred pounds per year. All his other expenses were also paid by his son and this was just pocket money. Novello never talked much about his father, but he respected him and made sure he enjoyed some of the fruits of his success. As much as this doesn't sound like a King's ransom in today's terms, at the end of 1919, it was a great deal of money.

The end of the New York holiday arrived and they embarked on the Mauritania for their transatlantic crossing to Southampton. Clara was secretly dreaming of her return to New York and was determined she would become the prominent teacher of singing and piano. Novello and Bobbie were oblivious to her plans and enjoyed the glamour of first class travel, dressing for dinner, and meeting the elegant men and women on board. Whilst in mid Atlantic Novello would receive a radio message which would astound him, and cause much debate between Clara and Bobbie as to how he should respond. It was a bolt from the blue, but fate was once again playing its part in Novello's life.

Possibly for the first time in their long relationship, Bobbie's instinctively shrewd judgment of Novello's capabilities, and of matters concerning his career came to the fore. Although their relationship was at this point in its infancy, Bobbie possessed an understanding of Novello's character which for many couples would take years together to acquire. This allowed him to reason with Novello when his petulant or obstinate streaks reared their heads; not to mention Novello's bouts of insecurity at this time about his future direction.

Louis Mercanton, a film director, who collaborated with the Lumiere Bothers in Paris, was in London to hopefully cast a film he was preparing to shoot in Sicily. Mercanton had called into the offices of agent Daniel Mayer and had proceeded to look through photographs of suggested leading actors. By chance he happened to catch sight of a photograph of Novello, who Meyer represented at this time. After looking at the photograph for some minutes his mind was made up. The man he wanted had to look Sicillian, and Novello did. Meyer informed Mercanton that Novello was a composer and not an actor, but he didn't flinch in his reply: "I can teach him that [acting] if he has any brains at all." He wanted Novello because of his dark romantic looks which, in his judgment, would work perfectly for his silent film. And more importantly, would add considerably to the films appeal to women. Thus the offer was sent by wireless message to Novello mid Atlantic on the Mauritania.

Novello was understandably scared and apprehensive. After all he had never been involved in any screen acting or even stage acting at this point. Would he be able to pull it off or would he make a complete fool of himself. Clara, surprisingly, eventually encouraged him to accept. She worried this might affect his career as a composer, but also understood the contract would be worth a great deal of money to her son. After much deliberation, Bobbie took control of the situation and looked at the whole thing with a calm logic. In his opinion Novello was perfectly capable of making a success of this film as long as he worked hard and was dedicated. He could also help with some technique advice from his career as a stage actor, and would support him in whatever way he could. Finally, it would be foolish to turn down such a golden opportunity - who of them knew where this could lead? Bobbie was right, and Novello sent a message back to London accepting the offer. Today this story does seem rather far-fetched. It is unheard of for someone in today's cutthroat film industry to be offered such an opportunity with no prior experience in the medium. But, one has to remember that the industry was in its infancy and had yet to evolve a system that would serve it appropriately. Mercanton, like many others making films in the silent era, were breaking new ground and were generally men who worked on their gut instinct. Mercanton had cast his leading man for *The Call Of The Blood*, Novello was a gamble he was prepared to take.

On his return to London, Novello made arrangements for himself and Bobbie to travel to Paris and meet Mercanton. It proved successful and they traveled to the location. The film was shot in Sicily and he worked hard and learnt fast the art of film acting. He received what was then considered to be expert guidance from Mercanton, and Bobbie was at his side to assist and reassure when necessary. The plot of the film was fairly predictable for the time and is worth mentioning in some detail simply because it was Novello's first film. *The Call Of The Blood* was based on a famous novel by Robert Hichens, who had also penned the likes of *The Garden Of Allah*, which gives a fairly good indication of the flamboyant and romantic content involved. The story was pure melodrama and centred around a plot of intrigue and betrayal. Novello's character was Maurice, and his new English bride, Hermione. Whilst on honeymoon in Sicily, Hermione is called away to nurse a sick relative. Whilst she is gone, Maurice has an affair with a local girl, Maddelena, and seduces her. Her father discovers the de-flowering of his daughter and exacts revenge by killing Maurice. Hermione returns to find her husband laying dead on the mountainside. Maddelena is also dead. As the story nears its conclusion, Hermione is seen laying flowers on their respective graves in forgiveness.

The final scene is Hermione leaving with Emile, once betrothed to Maddelena, whom she is about to marry. Interestingly, whilst on location in Sicily, Novello and the film crew were embroiled in a real life drama. They were held up and robbed by bandits in an episode that Novello described as "terrifying." He stored the memory and would recreate such events in a more glamorous and dramatic way in years to come.

Initial reviews for the film were very positive. *The Sunday Times* reported that "the success of the film is really due to Mr Ivor Novello," remarking that his characterisation of Maurice was a fine interpretation and that, "it also carries conviction with it - no mean success when psychology can only be conveyed by gesture and facial expression." Novello wrote to Marsh whilst in Rome after filming to inform him "apparently I'm thought to have a marvelous flair, and a great future and fortune, and really, Edie, it does seem to come so easy." It is interesting to note a hint of insecurity and sense of disbelief on Novello's part, and almost begs reassurance from his mentor. Even on his travels, Marsh assisted with his considerable influence. He managed to secure Novello and his entourage accommodations as a guest of British Embassies where, Novello reported back, "we were treated to unending luxuries."

Novello made a satisfactory screen debut and it brought him to the attention of an international audience. The camera enhanced his looks, as it does for some, and quite possibly due to his lack of any stage acting experience made him seem far more natural. Most actors employed for the screen at this time were stage performers, therefore their gestures and dramatics in front of the camera, although appropriate for the stage, seemed over the top and exaggerated. Film acting is about restraint and thought processes, a technique that few had developed, or even understood, at this early stage. Having no stage acting experience would have worked in Novello's favour considerably. There are times when, compared to others he shares the screen with, he seems quite naturalistic and relaxed. He does have moments of over-the-top facial expressions and gestures, but probably due to Mercanton's direction and assistance from the likes of Bobbie. That said there is a sense of real sincerity in his eyes which seems to leap out of still pictures of the film; and no doubt did the same during its initial cinema release to captivate and connect with the audience at the time causing "quite a flutter among fair film-goers," as succinctly stated by *The Illustrated*

Chronicle.

Novello's popularity was steadily rising, and this article from *The Daily Sketch* is remarkable for the personalities mentioned: "A number of well-known people were present yesterday evening, by invitation of Ivor Novello, to see the release of the new and thrilling film *The Call Of The Blood*...The Duke and Duchess of Sutherland, the latter in her girl-guide uniform, Lady Diana Cooper, Lady Dudley, Lady Churston, Mrs. Winston Churchill, Lady Howard de Walden, in a chinchilla-trimmed suiting, were a few of those present." Attitudes had changed since the end of the war, but attracting aristocrats and the wife of a prominent politician to a publicised event was a considerable achievement; and probably as a result of Marsh's influence within the establishment. Most of the upper classes looked down on theatre and film personalities and would have rather died than attend performances, never mind socialise with them too. Novello was also shrewd, he knew how to charm them all, and made no social distinctions.

Novello went on to make several films during the 1920s. After *The Call Of The Blood* he quickly embarked on *Miarka* (1920) and *Carnival* (1921) which in many respects were in a similar vein in terms of plot and character type to his first. They were light, frothy and capitalised on his looks, with the perfection of his profile on the screen becoming more famous than his characterisations. This prompted Coward to make his precocious remark: "There are only two perfect things in this World. My wit, and Ivor's profile!"

His next film was *The Bohemian Girl* in 1922 which was not a particularly good subject for film, simply because it dealt with Grand Opera - fairly tricky for the silent screen! However it was a moderate success simply by the fact that Novello was actually in it, and thus enabled his growing army of fans to continue with their respective fantasies. A few things are worth mentioning because it has relevance to the future. He co-starred with Gladys Cooper for the first time, and they subsequently became great friends. Gladys Cooper was a great beauty and aspiring actress of the time, who would star in other films and plays with Novello. Constance Collier and Ellen Terry were also in the film. Constance Collier would collaborate with Novello for his first stage success in the not too distant future. Novello's character in the film took part in a Gypsy wedding ceremony, a scenario he would adopt in the future for his first musical *Glamorous Night*. The films release in America prompted the *New York Tribune* critic to declare that "Ivor Novello seems bored with the whole thing," and added with sincerity, "though there never has been such a gorgeous profile on the screen."

The *New York Evening Mail* were a little more forthright in their critique and declared that Gladys Cooper "is lovely to look upon as the Bohemian Girl, but her lack of experience in the films is obvious: she has yet to learn how to register emotions," but added that, "Ivor Novello gives every indication of becoming another Valentino. He is not only one of the best looking men on the screen, but he is also a finished actor."

Novello was delighted to receive such praise from the press, but he was also the first to criticise himself, and remained modest about his achievements. Indeed, he knew that in reality he was as much a novice as Gladys Cooper, and worried he would suddenly be found out as not being a real actor but a fake. Seeing yourself as others see you is something we would all like to be able to do, but Novello could only see the things that were wrong with his efforts. During his times of insecurity and melancholy Bobbie would be there to shore him up. He also had fears that his sexuality would become known - he was the first to realise that it would make a nonsense of his "screen lover" image and end his lucrative career. Bobbie, as ever, was the voice of reason and allayed his fears. He was protective of his lover and loyal to the last.

Making a comparison between Novello and Valentino was appropriate and can help the reader to appreciate Novello's popularity, looks and the screen charisma he created during the 1920s. Cinema magazine polls in England rendered Valentino and Novello almost neck-and-neck in the popularity stakes.

Never one to miss an opportunity, and even though he was busy making films, Novello also composed the music for several West End revue shows. Many have said he found composing relatively easy, and had a habit of pulling melodies out of thin air when in the right mood. His collaborators and lyricists for these songs were numerous but included, with Marsh's influence, Robert Graves, PG Woodhouse and even the deceased Walt Whitman. The latter Novello never met as he died in 1894, but set his poem

O Tan Faced Prairie Boy to music. For the first time he was commissioned to compose an entire score for a revue titled *The Golden Moth* which opened at the Adelphi Theatre in 1921, swiftly followed by music for another revue *A to Z*, at the Prince of Wales Theatre, also in 1921. The cast list for these revues make interesting reading and included Jack Buchanan, Gertrude Lawrence, George Hestor, Herbert Mundin, Herbert Ross and Elizabeth Pollock.

Fate and Novello managed to collide in the most unusual places with even more unusual results. This time it was the Savoy Grill. The arte-deco lobby of the Savoy Hotel, along with its bars, buzzed with the elite as they paraded the public rooms and restaurants, all designed to allow its clients to "make an entrance" with elegant excess. Staff in pristine livery glided unobtrusively in the background, and pandered to their every whim with silent efficiency. Celebrities adorned the restaurants like sparkling chandeliers, at least the women and their jewels did, and it was most definitely the place to see anyone who was anyone and, more importantly, to be seen. Novello and Bobbie loved to dress for dinner, hold court at their favourite table, and listen to the tinkle of expensive china and crystal whilst the tittle-tattle of gossip whispered its way from table to table. On the surface an elegant and sophisticated world, but beneath the chic facade it was a deliciously wicked and bitchy place. It would also be a fortuitous one for Novello.

One evening in 1922 an American was dining with a friend in the Savoy Grill. His name was DW Griffith. The famous director, who rose to prominence through films like *Birth Of A Nation*, had done much to develop films into a sophisticated story-telling art form with his innovative production ideas and editing techniques. He suddenly spotted Novello in profile across the room. He asked his companion who he was. On being told it was the film star Ivor Novello, Griffith declared: "That's the actor I want as leading man for my next film." He insisted his companion introduce him. Before he knew what had happened, Novello found himself signing a contract to make his next film *The White Rose*, with Griffith as director, in New York.

As the 1920s progressed Great Britain was still recovering from the economic after effects of the war. Society was still divided between those who were wealthy and the struggling working masses. Disillusionment among those men who had returned from the war was rife. They had been promised a better life as a result of their sacrifice, but the reality was unemployment and hardship. The country was economically stretched to breaking point, and as a result income tax thresholds started to lower to help swell the Chancellor's purse. The hedonistic world of excess at the Savoy Hotel, and its Champagne lifestyle, were as far removed from reality as the public could possibly get. Indeed, most would not have been able to even imagine the lifestyle enjoyed by the wealthy few. Attitudes were beginning to change dramatically, especially among the younger generation. They no longer wanted to be stifled and suppressed by outdated Victorian values. Life was too short, as they knew only too well, and they wanted to have fun without feeling guilty. The life they wanted was liberated, loser and devoid of the morality corsets imposed by an older generation. All these developments were reflected in the fashions, music and dance. The age of the Flapper and Jazz had arrived with a vengeance and, for the most part, been warmly embraced by most. Novello for his part became an object of desire and lust, a position he was happy to take full advantage of. Strangely, he never succumbed to the music of the jazz age, although he did compose songs of the genre a couple of times, but instead he remained old fashioned in a "Merry Widow" kind of way. In the future it would serve him well.

For many the cinema was a way to escape daily routine and drudgery. It became a window to another world and enabled the viewer to enjoy their personal fantasies involving those portrayed on the screen. As entertainment it stood alone in terms of audience numbers. The theatre tended to cater for slightly more high-brow tastes and took itself, on the whole, rather more seriously, whereas the music halls were perceived as a vulgar, low art form by many, and had begun their journey to extinction. These conditions allowed Novello to establish his celebrity; indeed, he would eventually amalgamate these art forms and create a genre of his own in terms of theatre productions, which would bring the masses stampeding to the theatres where he performed live.

Not clever planning on Novello's part, although Bobbie would have managed the situation to take full advantage, more a case of technology and history creating fertile ground for his development. It has to be said, there must have been times when he had to pinch himself just to make sure it was all really happening. In the space of a couple of years he had developed from a composer of songs to a respected film star with a global profile. In England he had a fan base that ran into hundreds of thousands and he had never had an acting lesson in his life. Now he was sailing to New York to play the lead in a film by the world's most famous director. For Novello in his mid twenties, it couldn't get any better.

December 1922 saw Novello, accompanied as always by Bobbie, sail to New York to film *The White Rose* for Griffith. Bobbie was shrewd enough to realise that Novello's film career could be extinguished if his homosexuality became common knowledge among studio executives. There was rumour and speculation as to why Novello hadn't married in the press and film magazines; no doubt aided by gossip and sour grapes borne out of jealousy. To deflect this potentially harmful situation Bobbie decided the best form of defense is attack. The solution decided upon involved Gladys Cooper. She agreed to follow Novello to New York. Information was leaked to the press that Novello and Gladys were to marry on her arrival, and it predictably made the papers on both sides of the Atlantic and caused much hysteria among Novello's fans. It served its purpose and immediately silenced any gossip regarding Novello's unmarried status. It was a shrewd move.

On her arrival in New York, Novello met Gladys at the pier and happily posed for photographs with his intended wife. They continued with the charade unabashed. Eventually it was announced they had decided to part for reasons various, including a supposed intervention from Griffith. *The New York American* newspaper reported:

"Gladys Cooper, considered the most beautiful woman on the English stage, sailed from England Wednesday, bound for New York. Her sole purpose in making the trip is to marry Ivor Novello...who Griffith imported to star in his new production *The White Rose*. Griffith gave some advice. He is reported to have said: 'Ivor, although there is no clause in our contract that can keep you from marrying, I wouldn't do it if I were you...wouldn't it impair your value as a star if it were known you were married?"'

It was a charade, but a glamorous and fantastical charade that finally silenced the gossips. Novello could now say with honesty that he wasn't married because it would upset his fans - and his first devotion was to them. Game, set and match for Bobbie for pulling off such a public relations success. No doubt he was also relieved at not having to share his lover with a wife in tow - even a pretend one!

Novello, Bobbie and Gladys always said they never planned any deception, that the press had concocted the "marriage story." If that were the case, it seems rather odd they would play along with the situation so convincingly. It was a publicity stunt aimed at deflecting attention away from Novello's homosexuality. Gladys was, it can be fairly certain, happily involved from the start. Her intentions were honourable as she wanted to help protect her friend in whatever way she could. Griffith would have been happy to collude with them to protect his investment. No doubt they enjoyed the situation immensely, not to mention the free positive publicity it afforded all of them. Thankfully they didn't go as far as some when faced with this situation. Many years later, during the 1950s, Rock Hudson attempted to dupe the public, prompted by a nervous studio amid rumours and gossip, by embarking on a sham marriage to deflect attention away from his homosexuality. Like Novello, Hudson had a romantic image and lucrative career to preserve. In the 1920s the public were far more naive, and although perhaps not impossible in the 1950s, it would be far more difficult to hide the truth from the more cynical and media savvy public of the 21st Century.

The White Rose was released in 1923 and had a predictable boy meets girl, boy seduces girl, and finally reproaches himself for his actions that causes hurt and despair. Novello played a young trainee priest opposite Mae Marsh's manipulative waitress. The critical reaction was less than positive. *The Times* declared: "Ivor Novello is properly irritating as the priggish young clergyman."

The American press did declare Novello to be "a sincere actor with a pleasing personality and good looks, [that] will appeal to American audiences," at least in the opinion of the *New York Telegraph*. The Chicago press were not impressed with the film, but full of praise for Novello saying he was "the handsomest man in England." When Novello did an interview with the *New York Evening Telegraph*, who echoed this remark, Novello pleaded thus: "Please, please don't write me up as the handsomest man in England." Genuinely embarrassed by such protestations, he tried to elicit the cooperation of the interviewer by adding: " Promise me you'll cut out all that rot?" False modesty on Novello's part? No, I don't think it was. The trouble with Novello was his inability to see himself as others did. All he could see when watching his performances, which is disconcerting when your image is magnified to such a size, was all the things he could have done better. Watching himself would invariably make him cringe with embarrassment, and make him wonder what an earth anyone saw in him.

DW Griffith was at the end of his illustrious career and *The White Rose* speeded on his demise. Although the film had been a critical disaster, it did little to diminish the enthusiasm which Novello's faithful fans greeted him. In fact, none at all. Before Griffith fades out of the story it is worth mentioning the law suit brought against him by Novello. On signing the original contract, Novello had agreed to appear in six more films for the director. No doubt Griffith was protecting his interests, and it also gives an indication of his expectations for Novello's film career. Due to the rapid demise of Griffith's career, these films were never made. Novello sued the director for lost earnings, calculated at $700 per week, then multiplied by the average number of weeks for the six films. The total came to a substantial $11,000 Dollars. Disputed by Griffith, it came to nothing. However, it does demonstrate Novello's growing tenacity and business acumen at the time; no doubt aided by Bobbie and Marsh.

In 1923 he was again teamed up with Gladys Cooper for the film *Bonnie Prince Charlie*. "As the young Prince whose handsome features won the hearts of all," declared *The Daily Telegraph*, "Mr Novello is the very man to fill the part." Indeed he was, but the film was not a success. It did have "moments of charm" but not enough to do either Novello or Gladys any justice.

On Gladys, the *Encore Magazine* did offer some back-handed praise for her performance: "Miss Cooper's delineation of the character was obviously painstaking," but seemed a little mystified, considering it was a silent film, to discover, "the preliminary attempt to establish atmosphere by the introduction of a solitary piper as rather futile."

Whilst working on various films, and composing music for West End revues, Novello felt he had not yet achieved his greatest desire - to become an actor on the legitimate stage. As much as he enjoyed films, apart from the boredom between takes, and the early mornings which he hated, he wanted to experience the immediate rapport with a live audience. Insecure about his absolute lack of technique and experience in this area worried him. Bobbie, having been a stage actor since he was a child, was able to offer support and advice. It has to be said that those friends around him added to his fears by declaring earnestly that he should be satisfied with his success in films and as a composer. Although the advice was given with sincerity, it did little to allay his understandable fears when told he could "make a fool of himself" and pointing out rather bluntly that "stage acting was beyond his abilities." Bobbie of course countered this kind of negativity with reassurance, and right on queue an opportunity suddenly presented itself.

Bobbie had been cast in a play titled *Deburau* , a predictable melodrama of the time set in Paris in the early 19th Century, to be presented at the Ambassadors' Theatre; in many ways a theatre perfect for a novice as it is small and intimate. The management had yet to cast a small unnamed part and Bobbie suggested Novello. They approached him with the offer, and he accepted. His contract stated:

"Rehearse and play in the comedy entitled *Deburau* at a West End London Theatre on such occasions and for such period as the Managers may elect to continue the performance of the said play in the West End of London."

His salary was fifteen pounds per-week and the play opened on 3rd November, 1921, and ran for 28 performances, far from a success, but served its purpose. The result was a positive couple of lines for Novello in an otherwise harsh review that declared: "Mr Novello as the young man…put into his wooing the respectful ecstasies of 1840. He did very well…"

From this he was engaged to another role, at the Kingsway Theatre, for Benrimo Management for a salary of twenty five pounds per-week. The play was titled *The Yellow Jacket* (1922), an oriental odyssey, and again was not a great success but fared a little better than the first. He played the absurdly named character Wu Hoo Git opposite Ann Trevor as the equally ridiculous Plum Blossom. He was again mentioned by the critics for his fledgling performance: "Mr Novello, a frank and good looking romantic youth, showed too obviously a sensibility to the absurdities of the part," reported *The Sunday Times*, going on to add he, "forced the pace emotionally, and occasionally lost the heroic in the effeminate." Novello was understandably bruised by such remarks, but something was happening which soothed his sensibilities and, as he put it, at least he'd been noticed!

The most remarkable thing to happen during these early stage appearances were additions to the audience. So many women who had admired and fantasised about him from his screen persona, were turning up at the theatres to see him in the flesh. By the time he was appearing at the Kingsway Theatre, they were, much to the consternation and annoyance of the more serious playgoer, applauding his entrance on stage; moreover, he was even more amazed whilst leaving the stage door after performances to discover a throng of women waiting for his autograph. This was even picked up by a critic from *The Sunday Chronicle* who assumed "it was the engaging personality of Mr Ivor Novello, who has taken up acting in deadly earnest, that helped to fill the Kingsway with such a 'precious' audience on Tuesday night...he played the young lover exceedingly well."

Bobbie and Novello must have realised around this time the potential and impact Novello's persona and presence were making. Shrewdly they could see the potential of attracting his cinema audiences to the theatre; where they would prefer to see him live in person and talking. It has to be remembered that this was breaking new ground in terms of audience cross over, and a star like Novello capitalising on his film career to realise his aspirations for the stage was unique. More interesting is how Novello, at the age of 28, and never having undertaken any training for the stage, could perfect his technique in this medium so quickly. Admittedly he developed his technique and became more proficient as time went on, but he grasped the basic principles so quickly and with such determination it was admirable.

The matter of his "effeminacy" as stated by some critics seemed of little consequence to his status or legion of female fans. In a sense it enabled them to connect with him on a different level perhaps? After all, many of them had experienced at first hand, and heard stories about, the brutality of the war; not to mention the general harshness that was everyday life for the middle and working classes of the time. To see this handsome and gentle man on the screen or stage must have awoken desires within his fans to find a man who possessed such gentle and considerate qualities. He managed to portray a naïve, little-boy-lost quality that awoke the maternal instinct in many women whatever their age. Ultimately it all worked in Novello's favour and enhanced rather than diminished his appeal. Novello was one of a kind and totally unique, indeed there has never been anyone before, or since, who could match his abilities or qualities. The West End managements and money men were quick to catch on to Novello's unique appeal, and take full advantage.

Benrimo Management, seeing this box office potential, rushed into production of another play titled *Spanish Lovers* (1922). Novello played the character Javier, who marries a girl who loves someone else, he lets her go eventually, then dies from a wasting disease. Pretty flimsy and predictable romantic melodrama - but a good vehicle that adequately exploited Novello's abilities. It allowed him to make the most of his looks and romantic appeal and satisfied all those "precious" fans flocking to see him. Interestingly the press reviews give an indication of his progress in mastering stage technique. *The New Statesman* reported he "played the part of Javier with pathos and languishing grace" which at last began to silence his critics. *The Sunday Times* gave him an equally good mention and went as far as to say "he made a big step upward as an actor by his handling of this part," going on to describe his performance, "as poetic, as courageous, as graceful and vigorous as could be expected of him."

As busy as he was making films, Novello continued to appear in stage plays. 1923 saw him teamed with Gladys Cooper again. The play was called *Enter Kiki* It was generally slated by the press but again they found something positive to say. "Ivor Novello walked through the piece with more surety than he has yet shown," declared *The Daily Mirror*, " and now and then acted with considerable force." *The Times*, much to Novello's delight, declared that "the most successful performance of the evening was that of Ivor Novello."

By 1924 his career was progressing in all directions amazingly well; much to the surprise of many he had mastered the art of composing, film acting and now the theatre. To those in an industry where artists were generally known for one talent, Novello truly was a conundrum indeed. His fans were numbered by the thousands and he drew them to the cinema or theatre with apparent ease; indeed, he drew admirers into the theatre who previously would never have gone there. Even more astonishing was his seeming ability to be critic-proof, those who filled the cinemas and theatres didn't care what anyone's opinion was but their own. Never before had anyone had so many strings to their career and been so successful. All those aunt Mabels were well and truly hooked by his hypnotic charm and charisma; and able to indulge their own romantic fantasies wrapped around his persona.

Novello's biggest success both for stage and screen would be a play he conceived in collaboration with actress Constance Collier called *The Rat*. Ironically it started life as a screen play written by Novello, which was subsequently sold to a film producer who promptly went out of business. The rights reverted back to Novello and he showed the script to Constance. She immediately saw the potential of the script but as a stage play for Novello, and they set about rewriting it together. Novello at this time remarked he had "little experience in crafting a stage play" and welcomed Constance's considerable experience in this area. Rather odd considering he had been experimenting writing for some years, *The Fickle Jade* as example, and had absorbed so much, and learnt so much from the ever present Marsh, not to mention his considerable experiences working on both stage and screen. It is more likely he felt more secure embarking on his first stage play as author in collaboration with his friend. He relished working with Constance and would have enjoyed the experience less without her assistance. Bobbie, as ever, encouraged and advised where appropriate and kept Novello's feet firmly on the ground. It would prove to be a stressful and demanding project, where almost everyone they knew to a man or woman advised against what they perceived to be the makings of a disaster for both their careers.

Rather than deter them, this negativity spurred them on. Marsh was the exception and all in favour of the project, and offered his assistance in being a sounding board for the script. Once the stage script of *The Rat* was drafted they would read it aloud to Marsh, who would then offer constructive criticism and suggest possible alterations. Marsh was impressed by Novello's seeming flair for effective dialogue and determined this was an area he would help his protégé to develop further. Secretly, Marsh was of the opinion that Novello was "still lacking in a sense of purpose and drive" due to the relative ease of his "early successes" and that his real talent was "latent as yet." He hoped this production would help him grow and mature. Novello was determined, he informed Marsh, to write and manage his own stage productions in the future. This news must have pleased Marsh. Constance was thankfully adept at working out plot and structure and curtailed Novello's flamboyant and theatrical suggestions with panache. Eventually the script was finished and ready to go into production. Only one problem remained - money.

Novello proved to be better at spending his money than he was at saving it. In spite of the vast sums he had earned from composing and films, he didn't have enough to fund the initial production of *The Rat*. Marsh came to his rescue with "a loan from the 'murder money' towards the costs of production," in addition to which Novello contributed a small amount he had available. Marsh had also agreed a contingency plan with Novello and "undertook to make a translation of Bernstein's play *Israel* to fall back on if need be." Novello and Constance started work on *The Rat* whilst Marsh began translations of *Israel* from its original French.

The Rat went into six-weeks of rehearsals ready for its premiere at the Theatre Royal, Brighton on January 14th, 1924. The play catered for all Novello's assets in terms of his looks, abilities and set out to capitalise on all those aunt Mabels and their desires. The story was romantic and bizarre. On reading the script today one wonders how someone with Marsh's literary talents could have given his approval; even less risk "murder money" by way of an investment in the production. However, at the time, and as a vehicle to showcase Novello and his unique personality, it becomes less puzzling. In essence it catered perfectly for his growing number of fans, who would have paid money to see him do anything - even badly one assumes. The other great bonus for those fans was sound. In the theatre they could also hear Novello speak, unlike his image on the silent film screen. His voice was melodious, gentle and had a touch of the Welsh accent of his birth; all underpinned, it has to be said, with a slight camp or fey quality.

Novello and Constance also presented the play under the pseudonym of David L'Estrange for reasons of their own. Perhaps the negative comments that had showered down on them had made them more insecure than they already were. Perhaps it was just a delicious joke, concocted to amuse them in its secrecy. If it was the latter, it was in vain because everyone, including the press, were perfectly aware of who the authors were. The posters for *The Rat* capitalised on Novello's films by declaring "The world famous film star," underneath his name in capital letters a foot high.

Rehearsals were tiring and strained for the most part. At one point Novello nearly abandoned the project, at another Constance did too, but eventually all went smoothly and opening night loomed. The dress rehearsal was a disaster and a sense of gloom descended again over the cast, this in spite of a sell out for the first night in Brighton. Their collective fears were unjustified. In spite of a few first night glitches it was received with standing ovations and hysteria. The following day the run was extended to keep up with the demand for tickets. It was a sell out and the critics were baffled as their opinions demonstrate:

"Mr Ivor (David) Novello and Miss Constance (L'Estrange) Collier are responsible for *'The Rat'*," reported *Queen Magazine*, "and no single unassisted mind could conceivably put together so much stock situation stated in so many hoary platitudes as the combined efforts of these two clever people. They must have written *The Rat* with tongue in cheek all the time…Mr Novello is the Rat all the time, and six or sixteen or sixty lovely ladies in the cast kiss him with intention at and in-between the various curtains, and he dances, and laughs, and stays, and makes love, and even goes mad and babbles of green fields, and the audience is swayed by his joys and sorrows, and it is all incredibly humiliating to the intelligence and exciting to the emotions of the crowd. It must be seen to be believed."

The London Opinion newspaper reported: "As a work of art the value of '*The Rat*' is about nine pence at a liberal estimate, but as a box-office attraction I should think it ranks at about one thousand five hundred pounds per week."

Novello as the Rat sashayed his way through the scenes in the White Coffin nightclub and seduced all the women, treated them badly, and thoroughly enjoyed himself in the process. His fans stood in line for "returns" and cheered him to the rafters - critics were baffled and attempted to express it by stating "there are bad good plays, so there are good bad ones, and *The Rat* is not at all a bad good bad one," and in a state of exasperation advised, "perhaps a pinch of salt should be given away with every programme just to show that it is only a bit of fun."

The Rat moved against all the odds into London's West End. It enjoyed a considerable run at the Prince of Wales Theatre and changed forever Novello's fortunes. The film (1925) would follow quickly, adapted straight from the stage play, which in its turn filled cinemas around the country increasing his popularity ten-fold.

"Quite frankly I think '*The Rat*' established him as a box-office name. When Griffith took him for *The White Rose*, it was just for his lovely profile," according to Michael Balcon, " but to me a box-office name means only one thing: does it draw money at the box-office? And until *The Rat* I don't think he did."

In terms of theatre and film Novello had with this one project changed his status within the respective industries. He was now considered a force to be reckoned with. He would take full advantage of his newfound power and transform himself into an actor-manager and playwright. Marsh still had concerns about Novello and was as baffled as the critics at some of his more bizarre behaviour. He recalled being invited for lunch at "the flat" by Novello one day during the West End run of *The Rat* . On his arrival he found Novello with "barely any clothes on" and as the lunch proceeded observed him " leaving the room and coming back with another piece of clothing on," adding in his bemusement, "this continued until he was fully dressed." But it didn't end there because, much to Marsh's eventual amusement, Novello left the room again and returned practically naked "with a huge purple cushion on his head" stating he "was a Maharaja" or sum such person. Marsh was truly worried these eccentric exhibitions were in danger of damaging his protégé's career, reputation or even his sanity. Fortunately, Novello was becoming well protected by a few who were now closing ranks and devoting themselves to him.

Marsh was pleased with the success of *The Rat*, but a little disappointed that all his efforts in translating *Israel*, for Novello to fall back on, were wasted. His translation was, he remembered years later, "forgotten and subsequently lost." For Novello the latter half of the 1920s would be frantic. He would find himself "viciously booed" alongside Noel Coward, persuade Lily Elsie to make a West End comeback, and make a film with a young director called Alfred Hitchcock.

In Search of Ruritania

NOEL, ALFRED & ELSIE

"Mr. Novello, one felt, could have explained anything and everything from Lord Beaverbrook's politics to the esoteric mystery of the Black Bottom."

James Agate - The Sunday Times

Heartened by the success of *The Rat* Novello threw himself into stage and film work with seeming abandon. There were those who argued his persona was the reason for his success rather than any great acting talent he might possess, and in some ways this was probably true; indeed Novello was the first to recognise his own limitations. However, up to this point in history the theatre had been the aristocracy of art forms and was jealously guarded by traditionalists, with mainly high-brow attitudes, who were loudly sneering at Novello and his exploits. Novello, for his part was laughing, quite literally, all the way to the bank.

In the fast changing world of the 1920s it was the cause of much consternation and bemusement to see a whole new order emerge from the settled dust of the First World War. Cinema was now becoming dominant and attracting the most in terms of financial investment. During a ten-year period from the mid 1920s to the mid 1930s cinema audiences in Britain would grow at an incredible rate until 20 million per-week were attending "the flicks", as it was affectionately known. A boost to British films, and thus by default Novello's career in films, was Parliament's

Cinematographers Legislation. In a bid to compete with the ever increasing dominance of Hollywood, the legislation made it compulsory for Cinemas in the United Kingdom to ensure 5% of films screened were British made. This figure would slowly increase to 20% in the coming years. The result was a great demand for British films which served Novello's career beautifully. Theatres, as a result, struggled to compete. London's West End theatre still relied on a select small percentage of the populace, mostly upper middle class, along with the lower echelons of the aristocracy, to part with their money via the box-office. Theatre was still a place of manners and etiquette, where ladies arrived elegantly gowned and gentlemen wore white-tie and tails or black-tie evening dress, depending on the occasion. It was elitist and full of social pretensions, only the gallery and pit attracted those of a lower station who would gaze at the audience, as much as what was happening on the stage, as part of their amusement and entertainment. Novello came along and things began to change for the first time, and some of the old guard resented it.

For some of those producing theatre productions in the West End it was an even greater travesty. They viewed theatre as a high art form that, by its very nature, was not mass entertainment. Novello stood for everything they despised about low-brow art forms, music halls were bad enough, and were tolerated because the common masses needed some divertissement, but they knew their place and didn't encroach on real "theatre" territory. Novello had established himself in legitimate theatre and worse, was attracting hordes of those who hitherto never went to a theatre; and in probability wouldn't have been welcomed. Whatever their protestations, the old order of things was in decline and the new laying solid foundations which were immoveable. The younger generation was liberated and exerting the full force of change, a change they demanded and wanted. The old guard didn't stand a chance of halting a progress that eroded their comfortable world, but they would fight it whenever possible and for as long as they could.

Novello, for all his faults, actually did the theatre a great service by attracting the multitudes that were the cinema audience through its unfamiliar doors. It aided the survival of the theatre and provided much needed revenue to sustain the fabric of the buildings. There are those today who express similar high-brow opinions, regarding musical theatre and its domination of the West End to the supposed detriment of serious theatre. But without the likes of Lord Lloyd Webber and Sir Cameron Mackintosh, the theatres in the West End would have struggled to survive. In essence they are doing today what Novello did from the 1920s through to the 1940s. By attracting new audiences, they provide the vital income needed to ensure these theatres survive for future generations. Most importantly they are providing an entertainment the public wants, as did Novello in his way, and the public will always vote with their feet if not satisfied. Novello cared about "filling the plush" as he would say, or in other words playing to a full house. He could see little point in creating something that had no popular appeal, but perhaps great artistic high-brow distinction, which only a handful would be interested to see.

The younger generation in Novello's 1920s now became more vocal and demanding and were not prepared to be "kept in their place" any longer. They wanted an equal voice in how society functioned and were prepared to fight for it. Women were also becoming more independent and had finally secured the vote, thanks to the sustained efforts of Emiline Pankhurst and her suffragette movement. Indeed, the seeds of liberation for women were sown in this period and slowly began to germinate. Social evolution was in part responsible for catapulting Novello to the fore, and no one was more shocked than Novello to find himself in such a position of prominence.

Following hot on the heels of the film version of *'The Rat'*, Novello starred in a hurried sequel *Triumph Of The Rat* in 1925. The best that can be said is that it was a shrewd move financially, but not artistically. Whichever way you look at it, it was a blatant effort to cash in on the original's success while still fresh in the minds of the population. As such, it worked and added to Novello's ever expanding bank balance. His next stage venture was *Old Heidelberg* (1925) at the Garrick Theatre. Novello played the young student William Kendell and the part involved much soul searching and "making love to" his co-star Dorothy Batley. Novello, of course, milked the drama for all it was worth and satisfied his fans in the process. *The Sunday Times* critic, James Agate, declared the play too long, and as a result "the evening was half spent before Mr. Novello was called upon to begin acting, which in the end he did gracefully and at times movingly, even to the point of surviving a uniform reminiscent of a municipal bandsman from Southend."

The play would eventually be turned into *The Student Prince*, and enjoy far greater success as a musical. A similar fate would be the future of another play Novello starred in with a young actor making his West End debut: Charles Laughton. *Lilliom* (1926) had a previous incarnation as *The Daisy* a few years earlier but had flopped. This new version was presented at the Globe Theatre and brought Laughton to the attention of the public, but only managed a brief run. Novello played a fair-ground barker who bullies his girl, dies in a fight, and ends up repentant in heaven. Sound familiar? Many years later Rodgers and Hammerstein would turn this into their famous musical *Carousel*. Hard to imagine Novello pulling off such a brutish and cynical characterisation, with many believing he was badly miscast in the role. That said, he enjoyed the experience and used it to his advantage in terms of continued development. James Agate of *The Sunday Times* summed it up thus:

"Surely it must be obvious to everyone that this hulking brute must be a brute who hulks and that to present him with the aquiline grace and Latin effrontery of Mr. Novello at his most accomplished is to court disaster. As a blustering, throat-slitting bully this charming actor failed charmingly…The fellow should be totally unable to explain himself, whereas Mr. Novello, one felt, could have explained anything and everything from Lord Beaverbrook's politics to the esoteric mystery of the Black Bottom."

"If one is to fail at all, all the better to fail charmingly," Novello was heard to say without any obvious dint to his confidence. As for Beaverbrook's politics, he could have explained them quite well indeed. Marsh enjoyed being at the very epicentre of government, and would no doubt have discussed much during his daily visits to "the flat" on the way to Whitehall. The Black Bottom, the new dance craze, was indeed enjoyed by Novello. He was heard to quip he "loved doing the Black Bottom, but devoid of a Southend bandsman's uniform!" with reference to Agate's remark in his review for *Old Heidelberg*.

As for Laughton, he managed, with help from Novello, to establish himself in circles which would benefit his career in the future. Recently graduated from RADA, *Lilliom* was his first break into theatre. Novello, on seeing his potential and obvious talent, insisted that Laughton be paid a decent salary for his engagement. It has to be said that Laughton and Novello had one thing in common: their homosexuality. No doubt it created a bond between them, one that would allow Novello to impart the benefit of his experience to the young actor. Novello's hunch regarding his potential was proved to be right, and Laughton went on to be an international figure and respected actor.

Two other plays Novello appeared in during 1925 were *Iris*, with Gladys Cooper, and *The Firebrand* with Constance Collier. Neither were particularly good, but catered for his romantic appeal within a predictable, unbelievable plot, but it didn't stop Novello's female followers from turning up in droves. The still pictures that survive reflect an image of Novello sporting what can only be described as camp attire, especially the lycra-type jump suit, which leaves little to the imagination, adorned without embarrassment, presumably, in one scene of *The Firebrand*; alongside an equally eccentrically gowned and posed Constance Collier. A still photograph featuring Gladys Cooper and Novello from *Iris* is one of the best pictures of Novello with which to appreciate his looks and appeal at that time. In many of these pictures it seems as if Novello could have traveled back in time to pose for them. His contemporaries are "of the period" in the way they stand and pose with an air of melodrama, and somehow he is at odds with that. Maybe it is this natural quality that made him stand out from the crowd?

Clara's opinion of her son's involvement with the theatre and films was predictable. She disapproved of his decision to abandon his career as a composer because she still fervently believed that was the area to which he should devote himself. Neither was she shy in her ability to voice her opinions to her son. Many arguments ensued between them but Novello was adamant he would not be swayed from his present direction. The other side of the coin was her ability to bask in the reflected glory of her son's achievements; which also created an opening for her to use the Novello name to her own advantage. Her zest and energy were ever boundless, matched only by her self-obsession. Sadly her lack of any financial responsibility managed to rear its head again, forcing her to rely on him to once again bail her out.

Her expedition to New York had resulted in Novello receiving a telegram from Clara's attorney outlining the serious debt she had managed to accrue. Clara had obviously instructed him to contact her son with the sordid details, as her creditors were pressing her for settlement. Novello, no doubt exasperated, cabled back and asked for the full details and then arranged for the money to be transferred. His one condition, which infuriated Clara, was that she relinquish the apartment in New York and sail back to England immediately. She had no choice but to agree, but her son received the full force of her wrath once she returned. In spite of the tears and tantrums that ensued, Novello discovered he no longer reacted to Clara's attempts at emotional blackmail, deathbed scenes, or considerable temper. Instead he was firm but kind to his mother's errant ways. It wasn't the first time she found herself in trouble, and it wouldn't be the last time her son came to her financial rescue. To Novello's credit, he always declared that without his mother he wouldn't have achieved so much and thus begrudged her nothing.

Marsh was still championing his protégé and attempting to further educate his mind, and offering support and advice where necessary. Bobbie was ever present and invariably taking small parts in either the plays Novello was cast in, but also roles he was offered in his own right. He was more and more becoming a managerial figure in Novello's life, and Novello in turn depended on him for objectivity with his career. Bobbie was now manager, lover and friend in equal measures. Another figure that was prominent in Novello's life was a friend from his school days. His name was Lloyd Williams, and had been Novello's secretary since *The Rat*. Williams would also oversee the domestic staff and the smooth running of Novello's household. His chauffer Morgan, an actor who had been in the cast of *Old Heidelberg* where he met Novello, had also joined his staff and would, along with all his close associates, remain with him for the rest of his life.

Coward had become ever present in the circles that Novello found himself the centre of. Having at last got a foot on the ladder of fame, with the success of his play *The Vortex* (1925) he was beginning to climb it with his usual impatience. They enjoyed a close friendship and in spite of those who say they were rivals, they were not. Ironically, however, it was Coward's stage play *Sirrocco* (1927) which convinced Novello he would fare better by writing and presenting his own plays in the future.

The plot of *Sirrocco* was an unusual one for Coward when compared to his more biting drawing room comedies. A romantic and highly dramatic piece about the exploits of a married English woman alone in Italy. She is seduced by a handsome local and a passionate affair ensues. It all predictably ends in jealousy, betrayal and violence. Novello, at Coward's request, was cast as the Italian lover with Frances Doble as the errant English woman.

Coward at this stage of his career was fairly new on the scene and had not endeared himself to many due to his precocious and, some considered, his extremely arrogant behaviour. His biting wit could be personal and hurtful, leaving most with the opinion he needed knocking down a peg or two. Compared with Novello he seemed utterly without charm or the normal social graces; indeed they were poles part in terms of character. Whereas Novello was always incredulous at his good fortune, Coward expected nothing less than celebrity status, even before he had it. Such was the belief in himself. It is difficult to imagine two vastly different characters, even more so they should become firm friends. Many a time Coward would arrive back stage and, wagging his finger in Novello's face, lecture him on what he perceived to be his shortcomings. Novello, invariably, smiled and nodded during these diatribes, and then took absolutely no notice whatsoever. Novello, with much good humour, knew how to deal with his pompous friend, a friend he admired and loved unquestionably, but one who didn't understand his way of doing things. And never would.

Amongst a fraternity of the theatre-going public, along with some working in the industry, Coward had been a cause of irritation. The subject matter of his first success, *The Vortex*, had been too near the bone for some and a little too realistic; not to mention distasteful in its wanton characters, drug addiction and lack of morals. Not that many didn't know these things went on, but more because Coward was prepared to depict how frayed the fabric of society was underneath the perfect façade it presented to the world. Novello played the part of Nicky in the silent film version (1927) with his usual aplomb, although it was a fairly watered down version prompting a critic to state "the most successful of stage plays is not necessarily fit for the screen."

It was reported that from the moment the curtain rose at Daly's Theatre, the *Sirrocco* first-night audience were shrouded in an uneasy, restless atmosphere. When Novello's character grappled with his lover on the floor, hysterical laughter and jeering broke out. A humiliating experience for Novello and Doble. This eventually turned into open hostility during the third act and resulted in the entire cast being subjected to booing and jeering on an unprecedented scale. When the final curtain fell, all hell broke loose and violent confrontations amongst audience members ensued along with further booing and jeering for the cast. Coward was mortified and took it in good stead and refused to be intimidated. He foolishly stepped centre stage to make a speech and was drowned out by the hostile jeers emitting from the audience.

Marsh was present in the audience and admitted to "squirming in my seat" fraught with anxiety at how it all would end. "It was the first and only time Novello and Coward were viciously booed by an audience," declared the distressed Marsh. He would join the playwright and his leading man at "the flat" for a post mortem as to what went wrong. This, he reported, went on until dawn, where they were convinced their respective careers were over. It was a frightening experience and brought them both down to earth with an almighty thud. Coward, recalling the event in his book *Present Indicative* said:

"Ivor's behaviour throughout was remarkable. With full realisation that all his trouble and hard work had gone for less than nothing, his sense of humour was still clear and strong enough to enable him to make a joke of the whole thing. Nor was he apparently in the least ruffled by the inevitable press blast the next day. He made no complaints, attached no blame or responsibility to anyone, and accepted failure with the same grace that he has always accepted success."

Coward's memory had become glamorised, in true Novello fashion, by the time he penned the above many years later. Marsh's version seems to ring true, but once the initial shock wore off, and it was realised that their careers weren't destroyed, a lighter shade could be applied to the recollection of events; and no doubt the humour of the situation was easier to see with the benefit of hindsight. If it served no other purpose, it convinced Novello he would indeed be better placed writing and performing in his own plays - a thought which was encouraged by Marsh and Bobbie. Which is exactly what he did eventually do, accompanied no doubt, by Coward's regular finger-wagging visits to his dressing room on first nights!

Film work during this period was on-going for Novello. Michael Balcon introduced him to a young director who was about to embark on his first film for Gainsborough *The Lodger* (1926). The director in question was a young Alfred Hitchcock. The screenplay was adapted from a novel by Marie Belloc-Lowndes and had also been adapted for the stage - where it came to the attention of Hitchcock. It appealed to him because he could see the suspense potential in the story, which he could interweave with ideas of his own regarding filming and editing. Interestingly, Hitchcock had worked in the German film industry, which was later recognised as the birth place of the film-noir genre, where he had made two experimental films. These early experiences would have a profound effect on the young Hitchcock and he would go on to adopt some of the techniques he witnessed.

Novello was under contract to Gainsborough Pictures at the time, Balcon suggested him to Hitchcock, and he was cast as the mysterious lodger. *The Lodger* in question takes up lodgings with an east-end family, in an area where a series of murders have occurred, *Jack the Ripper* style. He is suspected in a fairly trite "is he?" "isn't he?" kind of plot. It turns out he isn't the murderer, after much melodrama, staring eyes, mass hysteria, and a mob that nearly kills him - all swathed in a London pea-soup fog.

Viewing the film is an odd and often disconcerting experience. Novello seems to glide through the film shrouded in perpetual fog as far as his character's intentions and emotions are concerned. With glacial, staring eyes one wonders whether he can see anything at all, including the other characters involved. It is an odd detached performance at times, which gives the impression that maybe Hitchcock was concentrating more on experimentation for his style, allowing it to develop and dominate, rather than that of his leading man's character. Novello comes across as eerie and melodramatic in the extreme, fairly leaping out of the screen and creeping over the viewer's flesh rendering it clammy and cold. Novello's naturalistic screen presence is replaced by a stilted, unsure and exaggerated performance; then as if he is sleep-walking through a scene not quite sure of where or who he is. Novello's performance at times brings to mind a caricatured pantomime villain appearing by way of a puff of smoke, but devoid of stage trap doors and twirling moustache. Much of this is down to the direction, and script requirements, as his character appears guilty of the crime as soon as he makes his first creepy, and extremely foggy, entrance. As much as the film did Novello an injustice, it does have all the early signs of Hitchcock's style, tentatively and crudely emerging, to be refined in later films. Many years later Hitchcock would admit freely that:

"It was the first time I exercised my style," Hitchcock recalled years later, " In truth you might say *The Lodger* was my first picture."

It was curious to see a screening of this silent film, accompanied by an orchestra, projected onto a large screen for which it was intended. It did add something to the overall effect and seemed to work better than seeing it on television. Novello draws you into the story in spite of the faults one can find with his performance, demonstrating an almost hypnotic quality. His eyes are, at moments, full of sincerity and thoughts appropriate to his characterisation. It is obvious he tried his best under difficult circumstances. Novello hardly ever mentioned Hitchcock or his experiences working with him. That would seem to say it all. On its original release it was, against all expectations, a great success and certainly established Hitchcock as a talent to be reckoned with.

Novello and Hitchcock didn't particularly get along that well. Hitchcock was not enamoured with, or comfortable in the company of, homosexual men and found Novello's particular "camp" style off-putting as a result. They did go on to make another film together *Down Hill* (1926), which was an adaptation of Novello and Constance Collier's stage play of the same name from 1925, but only because they were both under contract at Gainsborough, with Balcon calling the shots.

Down Hill told the story of Roddy, a public school boy, who takes the blame for his friend's dalliance with a shop girl who becomes pregnant and subsequently his life goes predictably down hill. Sandy Wilson, in his book *Ivor*, describes vividly the penultimate scene where Novello's character realises the grotesqueness of his situation:

"Roddy, again penniless, reduced to working as a gigolo in a Montmare night-club is the highlight of the film. Pale and expressionless, he steers a succession of ageing ladies round the floor on the instructions of a grotesque Madame. A weird woman, with glaring eyes, asks him to her table and, touched by her apparent concern, Roddy pours out his heart to her. At another table an elderly roué has a seizure and when the waiter pulls back the curtain to give him air, the room is flooded with daylight and Roddy looks around with growing horror as the customers are revealed in all their ugliness…Ivor's vivid face is at once beautiful and horrifying, and equal to anything in the most acclaimed 'art' films of the period," concluding that *Down Hill* is superior to *The Lodger*, "simply because the variety of scenes and situation gave so much wider scope to the genius of Hitchcock."

Towards the end of the film Novello's character gives his all whilst entombed on a ship. The dream sequences and his scary descent into delirium and seeming madness are fascinating to watch. Again he hooks the viewer and hypnotises them, drawing them into his mind and thoughts. At times it is quite unnerving and, it has to be said, eerie. It isn't hard to imagine his female audience in the darkened cinema gripping the arms of their respective seats, wishing they could rescue him and take him home. It also gives an idea of his charisma and a hint of the experience of seeing him performing live at a theatre.

The Observer's critic, St John Ervine, on viewing the scantily clad Novello as Roddy in *Down Hill's* school changing-room scene, noted that "when Mr. Novello washed his legs, one heard the sound of indrawn breath coming from the maidens… Here was a thrilling spectacle to be described with the utmost particularity on the morrow to the unfortunate maidens who had missed it," concluding, with one imagines tongue-firmly-in-cheek, "His knees, his shins, even his thighs, and his dear little wiggly toes…Not in vain had the maidens stood in ques for hours!"

Again it was a silent film, and perhaps enabled Hitchcock to experiment with his visual technique, before he could enhance it with the addition of sound. For the young director, the combination of skills he acquired in German film studios, which would soon be destroyed by the rise to power of the Nazis, combined with his early days on British silent films, aided his progress and helped to develop his talent as an innovative and unique film director. Had his relationship with Novello been a more positive one, perhaps they could have developed their association and helped each other along the way. It was a lost opportunity for both of them, perhaps?

Novello carried on unperturbed by the highs and lows of the past months. He was resilient and ever optimistic in public, but the truth was he still fought privately with his insecurities and other demons. Those close to him began to notice his odd behaviour and bouts of depression. One minute he would seem happy and relaxed, in the next moment he would become frantic with activity, then swoop the next moment into silent depression. He attended parties and enchanted everyone, but would suddenly whisper to Bobbie he wanted to leave immediately for no apparent reason. Eventually he gave up going to such occasions unless he absolutely had to. Underneath he was full of apprehensions and anxiety, which manifested itself in a lack of confidence and sometimes shyness when around unfamiliar people. Bobbie came to recognise the signs and made sure he was always on hand. However, Novello absolutely loved giving parties at "the flat", and would entertain his guests until dawn with effortless energy. When in control, and in his own safe environment, Novello was a different kind of party animal. He had moments when for no apparent reason he would disappear and the guests would ask where he was. Bobbie would assure them he was fine. After a short while he would reappear as if nothing had happened and once again become the centre of attention.

Bobbie was a loyal friend to Novello and it is difficult to find anything he recorded about their long relationship. Looking at the situation as an observer many years later, it must have been terribly difficult for him at times. He was observed to be a very shrewd, witty man and the only person who really understood Novello and his moods. He was also Novello's voice of reason and practically never, once a dilemma was debated, did he go against the advice of Bobbie. And never once did he have reason to regret his advice. Bobbie for his part had had a successful career as an actor since he was a child, but since meeting Novello his own career had slid into the background. Novello did write small parts in most of his plays for him, but that must have been difficult to accept initially. There have been those who claimed that Bobbie "was not very good" as an actor, punctuated by "but Ivor always wrote him a little part to play." That must have been terribly hurtful. However much you love your partner, it can still cause friction and discontent to hear such remarks whispered behind your back. Besides, how could Bobbie compete with Novello's celebrity, it would have been impossible. By the end of the 1920s Bobbie had become resolved, if not content, to allow his own career to fade into the background and support Novello in whatever way he could. Novello was, it has to be said, very lucky to have him by his side. They obviously enjoyed an "open" relationship as far as sexual partners were concerned, we forget that the 1920s and 30s was a very promiscuous and hedonistic era, but they remained a devoted couple to the last. Bobbie, in many ways, has been an unappreciated protagonist in the story of Novello's life and career. He did some foolish things once Novello had died, but then at that point his world had been shattered and he found himself cut adrift and alone.

Novello embarked on yet another film project in 1927, one which would satisfy him in three very different ways. *The Constant Nymph* was a successful Novel by Margaret Kennedy which had been adapted into an equally successful stage play. Noel Coward had been cast as the male lead, Lewis Dodd, for the stage version but hated the part and promptly had a convenient nervous-breakdown and left. John Gielgud, his understudy, took over to great acclaim. The romantic story is about a young composer who becomes the object of a young girls passion. Novello was intrigued by the play and would have liked to have played it on the stage.

The film version was quickly planned and casting began. Set in the Austrian Tyrol, where the location shooting took place, with the interiors shot at the Gainsborough Studios in Islington, it had high production values from the outset, although it would be a silent film. Basil Dean approached Novello and offered him the part of Lewis Dodd. He turned it down initially, annoyed he hadn't been asked to do the stage version. In the meantime he had been to see a house near Maidenhead, which he fell in love with.

"At that time I was terribly keen on playing Lewis Dodd," recalled Novello during an interview for *New London Magazine*, "but when the play was cast, to my bitter disappointment I was not offered the part. Later, when Basil Dean started work on the film version, he had great difficulty in finding a Lewis Dodd for the screen. He tested fifteen actors without success and finally approached me. My reply was to ask for a big salary and I named the exact price of the freehold of Red Roofs, even to the odd shilling. So with one film I was able to achieve two of my ambitions: to play Lewis Dodd and to own Red Roofs."

Novello had cleverly exacted his revenge for being over-looked for the stage production, and managed to secure the large fee as a result. He then purchased the Maidenhead house, from his friend John Gordon, on the 11th November, 1927, and paid four thousand one hundred pounds, fifteen shillings and sixpence for the property, which included the main house and two cottages for staff. He considered calling it *The Constant Nymph* but Bobbie thought that was a ridiculous name for a house, so suggested Red Roofs on account of the red tiled roofs. So Red Roofs it became.

The Constant Nymph was also a landmark for Novello in terms of his performance and characterisation. That he had an obvious passion for playing Lewis Dodd and for the overall story is without question, and it was the film where he finally demonstrated his abilities as an accomplished screen actor. The stills from the film reflect his naturalistic and relaxed demeanour, and it has to be said his attraction physically. It is Novello in his prime and at his best. The tragedy for the film was that its release came after the introduction of sound, therefore it didn't enjoy any success at all - with audiences as fickle as ever, over night they were only interested in sound pictures. Ironically, there had been debate during the pre-production stage whether or not it should be a sound film. Sadly for posterity it was decided against due to the increased costs involved.

Basil Dean declared it to be "a very good silent film indeed," adding that "talkies had just come in…its commercial future was very much in doubt." However, the bigger tragedy was yet to come. Warner Bothers bought the film rights for a re make in the 1940s starring Joan Fontaine and Charles Boyer. Part of the condition was the destruction of all copies of the first film. Thus Novello's efforts, and those of all the original cast, which included a young Elsa Lanchester, were burnt and lost forever. But one never knows, maybe a forgotten copy is laying undiscovered in a dusty attic somewhere? Stranger things have happened.

Fascinating as Novello was to his fans at this time, not all of those close to him were quite as confident in his abilities. Apart from Bobbie and Marsh, those around him seemed quite negative about his talents and did everything they could to persuade against attempting to further develop his career as a playwright. No doubt such comments were borne out of a genuine concern for Novello, but it must have made him at times feel quite insecure and anxious about his potential; not to mention annoyed and frustrated! Having successfully developed his acting career with, it has to be said, positive encouragement from critics like Agate of *The Sunday Times* who, although honest and at times harsh, always seemed to find a positive comment for Novello. It is obvious they too had become spell-bound by his persona and one can sense them almost willing him to succeed. It is possibly the one vital ingredient with Novello that some of those close to him failed to add to any equation of his future potential. His unique personality.

At this point he had been employed in various plays penned by others with varying degrees of success. These outings had enabled him to establish himself and develop as an actor, and no one could dispute his ability to fill the theatres with his fans. That fact alone allowed him to continue undeterred. However he had written two plays himself in collaboration with Constance Collier, and they had been successful beyond anyone's expectations. Indeed, hadn't he been warned by those same people not to embark on those productions for fear he would humiliate himself publicly? The opposite had in fact occurred.

Novello was very aware of his limitations, but as acutely aware of his strengths, and used that self-awareness to his advantage. Anything he had written to date was fashioned and structured in such a way as to capitalise on his capabilities, sense of comedy, and thus entertain his fans. He had no delusions that what he had created was in any way intellectual high-brow art, but they serviced his abilities and satisfied his fans which is all he really cared about. With those thoughts firmly in his mind he set about writing his first play alone. Coward was horrified and did everything he could to persuade him not to do it. Novello appreciated the advice, but went ahead anyway. Novello would always be a conundrum to Coward, simply because he was always baffled at how Novello managed to make huge box-office successes out of material which he considered to be trite and inferior. In one way Coward was right, as those plays are now considered to be awful, but with Novello's personality, and in their time, they served their purpose as intended. Without Novello, it seems they are meaningless and have no life.

Novello set about writing *The Truth Game* with an eye to achieving a long held ambition. He had always admired the Edwardian actress Lily Elsie, and had been entranced when he watched her in *The Merry Widow* at Daly's all those years before. He would write the lead part for her in his first solo play, and decided to do everything in his power to persuade her to play it. He was aware that she had retired from the business many years earlier, but maybe he could persuade her anyway.

Lily Elsie was an enigmatic character and in some ways a forerunner to Garbo, by definitely wanting to "be alone" most of the time. This was not a demonstration of haughty grandeur on her part but a genuine insecurity and shyness. She never enjoyed performing and was always racked with nerves. On becoming the Edwardian equivalent of a celebrity with *The Merry Widow*, she found it impossible to deal with being known by everyone, wherever she went, and it affected her nerves badly. Withdrawing into herself she became rude and surly when recognised, but it was all a reaction to her own fears and insecurity. As a result, and quite unfairly, she developed a reputation for being "difficult" and "impossible to work with" in the industry.

Elsie was born on 8th April, 1866, in a suburb of Leeds. She grew up mainly in the north of England and found herself performing in music halls and pantomimes in the latter years of the 19th Century. Known as "Little Elsie" she was described at the time as a child with "a sweet voice" and she delighted with a ballad called "Dear Heart" where she sang "the highest notes with ease, and renders the exacting song with good articulation and perfectly in tune." The audience were listening "with rapt attention" to her efforts. She eventually found herself in London as a chorus girl at Daly's.

Her introduction to the West End and Daly's didn't go altogether smoothly. George Edwardes, Daly's Manager, sacked her after watching her break from a routine and flirt with members of the audience by patting a balloon in their direction. It seems a ridiculous punishment for such a trivial misdemeanour, but it does give an insight into the controlling and strict regime endured by Daly's chorus girls at the time. It is also worth noting that such an innocent action could have been misconstrued at the time. Any suggestion of improper behaviour by chorus girls, and flirting or contact with the audience in any form, could have resulted in accusations of immoral behaviour by the licensing authorities. Daly's was a fairly respectable establishment and had moved away from the more coarse image of music halls. Promenading in music halls provided a thinly disguised opportunity for men to pick up prostitutes. The promenade in question was situated in the front of house area, and was a popular haunt for male audience members and some chorus girls who supplemented their meager wages by selling their sexual favours.

Elsie found herself without a job and struggling to survive in London alone. A few weeks later she happened to bump into Edwardes on the street, who discovered her plight and regretted his actions. They managed to resolve their differences and she was again employed in the chorus of Daly's. She then appeared, under Edwardes management, in a Chinese musical titled *See-See*, at the Strand Theatre, where she appeared with oriental eye make-up and hair and appropriately costumed. Amazingly this fact alone brought her to the attention of the press because she created, through her own efforts, a sense of realism to her role. For musical comedy it was a first, for up to that point no one had bothered with such authenticity in their characterisation or appearance.

Edwardes then asked her to play Sonia, the lead in Lehar's *The Merry Widow*, which he had taken her to see in Germany. Elsie's reply was "oh, no, I couldn't possibly!" On being asked why, she informed Edwardes she didn't feel she was "good enough as a singer or actress" to attempt such a demanding role. Her insecurities were always to the fore and she could only see what she perceived as her faults. She disliked her too thin figure, her plain features, and considered her voice too small and untrained. Edwardes did attempt to find someone he could cast as Sonia, but at the back of his mind he couldn't erase Elsie's charms and talent. "She has never done anything to speak of," Edwardes commented at the time, "but I know she is clever and I believe she has a great future in front of her. I believe she can play the part of Sonia and astonish them all."

Astonish them she did. Her portrayal of Sonia was superlative and is still talked about today in theatre circles; her performance still considered definitive. Which in itself is quite astonishing considering the passage of time and the fact her name has slowly disappeared from the minds of the general public. An indication of her character and temperament is her remarks made on the opening night of *The Merry Widow*. Standing in the wings listening to the deafening cheers of the audience, she turned to a colleague and asked sincerely: "Do you think I was any good?" When it was pointed out to her the cheering was for her she replied: "Oh, no, it can't be. It must be for the costumes!"

Indeed the costumes were lavish, designed by Lucille, Lady Duff-Gordon, a famous aristocratic socialite who would a few years later become infamous around the world when she and her husband commandeered a lifeboat and subsequently survived the sinking of the Titanic. Heavily criticised for being one of a handful of people in a life boat which could hold up to forty, exacerbated by her refusal to allow the crew members to return and pick up survivors perishing in the cold sea. But in 1906 she was as yet untainted by such allegations.

"That season was a brilliant one," she recalled in later years, "perhaps the most brilliant of the series which brought the social life of pre-war London to its peak. And just when it was at its zenith a new play *The Merry Widow* was launched with a new actress, who set the whole town raving over her beauty and a waltz that set the whole world dancing to its fascinating lilt."

Enjoying the "fascinating lilt" was a certain teenage boy who was hanging over the rail of the gods cheering with them at Daly's, something he would repeat on many occasions during the run of *The Merry Widow*. For the young Novello, Lily Elsie stood for everything he admired about the theatre and female talent. He would never forget those visits or how they made him feel. In the future he would always remember the excitement of being part of the audience, and would always structure his own productions in a way that recreated those feelings. In an industry where so many become jaded and chose to forget what it's like to be on the other side of the proscenium, Novello never did. It would turn out to be one of his greatest strengths.

For Lily Elsie, the consequences of her fame was not one she particularly enjoyed. She hated being recognised and was still nervous to the point of illness prior to every performance. As a result, she started to miss matinees and then some evening performances. This caused some fairly predictable but unfair press gossip that labeled her "a part time actress" with ideas above her station. Ironically, one of her greatest strengths was her genuine self effacing attitude about her abilities. It would also prove to be her greatest weakness. Her nerves were often fraught and she had several bouts of nervous collapse; indeed, these were the early signs of her eventual decline into paranoia and severe mental health problems.

By the late 1920s, Elsie had been absent from the business for several years. She had been introduced to Novello by Mrs. Asquith at Downing Street years earlier, and had no doubt been aware of his rise to prominence in the years that followed. She was flattered when her manager relayed a message from Novello asking if she would consider appearing in his new play *The Truth Game*. The offer came at a time when Elsie was sorting out her life after her marriage collapsed, and was thus receptive to, and welcoming of, such an offer. That it came from the most famous man in England was a bonus. No doubt she was also glad to abandon her self-imposed exile in the Gloucestershire countryside, which she found a lonely place once her husband had left. Interestingly, as much as Elsie shunned the limelight and considered it intrusive, there was a part of her that craved the chance to perform. It would be a paradox in her life, one that would become ever destructive to her fragile mental health.

Looking forward to this new opportunity Elsie traveled to Biarritz, at that time a fashionable and exclusive resort for the rich and famous in the South of France. Her intention was to restore her health in preparation for Novello's play and her appearance in the West End. She wrote to Novello and confirmed their contract, but couldn't help slipping into an informal address. It is interesting in as much as it gives a clue to the informality of any contract between them, which was a reflection of the status Novello had achieved and her delight at the opportunity to "star" with him in a high profile London production.

Elsie's letters to Novello are worth including because they make interesting reading, and also because so little correspondence between them has survived. It also gives a hint of her character and business sense:

"Ivor Dear, I received your letter of July 3rd [1928] engaging me to play lead in your play *Taken By Storm* [Novello changed the title to *The Truth Game* later] at a salary of 150 (one hundred and fifty pounds) and a further increase of fifty pounds a week or 10 per cent of the gross should the play run over three months. Rehearsals to begin as near as possible September 15th - the play produced round about October 15th. I think this covers everything but of course it is very important to get the best and most suitable theatre possible. Do remember, Ivor dear, it is an intimate play and must have a lovely intimate theatre. How thrilling now I'm going to sign my contract with you."

Novello had hoped to get the Theatre Royal, Haymarket but discovered it would not be available. He settled on the Globe Theatre (now the Gielgud Theatre) on Shaftesbury Avenue. The cost was four hundred and fifty pounds per week with two weeks deposit as retainer for the theatre rental. Along with Elsie's salary of one hundred and fifty pounds per week, plus Novello's salary and those of other cast members, and the set and properties, it gives a good indication of the costs involved at the time. Elsie sent Novello another letter dated the same day:

"Ivor dear, here is my contract. At least it started by being my contract and then I started to talk to you in it. So like me! Just imagine this, you really engaging me as your leading lady (at least I hope I'm a Lady) It is strange, Ivor darling, isn't it? I do hope with all my heart you are going to have a grand success with it and that I shall help with you and all the others to make it so. Do get a lovely intimate theatre darling, please."

Considering Novello's knowledge of Elsie's singing talents, and his own considerable talents as a composer, it is even more interesting he never considered a musical presentation for the woman he had admired for so long. Inevitably it was probably due to his complete focus and obsession for being taken seriously as an actor at this time. One must remember that musical comedy and revue did not hold the same prestige as appearing in a West End play. At this point in time he didn't consider himself to be anything but an actor. It is also likely that Elsie wouldn't have considered a singing part at that point in her life. Posterity is perhaps the loser as it would have been interesting to see what his musical comedy ideas would have been like. It is known he composed an Operetta for Elsie titled *The Argentine Widow* and also made additions to *The Fickle Jade* with her in mind. Neither production ever saw the light of day, and the scripts and scores have never been found in their entire form.

With the cast assembled which included Constance Collier and Viola Tree, and the director Sir Gerald du Maurier, rehearsals for *The Truth Game* began. To say the production did not have a good beginning is an understatement.

Novello found himself embattled and frustrated almost from the start. Du Maurier never arrived for the start of rehearsals, so Novello and the rest of the cast carried on and utilised the time until he did appear. Frantic telephone calls were made by Novello trying to contact Du Maurier, then out of the blue he received a call from Noel Coward informing him that Constance Collier had decided to pull out of the production. Novello arranged for Ellis Jeffries to take over and then as quickly she decided she didn't want the part after all, and promptly left the theatre. Novello was understandably aghast at what was happening around him. Du Maurier then arrived and announced he didn't think the play was any good and advised Novello to cancel the production. On questioning his reasons, it transpired that du Maurier hadn't even bothered to read the play. Novello pointed out to him he should perhaps actually read the play before making such a negative assessment. Du Maurier answered patronisingly: "My dear boy, you won't even get to the end of the second act."

Furious but undeterred Novello battled on and declared he would recast and find another director. Graham Brown duly arrived at the theatre and after watching the first act declared: "What are you worrying about, this is charming." He subsequently took on the job. Lily Elsie had stood by him and assured him she thought the play was good. The pre production period was fast turning into fodder for a more intriguing play than *The Truth Game* with which it was preparation for. The whole situation was farcical and extremely frustrating for Novello. But it does demonstrate his tenacity and resolve to never take "no" for an answer when faced with adversity. A trait he had inherited from his mother, no doubt. Constance Collier was his friend, or so he had thought, and she chose to tell him of her decision to withdraw through Coward, which baffled and hurt Novello.

Behind the scenes there was much gossip and tactical maneuvering going on that Novello was unaware of. Many of his friends believed his idea to write a play in his own right and present it in the West End was simply beyond his abilities. They were pessimistic almost to a man and woman. Constance Collier, colluding with Coward, decided to pull out of the production in the hope Novello would cancel it completely. They feared certain disaster and were supposedly protecting their friend. Ellis Jeffries picked up on the negative gossip and suddenly saw herself involved in a flop which would not only humiliate her but damage her career. The psychology of theatre artistes was hard at play and the first thing it attacks is their insecurities. Du Maurier was also aware of the gossip and decided they were probably right and he should try and bring an end to it. As much as all those concerned seemed to be concerned primarily for their friend, it must have been a huge blow to Novello. He had committed himself to a great deal of money and would stand to lose everything - something he could ill afford to do. It must have also occurred to him that not many of his friends had much faith in his abilities, even after everything he had achieved. A lesser person would have retreated wounded and bitter, but not Novello.

It spurred him on, prodded and supported by Bobbie and Marsh, making him even more determined he would produce the play. Marsh was at Chartwell, Churchill's country home, keeping abreast of the unfolding drama and fearing "the venture would collapse" offered reassurance where he could . "My only comfort was when I thought of making a list of pictures I could sell," Marsh wrote, "to help if you were forced into cutting your loss." There would be no cutting of losses. Novello had engaged another director, cast Lillian Braithwaite to replace Jeffries, whilst Lily Elsie took it all in her stride and carried on with silent determination. Rehearsals went ahead and all began to come together, albeit slowly. Working against the odds, as they had lost nearly two weeks of valuable rehearsal time due to the fracas, it began to take shape and the first night seemed ever closer.

The plot was fairly predictable for the time, revolving around the themes of sex and money. Elsie played a wealthy widow, Rosine Browne, who finds herself involved with a charming adventurer, Max Clement, played by Novello, who is also impoverished. Rosine eventually falls in love with Max only to discover he is a distant relative. If she marries him it would mean he would inherit her fortune. She then switched her affections to Sir George Kelvin, and they announce their engagement. After further intrigues and pleading it all ends happily for Max and Rosine. Also included in the cast were Viola Tree, Mabel Sealby, Glen Byam Shaw and Frederick Volpe. Novello once again decided not to credit himself as author of the play, this time his pseudonym was H.E.S. Davidson. Unsurprisingly after all the problems that had ensued, he felt insecure in using his own name.

From the first night, October 5th, 1928, *The Truth Game* was an immediate success. The critics were favourable in their comments and Novello had succeeded with all the odds stacked against him.

"Lily Elsie and Ivor Novello are the most picturesque pair that feminine playgoers could wish to see," declared *Theatre World*, " and as women form the greater part of any given audience, their complete satisfaction with the entertainment is practically guaranteed in advance."

Cecil Beaton recalled a friend telling him that Elsie and Novello were so impossibly beautiful together in *The Truth Game* they were "like two fawns in a Sultan's garden, they should have eaten flowers."

Punch in their review did offer some praise for Novello's ability to create interesting characters and effective dialogue but suggested he could possibly refrain from swamping everything with sentimental baggage. 'Sentimental' was a word which would become very attached to Novello and his work, and further fuelled his detractors in serious theatrical circles.

The Times in their review were more down to earth in their appraisal. "The Third Act was all the more inane than it need have been," they opined, " and it is pleasanter to remember the earlier acts which are full of good humoured nonsense and the ingenious decorations of impudent dialogue." There are compliments to be found in the pompous tones of the reviewer who declared Novello to be in "high spirits" and Elsie to have a "charming grip on the not very subtle intricacies" of her character. In summing up it was decided "the play is shallow and scattered in its conclusion, but the trimmings are often very good fun."

The Truth Game ran for six months at the Globe Theatre, then embarked on a national tour, only to return for another West End season at Daly's Theatre. Much to the chagrin of those who had tried so hard to destroy the play's chances from the outset, it was a huge success both artistically and financially for Novello. The audiences in the provinces came in their thousands and filled every theatre it played. Novello could do no wrong in their minds and they took no notice of what critics said. It was also a turning point for him. Having survived the onslaught of negativity, he would never again allow such things to alter his course or change his mind. In many ways those who had worked against him had done Novello a great service. The experience made him much more confident in his own abilities, and determined to never again to allow others to chart his course. His next play was already completed, and he decided to credit himself as author for the first time.

Symphony In Two Flats tells the story of the inhabitants of two flats (apartments). In one lives Novello's character, a musician called David who goes blind, who then becomes entangled in an emotional ménage-a trios whilst writing a symphony in the hope of winning a competition. His love interest is Lesley (Benita Hume) and his friend Leo Chavasse (George Relph), who is also secretly in love with Lesley. In the flat below lives a mother (Lillian Braithwaite) and her eccentric daughters, Salmon (Viola Tree) and Beryl (Ann Trevor) who camp it up for comic effect as they all strive to find husbands. Their maid, Mabel, was played by cockney comedienne Minnie Raynor. She would appear in all Novello's shows until her death in 1943, and he considered her to be his "mascot" from this point on; although many of those close to Novello considered her to be anything but, and she would eventually be the cause of one of Novello's greatest personal disasters.

The production opened on October 14th, 1929, under the direction of Raymond Massey. Although the critics were unsure to say the least it ran for several months and again drew huge audiences. Novello's abilities may still be dumbfounding the critics but his fans couldn't get enough. Marsh declared that "the scene where the blind musician learns that it is not his symphony which has won the prize…never lost its shattering poignancy," and also felt it was a "measure of the progress the author has made" as a playwright. There were those who didn't agree, but then Novello was used to his detractors diatribes by now, and cared even less to take any notice.

"Each of his two separate plays has an odd effect of distracting from the other," reported an obviously baffled *Daily Telegraph*, "the people in the top flat are so unrelievedly intense, and the people below are so painstakingly comic, that one wishes they could be allowed to mix and so mitigate each other's crudeness…the material they are given is rather course in texture, [but] they keep us laughing almost continuously."

The Times, ever surly, remarked one is "driven to decide that the moral of the play is that you do not get to know people unless you happen to meet them. Nine scenes are a long journey for such a prize."

Hardly what anyone could consider to be critical endorsements for the play. The fact of the matter was it didn't matter. By this point one feels Novello could have filled a theatre nightly but just walking on and talking about the weather! Such was his popularity coupled with the steadfast devotion of his female fans. The Shubert brothers had seen the play and saw the potential in Novello as a box-office draw, and decided to capitalise on it for Broadway. They offered Novello the chance to present two of his plays on Broadway, both of which he would "star" in. Novello accepted and the finer details were agreed. Once again there were whispers of negativity by those who considered going to America would be Novello's undoing. He smiled, thanked them for their advice and concerns, and did it anyway.

For the Shuberts' it was no doubt a move born out of circumstances. The Wall Street crash of 1929 had sent the world's stock markets into free fall and billions of dollars had been lost; the perilous state of the British economy, still not recovered from the effects of the First World War, was badly affected too. The result was to plunge the United States and Britain into a depression which would see thousands in this country thrown out of work. Maybe Novello's eccentric typically English comedy was just what was needed to fill a Broadway theatre. He still had a profile in America due to his film work, and it was also economically viable way to place a production into an empty theatre. Circumstances and history were again playing their part in Novello's opportunities and fortunes. Preparations were initiated for the company to travel to New York, where the first play to open would be *Symphony In Two Flats*.

Novello had also been busy in other areas whilst appearing in his plays. He had composed music for a revue titled *The House That Jack Built*, produced by Jack Hulbert at the Adelphi Theatre. Other composers involved included Vivien Ellis, Arthur Schwartz and Sidney Baines. His film work had also continued but, as Novello freely admitted, more for the money offered than the quality of the films. *The Gallant Hussar* (1928) was described on the advertising material as "a charming love story with a background of

Hungarian military life." Predictable in its slushy romantic plot and storyline, it served Novello's fans with its dashing hero involved in love and intrigue. The reviews were luke-warm at best.

"This charming picture is convincing proof that fragility of plot is no bar to enjoyment. Fortunately the star is endowed with a personality suggesting innocent irresponsibility rather than ingrained wickedness: consequently he never forfeits sympathy."

One wishes that Novello would have, just for once, embraced a truly wicked and decadent character just to enliven his film repertoire. Sadly it wasn't to be. Some of the blame no doubt lies with Gainsborough, who were determined to milk his Valentino image to the last drop. Predictably Gainsborough were still attempting to cash in on their stars previous incarnations. *Return Of The Rat* was a sequel of such low standards in terms of any plot or storyline, one wonders why they bothered at all. Novello must have spent his time dreaming of Broadway and reading his vast payment cheque more than reading the script. Had he read it, he would have thrown in into the waste paper basket immediately. *Film Weekly* were pretty scathing in their comments declaring the story as "novelettish and unoriginal" while Novello's performance "as usual, relies more on his effective profile rather than acting ability."

One senses that Novello had started to tire of films at this stage, probably due to all his energy and passions being directed at his stage work. In many ways the films were an easy way to swell his bank balance, and brought him little in the way of artistic satisfaction. The fact he was still making silent films at a time when "talkies" were becoming common is also rather odd. Possibly this was down to the costs involved, costs which Gainsborough and other small British studios were unwilling to shoulder. It also has to be borne in mind that at this stage, many believed the "talkies" were a fad and that audiences would lose interest in them, and films would once again be silent. If nothing else it does highlight the naiveties and inconsistencies of the film industry and how even those involved were still experimenting and evolving the art form - even though they weren't perhaps aware of it.

A South Sea Bubble (1928) would be Novello's last silent film. It was a disaster commercially mainly due to its lack of sound and therefore limited release. It was also not a particularly good film and Michael Balcon declared "it was really a load of nonsense, indifferently directed…in fact it was a failure." Some stills which survived from the film depict a sophisticated and naturalistic Novello, which also manage to capture an element of his charismatic persona on the screen; also the glamour of his co stars Anette Benson and Benita Hume.

As the 1920s came to a close Novello could look back on the decade and marvel at his achievements. Fate seemed to work in his favour and seemingly he could do no wrong in the eyes of his fans. He was very satisfied indeed, and one suspects delighted he had proved all his critics wrong. Seemingly untouched by the global economic crisis which would bring devastating poverty to those both sides of the Atlantic, Novello set out to conquer Broadway and Hollywood. He would be among the few who initially managed to make the transition from silent to sound films. Along the way he would make some powerful friends in Hollywood, be utterly frustrated by the MGM moguls and their system, and be forced to consider his relationship with his father.

Novello's house Red Roofs at Littlewick Green near Maidenhead.

From left – Richard Rose, Anthony Bushell, Ivor Novello, Benita Hume & Lloydie reading the paper

Magdalen College, Oxford. Novello third from left, third row.
Sir Thomas Herbert Warren and Varley Roberts seated second row, center.

Picture taken circa. 1906

With thanks to Magdalen College for permission to use this image
and Dr. Robin Darwall-Smith

Lily Elsie – Edwardian actress & beauty so adored by Novello in Lehar's The Merry Widow operetta.

Lily Elsie & Ivor Novello in Novello's play The Truth Game
at the Gielgud Theatre 1929

"Like two fawns in a Sultan's garden,
they should have eaten flowers."

Cecil Beaton

Lily Elsie as Sonia in The Merry Widow
1907

Lily Elsie

Novello departing on the boat train from Waterloo Station.

Novello with Bobbie Andrews – his life partner at Croydon Airport 1937   to visit the Paris Exhibition

Beatrice Lille, Novello & Dorothy Dickson on board the Queen Elizabeth to New York

Novello & Bebe Daniels at the Arts Club, London 1943

Novello & Dorothy Dickson.

Dickson was his leading lady in Careless Rapture, Crest of the Wave and Henry V at the Theatre Royal, Drury Lane, London in the 1930s

Novello and Zena Dare catching the Queen Mary boat train at Waterloo Station, 1948

Novello as Rudi in The Dancing Years – finally able to portray the Nazis once the production returned to London's Adelphi Theatre in 1941

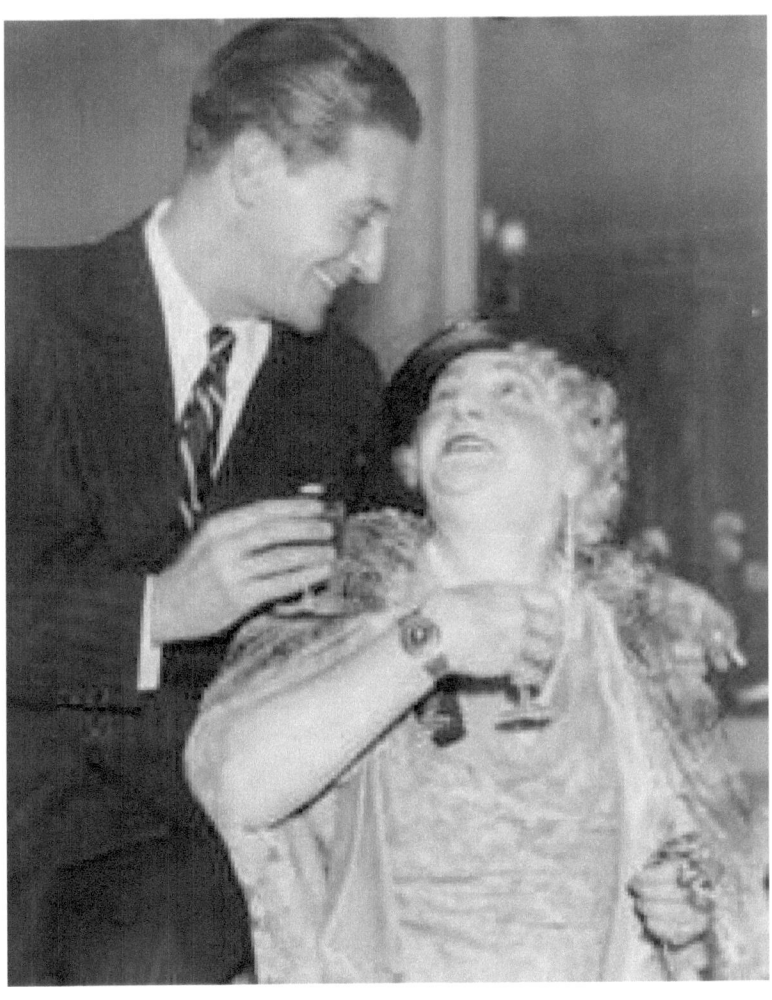

Novello with his beloved mother, Clara Novello Davis 1937

In Search of Ruritania

Novello with Olive Gilbert, Zena Dare and Sonia, a child he adopted, at his Jamaica home Wyndways

Olive Gilbert & Novello in Jamaica 1948

Novello at the time of his Hollywood career when he was credited with writing the immortal lines "Me Tarzan, you Jane."

Novello & Mary Ellis back stage at Drury Lane during the original run of The Dancing Years, 1939.

Novello, Olivier, Zena Dare, Olive Gilbert, Vivien Leigh, Vanessa Lee and Bobbie Andrews back stage in South Africa.

Olive Gilbert – photographed at the time of King's Rhapsody, 1949.

THE LAND THAT MIGHT HAVE BEEN!

"He was a beautiful man, an enchanting actor, and had the great gift of being a friend. He felt as I did, and do - In order to have a friend, you must be a friend."

Joan Crawford.

Novello arrived in New York full of optimism for the future and the possibilities that lay ahead. For a country still reeling from the devastation of the Wall Street crash which had seen billions of dollars wiped of the stock market, and resulted in hundreds, if not thousands, hurling themselves out of windows and from the top of buildings to a grisly death, Novello must have appeared an eccentric figure. The old order of lavish indulgence was at an end, prohibition was in place, and the unemployed stood in line for soup and bread on street corners. The depression was upon them and would exact a terrible revenge, most having to endure a poverty stricken existence.

Broadway was also suffering because of the economic collapse. Once wealthy investors and impresarios no longer had the means to gamble thousands of dollars on theatre productions for fun. Before the crash most had indulged themselves with little care of a return on their money, so plentiful were their reserves. But all that had changed. Broadway greats like Ziegfeld no longer had the power they once enjoyed. He, too, lost almost everything in the crash and would no longer be able to astonish audiences with his lavish and expensive *Follies* productions.

But life went on in the great city of New York and, in spite of the struggles, the theatre did survive and begin its long journey back to economic recovery. The Schubert brothers had been wiser than most. They still owned their theatres and had been sensible in how and where they had invested their money. Their prudence and skilful business acumen, which had never included a high-risk strategy, had in the end saved them and some of their investments. Their priority now was to generate an income through the box-office as soon as possible - their good fortune would count for nothing if they failed to create some kind of cash turnover. Theatres were expensive buildings when 'dark' and could eat money quicker than create it.

The Schuberts' took a chance on Novello hoping that his personality, he still enjoyed a film following in the US, would encourage audiences to come and see him live at the theatre; much as he managed to fill the theatres in England with his fans. The Schuberts' also reckoned Novello's slightly eccentric and very English play *Symphony In Two Flats* would be the perfect vehicle to launch him on Broadway. After everything New Yorkers had endured with the crash, something light and frivolous was perfect to help them forget the terrible reality. Having been successful in the West End, it was much cheaper to transfer the production to New York than create a whole new production. So that is exactly what they did.

Novello was delighted to be in New York and was full of optimism for the future. He wasn't oblivious to the economic depression and sympathised with those caught in its grip, but it didn't affect him directly. He was now quite wealthy, and due to his prudent business dealings, would continue to be so for the rest of his life.

Preparations thus began for the opening of *Symphony In Two Flats*. Rehearsals went smoothly at the Sam S. Shubert Theatre with an air of excitement and optimism reverberating among producers and cast. The very fact it seemed to be going so smoothly seemed to concern nobody; it is usually taken as a bad omen if the pre production stage doesn't include some minor turmoil or frustration. However, there would be trouble ahead for Novello and the play, which would nearly kill stone dead his Broadway career.

Opening on September 16th, 1930, the play and Novello received pretty tepid reviews. *The New York Times* declared the play and Novello to be "more mannered than substantial" and "coloured by preciosity," whilst the *Herald Tribune* opined it as "an ambitious and often interesting attempt that doesn't quite work out." These reviews combined with the heat wave that engulfed New York put an end to the play. It closed unceremoniously after 47 performances. Novello was devastated but, as always when faced with adversity, he refused to be beaten by the critics or the weather. It says much about Novello, not to mention his considerable charms and personality, that he managed to turn this disaster into a positive possibility. The hardheaded Shuberts' were obviously no match for Novello's personality as he managed to persuade them to go ahead with a second play, which he assured them would be a hit. If the same situation arose today, the author-actor responsible for such a flop, and making such a suggestion, would be laughed off Broadway. Even in 1930 it was remarkable he managed to persuade them and reached an agreement. But he did, and *The Truth Game* would be Novello's next play produced by the Shuberts' on Broadway.

In its long and distinguished history Broadway had never experienced such a bad season as that of 1930 - 1931. Even established stars like Fanny Brice, who would be immortalised years later by Barbra Streisand in *Funny Girl*, struggled to pull an audience into the beleaguered theatres, still suffering from the effects of the crash. Billy Rose had produced two revues for her to star in *Sweet & Low*, swiftly followed by *Crazy Quilt*, but in financial terms they no way produced the kind of revenues expected prior to the depression; that said it gives a good indication of Brice's popularity that they managed any business at all and broke even, then managed to make some money when they went on a nationwide tour. Brice had by this time discovered the true depths of Ziegfeld's financial collapse. She was a friend of his wife, Billy Burke, and through some sly maneuvers managed to arrange deposits of five hundred dollars a month into her old mentor's bank account without him knowing. Ziegfeld was never the most organised businessman, and never knew she had helped him financially. Her reasons were honourable, and she was the first to admit she would have never achieved so much in her career if it hadn't been for him. His death in 1932 saddened her terribly. Billie Burke, his widow, was left with massive debts she spent many years trying to clear.

It is without doubt that Novello was an admirer of Fanny Brice, and had seen her in the earlier heady days of *Ziegfield's Follies* at their best. For the New York theatre world, inhabited predominantly by homosexual men, Fanny was a goddess of fun and camp, and would hold court at nightly drinks and dinner parties. Billy Rose, her erstwhile husband, was not at all enamoured by her gay fan club and found it a disconcerting and humiliating experience. "She's up to her ass in nances," Billy was heard to comment, presumably with no pun intended.

Novello was introduced to Billy Burke at one such party and they hit it off immediately. At this stage Burke was attempting to rebuild her career in the hope it would help her ruined husband's finances. Novello had the perfect offer. He had to recast Lillian Braithwaite in *The Truth Game* as she had to return to England at short notice. Burke was charmed by Novello and, after reading the part, agreed to the deal. Novello was delighted and it was a real achievement in many ways. The Schuberts' and Ziegfeld had been sworn enemies for years due to a long forgotten broken contract, that they should agree to his wife being cast in *The Truth Game* was as much down to Novello's persuasive charms as it was to good business sense. Burke had been a hugely popular star in the *Follies* heydays, and her return to the Broadway stage would inevitably cause a stir; and no doubt enough intrigue among audiences to make them come and see what, if anything, she had left to offer. Contemporary audiences can see a glimpse of Burke's charms and talents still in Judy Garland's famous film *The Wizard Of Oz*, where she played Glinda the good witch. Back in 1930, Burke hoped her appearance in *The Truth Game* would rally her ailing husband's spirits, and also give him the opportunity to see her on stage again for one last time.

The first night of *The Truth Game* was December 27th, 1930, at The Ethel Barrymore Theatre. It was an immediate success and sold out for the three month run. Much of the credit for the success of the play is down to Billy Burke, she brought a grace and elegance to the part along with her enviable comic skills. Novello was a perfect foil and partner for her and they worked a rare magic together on stage.

"A superb example of what can be done with a thin story by brilliant acting and direction," declared *New York's Theatre Magazine*, "the author of this charming bit of fluff is the clever young Englishman, Mr Ivor Novello, whose acting in the principal male role is going to give many a husband something to think about for several months to come." They went on to add that "Miss Burke gives a show that is a constant ripple of joy."

The New York Times review, in unusual gushing mode, said: "By combining romance and riches Ivor Novello, who is a young gentleman of considerable sensibility, has turned out a perfect matinee comedy."

It is always interesting with Novello's reviews that predominantly they are always less enthusiastic about the substance of his plays, but always over enthusiastic about his persona and performance. Therein lies the secret of Novello's success one could argue. Had these plays been performed by someone without Novello's romantic good looks, however good the comic and acting abilities might be, one feels they would have been complete flops. It is almost as if he manages to hypnotize an audience with his considerable charms and delivery which thus completely overshadows anything which seems lacking in the literary or structural merits of his plays. Without him these plays have been rendered lifeless and impotent; which is the main reason they have not enjoyed any contemporary significance in terms of revivals, unlike Coward's plays which are regularly performed in repertory, the West End and on Broadway.

Novello for his part was at last satisfied. What could have turned into a humiliating experience with the disaster of *Symphony In Two Flats,* which for American audiences of the time was just too English and confusing in its eccentric characters, he had managed against all the odds to turn around with the overwhelming success of *The Truth Game.* Broadway success was his to savour and it also opened the doors for him to meet and socialize with some of Broadway and Hollywood's biggest stars.

New York in the 1930s was a very different place and making any kind of comparisons to the contemporary atmosphere of the city is pointless. Vaudeville and Burlesque were in their last throws of optimism in spite of diminishing audiences, made worse by the drastic economic decline which resulted in theatres being closed down daily, with artists being literally thrown onto the streets along with their costumes and props. Shantytowns were springing up in Central Park where those made homeless by eviction and poverty built whatever shelter they could and struggled to survive day by day. The whole economic collapse had created a huge chasm between those who had money and jobs and those who had nothing. Legitimate theatre struggled along with the best. Novello's luck kept him buoyant and he was fortunate to be in a position financially where the suffering of the masses hardly touched him. He was ensconced in the glittering world of the wealthy few high above Madison Avenue in the opulent apartments of those still rich and famous; along with those whose fame had not deserted them but their riches had. The likes of Fanny Brice had been hit hard by the crash but due to some shrewd investments she had not been completely wiped out financially like so many of her friends and colleagues. It is also pertinent to mention the quality of the plays produced on Broadway at this time. Today it is easy to look at some of these plays and compare them with the caliber of writing we now expect in contemporary theatre, but that is to do them an injustice. Again it is important to connect them with their place and time, having done that it is easy to see why they had an initial success; a success that was rooted in the social and economic values, and also what was considered escapist entertainment. Take away the mass media and the technological advances we are so used to, and one begins to see entertainment in the 1930s in a different light.

Delighted with his success, and that of his play, Novello threw himself into New York's social whirl. He was in demand and enjoyed a frantic social life that invariably went on until the early hours, if not dawn, on most days. His energy was boundless and he enjoyed wickedly delicious affairs with handsome homosexuals who flocked to get his attention. Not only was he good looking, rich and successful but he was not shy in letting it be known he also possessed a fairly voracious appetite sexually. And there were no shortage of takers among the theatre community to sample his delights. Bobbie was also back in England, so he had no worries of upsetting his lover with his promiscuous behaviour; indeed, in London, Bobbie was enjoying affairs of his own. Neither would ever feel truly threatened by their respective dalliances, they enjoyed casual affairs but always remained loyal to their firm partnership.

During the run of *The Truth Game* Novello was to meet two Hollywood newly weds who were enjoying their honeymoon in New York. Douglas

Fairbanks Jnr and Joan Crawford had married despite Fairbanks's parents, and especially his stepmother, Mary Pickford, having their doubts about Crawford. Pickford saw Crawford as an upstart and a common bar dancer. And worst, an opportunist who was only interested in her handsome stepson to further her career - she never went as far as to call her a tramp publicly, but she voiced such an opinion in private. Fairbanks Snr and Pickford were, it has to be remembered, the royalty of Hollywood and everyone was in awe of them. An invitation to their parties at 'Pickfair' were much sought after, but not often granted. Fairbanks Jnr was a young, handsome and very charismatic man. The attraction between him and Crawford had been physical from the start and, it has to be said, stormy. They could argue viciously in public and private, usually resolving the issue by falling into bed and venting all their energy in prolonged sexual gymnastics. They were a hedonistic couple and gloried in their sexual exploits, and enjoyed the company of other hedonistic souls.

There was an immediate attraction between Novello and the couple and they formed a friendship that would last all their lives. In 1996 I was fortunate to have conversations over the telephone with Douglas Fairbanks Jnr. He lived in New York and initially responded to a letter I sent him regarding some research I was undertaking on Novello. His memories and thoughts of Novello were very clear and he was eager to talk about him. Although it had been several decades since that first meeting with Novello he recalled it clearly and delighted in saying how "difficult it is for anyone today to understand the powerful charisma possessed by Ivor" and that he had a "magical and hypnotic" quality as a stage actor underpinned by "a wonderful sense of humour and razor sharp wit." As for his wife, Joan Crawford, he said "she really got on well with Ivor" and unusually for Joan, "she was able to forge a friendship with him that lasted until his death." They all enjoyed the social scene together and would party until the early hours. "We were all young with everything to live for - and we enjoyed life to the full. We all had admirers, but none of us had as many admirers as Ivor. He had a pretty wild time in New York and Hollywood."

As the run progressed Novello found himself captivated by others including Fred and Adele Astaire, Alfred Lunt and Lynn Fontanne, Clifton Webb and Hope Williams. He was also introduced to Ethel Barrymore. *The Truth Game* was playing in the theatre named after her. Hollywood's Irving Thalberg also paid Novello a visit during the run of the play. He admired Novello's Englishness and, true to form at the time, was snapping up anything on Broadway that could be written into a screenplay. Now the "talkies" had been developed and eliminated silent films the major Hollywood film studios turned to Broadway to find writers and actors for films. Novello fell into both categories and was among the few silent stars to also make the transition to the "talkies." Many of the silent stars found themselves discarded because they had unsuitable voices or lacked the ability to memorise and use dialogue effectively as part of their performance. Once again Novello found himself in the right place at the right time and understandably grasped the opportunity with relish.

Thalberg was the driving force and creative backbone of Metro Goldwyn Mayer studios in Hollywood. MGM had developed into the dominant studio that specialised in lavish films with colossal resources and budgets and boasted they had "more stars than there are in the heavens" at their disposal. The film industry's move to California's West coast had also allowed them to exploit fully the vast expanses of cheap land on which they could build huge lots to service their industry and thus eventually dominate the world's film markets. The move from New York to the East coast had also enabled them to escape the tax imposed on the industry in the then established state communities; indeed California had in many ways allowed the film industry to create their own rules and regulations and control the local economies which included the tax system therein. Novello's arrival at MGM was at the very dawn of the studios eventual power and control over the industry that would last until after the Second World War when the decline of the giant studio began, to be completely destroyed by the time Louis B Mayer died in 1951. But in 1931 it was a place where anything was possible and the passion and determination demonstrated by all was infectious and heady indeed. It was an affluent and highly charged creative atmosphere where beautiful people adorned every avenue; and talented writers, artistes and technical personnel were the best in the world. They all had the power of the latest technology at their disposal and they made full use of it to be creative and innovative in the films they produced. If this were not enough, it was bathed in an eternal golden sunshine that lit up this frantic, gorgeous and complex world and heightened its elegant demeanour to those looking on.

Thalberg was given free reign by Mayer to run MGM as he saw fit. Mayer was a shrewd business man and knew that Thalberg possessed what he could only be described as a Midas touch combined with artistic sensibilities all encased in a ruthless veneer of organisational skills. Thalberg had been fascinated by Novello and was quick to snap him up for MGM - but as a writer. Even though he had admired Novello's performances on the stage he saw him primarily as a writer and not an actor. Having bought the film rights to *The Truth Game* he set about having it adapted for the screen. This would prove to be the beginning of Novello's utter frustration with MGM and their procedures. Understandably Novello assumed he would write the screen adaptation of his play and arrived in Hollywood thus prepared to undertake the task. It is easy to understand his surprise to find that Thalberg had already had a screenplay version penned by two of his staff writers at the studio, a version that, as Novello realised as he read the treatment, resembled his original stage version not at all. Even the characters names had been changed and new ones added. This was, in Novello's opinion, a complete mess and he set about writing his own version for the screen. Ultimately it was all to no avail, as Thalberg insisted on using a version penned by his staff writers and it did not make a very good film at all. Novello suppressed his frustration for as long as he could but eventually even his good humour floundered in the face of such controlling management. As much as the world of MGM seemed glamorous and privileged to those looking in from the outside in reality it was far from ideal. Every aspect of the lives of those contracted to the studio was ruthlessly controlled and for some, and most definitely Novello, it inhibited artistic expression and freedom. During this time he did undertake the task of creating a screenplay for a planned film titled *Tarzan The Ape Man* and, much to the amusement of many in later years, created the infamous line "Me Tarzan, you Jane!" Novello's contribution as screenwriter to that particular film has been forgotten but then it demonstrates his ability to leave his mark even under the most trying of circumstances.

The actress Ruth Chatterton had sensed Novello's frustration at MGM and heard his very vocal disappointment at not being offered any acting roles in all the films that were being made around him at the studio. This again was down to Thalberg's opinion that Novello was predominantly a writer and not an actor. Chatterton had become firm friends with Novello and managed to secure him the second male lead in a film she was to star in titled *Once A Lady*. The story revolved around Chatterton's character Anna, a White Russian émigré. Disillusioned with her life married to an Englishman she flees to Paris and has an affair with Novello's character, Bennet Cloud. As character names go, it is quite ludicrous and makes one wonder who ever thought of such a ridiculous name! But choose it they did and Novello attempted to bring some sense of reality to his character but all to no avail. The film was a disaster and flopped spectacularly, which was a good indication of its failings even at the time; normally any film with Novello in it, however bad the plot and ludicrous the characters, would garner acceptable success and box office simply by his presence. But not in this case. *Picturgoer* opined sadly that:

"The strong cast, which includes Ivor Novello, would lead one to expect much more entertainment than there actually is in this picture...Technically the picture is very good, with elaborate settings; but no amount of these hide the deficiencies of a plot which weakens as it progresses."

In Hollywood terms it did Novello a great disservice, as he was never again asked to appear in a film made at any Hollywood studio. Chatterton's sincere and earnest desire to help Novello establish himself as an actor as opposed to a writer in Hollywood failed completely. Novello was beginning to feel concerned for his future career. MGM was, he felt, swallowing up his individuality and suppressing his best talents. It could, he reasoned with friends, if he did nothing about it, see the end of his career; a career he had worked so hard to build for himself. Thalberg was blind to Novello's frustrations and it has to be said his real abilities. It is more than likely that Thalberg just didn't understand what he possessed in Novello; and even less idea as to what, with some positive nurturing, he could have achieved with him in the long run. Novello's Englishness in terms of his humour and also his sense of the past and its values just didn't fit in with the American vision and ideals reflected in the films churned out by MGM and Hollywood generally.

For Novello's part he never enjoyed films as much as he did a live audience in a theatre. That was where his true abilities and passions were directed. Had Thalberg seen Novello as an actor first and last, then maybe his Hollywood career would have been more fruitful and rewarding for all concerned. Anything could have happened, and probably would have done, if Novello had had the chance to truly express himself in that difficult environment. It is no surprise, even today there are those who have phenomenal creative drive and vision who find themselves suppressed by those in positions of power who decide against giving their support; usually those who have no understanding of the industry and its demands. It is all a matter of luck, being in the right place, and being supported by the right people.

Novello had approached Thalberg and asked to be released from his contract. Thalberg refused and asked Novello to give it a bit more time, assuring him things would change. Novello rightly expressed concern that he was drawing such a large salary but not actually doing anything for it. Things didn't change and again he was left to his own devices where his anger and frustration festered until he was nearly mad with boredom. For him there was nothing worse. He did make up for it with his social life and enjoyed the parties and dinners he attended at Joan Crawford and Douglas Fairbanks's house; they ensured he was well looked after and able to enjoy the social whirl and have flings with attractive young men discreetly and away from the prying eyes of the press. His friendship with Crawford and Fairbanks would be enduring, and it was due to their efforts that he was accepted into the social world he enjoyed and offered him some distraction from the frustrations of his treatment by MGM. They had been there to meet him from the train the day he arrived in Hollywood and Crawford, who was becoming a dominant star at MGM, took him round the MGM lot and introduced him to everyone. Ramon Navarro was one of the friends he made during this time and there is no doubt they enjoyed a passionate affair which, owing to their charms and good looks, and ever wandering eyes, fizzled out into a life-long friendship. There were so many young homosexual men all willing to make the most of their opportunities; and it has to be said that Novello and Navarro would have been a good catch if only for a night or two!

Novello's other great achievement while at MGM was, against all the odds, to make friends with the elusive Greta Garbo. Garbo was notorious for not socialising or indeed even speaking to those working on her films. She was shy and reclusive even at the height of her fame. However, Novello was determined to meet her and one day heard she was in her bungalow on the

MGM lot. Against all advice and without further ado he strode into her dressing room and introduced himself. Her staff were horrified at his intrusion and waited for the explosion of temper from Garbo because he had slipped past them. To their complete amazement she was instantly charmed by Novello and requested they be left alone. This meeting lasted for nearly three hours, and during that time Novello had penetrated what many described as Garbo's glacial façade and made a firm friend. To her staff it was barely believable to hear the chattering and laughter emitting from her sitting room, and they were all of the opinion that Novello must be a very unique character to have endeared himself so quickly to Garbo. All of these friendships would continue once Novello had left Hollywood, indeed they all became guests at his London flat and at his country home Red Roofs.

The final drama played out in Hollywood would be a cause of great sadness for Novello. He received a telegram to inform him of his father's death in London. He immediately went to Thalberg and explained the situation, and that he finally had decided he wanted to be released from his contract. Thalberg commiserated with him over his father's death and reluctantly agreed to terminate his contract. Novello was delighted, but puzzled at Thalberg's seeming "reluctance" as he felt they were paying him handsomely but not actually using him at all. But it mattered not, he was free and couldn't wait to return to England. He made arrangements and within a couple of days he was on his way.

The death of Novello's father had a profound effect on him. It made him face his own mortality and realise that there was no time to waste. Never again would he allow himself to be so bound up by a contract it rendered him helpless and starved creatively, no matter how much money was involved. His relationship with his father had always been distant and somewhat strained, he was a man that had been almost completely overshadowed, if not dominated, by his mother. He had never considered how deep feelings for a father can run, so was surprised at his complete grief and devastation once the reality of his death had sunk in. He had a million thoughts about all the things they should have done, those they could have done, not to mention all the things he wished they had discussed and sincerely said to a parent that is no longer there for him. Novello was the first to admit he must have been a complete mystery to his father. Here was a father who loved sports and working in a steady job and enjoying the company of colleagues over a pint of beer. Indeed, everything that Novello hated. The greatest tragedy for Novello was his sudden realisation that he didn't really know his father; had never even made an effort to understand him or forge any kind of meaningful relationship with him. For the first time in his life he felt a slight resentment towards his mother for barring the way to his father's heart. But on reflection maybe that was unfair on his mother, after all his father had been happy for her to take the dominant role in their marriage, and he disliked himself for feeling such a negative emotion towards her. But then had his father been happy with second position? Novello was upset and angry and distraught that he would never be able to find satisfactory answers to such difficult questions. His father was dead, and his father had been the only person able to provide the answers.

He also wondered how his sexuality had affected his father and if it had been a cause of embarrassment or disappointment to him; if it had he had never said anything. They had never talked openly even about his relationship with Bobbie, but his father knew - he knew he knew. It was acknowledged and unspoken. Unlike his mother who chose to just ignore it and pretend it wasn't there, his father had been more perceptive; a perception which his eyes could express more than any words. As always Clara would rather fantasise and glamorise a situation she found difficult to comprehend, and she found that comfort by believing her son truly had relationships with all his female co stars on the stage and screen. As is often the case, Novello realised too late that he understood his father too little and had taken his presence in his life for granted, expecting everything to go on forever. He undoubtedly loved his father but didn't understand that love in all its details.

The physical cause of death was the result of a genetic heart disease that had blighted men in his father's line for several generations. Little was understood at the time about the genetic inheritance of heart disease, unlike today where it is much better understood and thus controllable to some degree. The official cause of death was coronary thrombosis and a weakening of the heart muscle. This defect will have been passed on from generation to generation where it inevitably caused an early death in otherwise healthy males. Novello's father was 59 when he died in 1931 and, unbeknown to his son, the same faulty genes had been passed on to him. The young Novello had already had a scare with his heart as early as 1914, but it had been passed of as a transitory affliction from which he seemingly made a complete recovery. The truth was that the defect was still there lurking in the shadows waiting for its moment to once again gain predominance over the heart. Had more been known about the genetic implications then, Novello could have received expert medical advice on how to avoid a similar fate for his own heart, but the link had not been made at the time. Novello had also become a heavy smoker by 1931 which would obviously set alarm bells ringing today, but at the time people were ignorant of the devastating effects of smoking on the heart and lungs; more so for someone with a potential time bomb ticking in their chest waiting to explode. Smoking was seen as harmless and a pass-time indulged in by almost everyone in the 1930s. It would be many years later when the full implications of smoking on the health would be revealed to an unsuspecting public. So, Novello continued his 100 cigarette a day habit blissfully unaware of the danger to his own heart and health; made worse because he had a liking for Turkish black tobacco cigarettes called Abdullah's, which were also devoid of filters.

His thoughts on Hollywood and its disappointments were ever present in his mind and added to the turmoil he felt about the future and what step he should next take. He would need to earn money as he had quite considerable financial obligations in England. He had been paid handsomely by MGM but he sent money to England to pay the lease on "the flat" and for the upkeep of Red Roofs, along with all the staff that were needed for both residences. He also paid the rent and upkeep on his parents' apartment along with their living expenses. Not to mention the many financial scrapes he resolved for his mother who still had schemes and dreams that were embarked upon without a thought to the financial risks involved.

He had truly believed when he first signed his contract with Hollywood and MGM that his ultimate success was assured, and that very fact would bring financial security. He had been proved wrong and it had been a disaster. Once again he pondered on the fact that to date he had been most successful when he put himself in charge of his career and destiny. Left to be a cog in someone else's machine invariably led to disaster for him. These thoughts accompanied him on the long train journey from Los Angeles to New York. It was a journey long enough for him to come to terms with his failure in Hollywood and face the world and his friends with a brave face.

Most importantly for Novello, he never allowed setbacks to deter or depress him unduly; that's not to say he didn't still crash into the depths of depression, more that he recognised this ability in himself and refused to allow it to be ultimately destructive. He would eventually pull himself up, brush himself off, and start all over again with a renewed enthusiasm for the next project. By the time he set sail for England he was desperate to see his home, Bobbie and his mother, and all his friends once again. He also made the decision to concentrate on theatre work in England and leave behind his hopes for an American dream.

His arrival back in London was greeted with much excitement by all those who had not seen him for over two years. Bobbie and Morgan the chauffer met him at Waterloo Station and whisked him back to "the flat" and a homecoming party. Within a couple of days it was like he had never been away, and as it turned out, he would never be away again apart from holidays where everyone went with him. Once the celebrations had died down, he had to develop a plan, in discussions with Bobbie, on what he would do next. He felt it was time to really make some definite decisions on the way his career would now proceed. Two years is a long time in theatre land and it must have felt like a lifetime since he had last appeared in the West End. No one had forgotten Novello, but it was difficult even for him to jump back in at the top.

Clara was overjoyed to see her son and seemed to have borne the death of her husband with her usual fortitude. Novello couldn't help but see a difference in her and she seemed to have aged and was less robust. He accompanied her to Golders Green cemetery to scatter his father's ashes in the garden of remembrance and was touched by his mother's genuine grief at her loss. It's not that he ever suspected his mother's love for his father, but she had always seemed so strong and independent and in need of no one emotionally. It was the first time he realised how much it mattered to his mother that his father's loyal support was always there for her. She missed him terribly and Novello decided that he would make sure his mother always had him to lean on, no matter what. After all, she had sacrificed so much and fought so hard to give him the best of everything. He could do nothing else but make sure she received the same by return - financial scrapes and all. It was only money, and he may have left it too late with his father but he would make sure the same wouldn't happen with his mother. Novello, for probably the first time in his life, began to grow up emotionally and be less self-obsessed and selfish. Life has a way of ensuring we all learn similar lessons.

GOSFORD PARK AND RED ROOFS MYTH & REALITY

"I remember Red Roofs so well and recall many happy visits."

Douglas Fairbanks Jnr.

Novello's return to London in 1931 after the disaster of Hollywood spurred him on to once again achieve prominence in the ever fickle world that is the West End. It would not be as straightforward as he might have hoped and he faced the initial months with some difficulty. Having decided to concentrate on stage work, and thus abandon film work for good, he was surprised to find that the film studio bosses in England were eager to utilise his services to satisfy his fans who had remained loyal in his absence. This was certainly not what Novello had in mind but had little choice, as he was the first to see the financial benefits of undertaking the film offers flooding in.

British cinema was booming during the early 1930s due to the increased percentage levies to screen films made in England imposed upon exhibitors as a way of combating Hollywood's ever increasing dominance of the medium; not least in this decision were the considerations of the box-office revenue which would remain in the UK as opposed to feeding the voracious appetite of Hollywood studios. It also ensured that those employed in the various studios, Shepperton, Ealing and Pinewood to name but a few, would not lose out to the monster across the Atlantic. The economy in the United Kingdom was still teetering on the edge and this kind of government legislation ensured that it's own economy would not suffer unduly; or in the very least shore it up until better days appeared. Cinema in the 1930s was big business indeed with millions purchasing tickets up to twice a week at the height of its popularity. Ironic then that finding himself shunned by the Hollywood moguls, and thus making the decision to abandon his dreams of Hollywood film stardom, he found himself in such hysterical demand by the British Studios.

Novello's aversion to films wasn't caused just by his Hollywood fiasco, or indeed his preference to work a live audience, it was also because of the routines and disciplines required by the film industry. At heart Novello was a night person, where he functioned far more effectively. The early mornings and boring hours spent between takes whilst filming drove him to distraction. He also disliked the coldness of filming as there was no audience to react to or respond from. It was becoming quite normal to create films in a very disjointed way, whereas the closing scene would be shot perhaps first and a scene in the middle of the film would be next etc. Breaking up the story in this way can be hard at the best of times and Novello found it frustrating in the extreme. He preferred to work from the beginning to the middle to the end, where he could get a feeling of, and create a flow of the character's experience as he progressed through the story. This is generally impossible, and became more and more difficult as the idea of multi location shooting and studio set shooting became more common. Financially it was impractical to film in his preferred, chronological way. Novello was also quick to realise that film was becoming more and more a Director's medium. Once the film was in the can, they could make or break, or completely destroy, an actor's performance. Being left to the mercy of the cutting room floor and the egos of directors and editors was, Novello felt, once again surrendering his need for the control of his performances and image. Only one place could that be possible, with a live audience in a theatre under his own management. His wish would fall into place, but only eventually. For now he decided to accept some of the film offers and earn some money, after all the fees he earned for films were far in excess of the paltry payments offered by the theatre.

The first few months were frustrating in many ways, but he was able to earn enough to keep everything afloat and, it has to be said, enjoy still a lifestyle that would have been far removed from those ordinary working people still suffering from the depression and its terrible depravations. It is during this time of re-establishing his career that seventy years later Novello would be portrayed in Robert Altman's movie *Gosford Park*. And seventy years later, I was working on a celebration concert at the Theatre Royal, Drury Lane, to mark the 50th Anniversary of Novello's death. One thing led to another and a telephone call from Bob Altman's office instigated a meeting that would result in my employment as the Novello Consultant on the movie. So the past and the present would meet and Novello would once again find an audience, this time his presence was embraced by a Hollywood system that had shunned him in his lifetime. For me the road that led to that telephone call from Bob Altman was a long, winding and fascinating one. It was a road which finally propelled me into the vortex of Novello's life, his past, and would instigate opportunities to meet some of the main protagonists who could still relay to me stories unclouded by any misinterpretation. They were a unique handful of people who by their very longevity had out-lived everyone but each other, and could still vividly recall their association with Novello and the past. Vital then that you are privy to this element of the story of Novello, for indeed it will help to create shape and form to the misty shadowy figure Novello has become, a mysterious figure not unlike his character in Hitchcock's film *The Lodger*, who appears through the mists of time into the 21st Century, giving a hint of his persona to those today who know very little about him. I will also continue and progress with his own story in his own time, but allow an interweaving of his past and my present to offer a differing perspective.

Novello's character in *Gosford Park*, portrayed by Jeremy Northam, was in fact the only factual character in the movie. Altman's decision to include Novello amidst the fictional characters of an upstairs and downstairs theme ensured at the very least a new recognition of Novello in history, and it also served the film well in as much as it firmly placed the action in the early years of the 1930s. Altman had admired Novello for many years and enjoyed his music from *Keep The Home Fires Burning*, his early satirical revue songs, to his more lavish scores for musicals like *Glamorous Night* and *The Dancing Years*; which in terms of the time and place of the film were yet to be written by Novello.

The atmosphere created by *Gosford Park*, and its portrayal of the etiquette and mannered hypocrisy of the time, was a perfect vehicle in which to portray Novello's character. He acted as a middle ground in terms of his place in the very society that enveloped him. Novello was in reality luckier than most early celebrities in that he was generally welcomed into the upper echelons of society, but more for his grace and charm than an appreciation of the commercial celebrity exploits he enjoyed. There was still an old guard in English society who were advancing in years, and who looked down on those populating the theatrical and cinematic worlds; perceiving them as vulgar and crass in spite of how much money they had acquired or how famous they had become. Within the film Dame Maggie Smith's character sums up this blatant snobbery perfectly in the opening sequences of the film where she encounters Novello briefly as their respective paths cross as they journey to *Gosford Park* for the weekend house party. Her haughty disdain, verging on disgust, towards Novello highlights the gulf between them personally and socially and also serves to put Novello firmly in his place for the viewer in terms of his social position at the time.

In reality Novello did attend such house parties but only those of his friends within society who accepted him as an equal. He would have, I am confident in saying, rather have stuck pins in his eyes than expose himself to such brutal bad manners and sycophantic hypocrisy as portrayed in *Gosford Park*. He would also insist that he could be accompanied by Bobbie and other friends, like Marsh or Coward. He was unique in that he made little or no distinction between people in terms of where they came from or how much money they possessed, or even their position in the aristocracy. He liked people if he liked them and that was that. His shrewd judgment of people was fine tuned and he hated sycophancy in all its shapes and forms; after all he was in a position to attract such insincerity and there are always plenty of people willing to take advantage of those with any connections or influence.

Placing Novello's character in the film between the upstairs characters and the downstairs servants was perfect. In a sense he was the lynch pin which created a bridge between the two very different worlds. On the one hand there are those upstairs who, he shrewdly judges, despise him and everything he stands for, but have to be two-faced and feign politeness to satisfy the demands placed upon them by society and their host; a host who is equally reviled by the same guests but due to his satisfactory position in society, not to mention wealth which they rely on, is afforded a grudging respect. Mainly because they need him financially more than he needs them. Novello's character seems to sense all of this and disengages himself from such petty and base snobbery by losing himself in his own world by playing the piano and, much to the disdain of some characters, entertaining them with his songs and piano compositions. The joke is all his, as he is actually deliciously sending up the very people who sneer at him and they are oblivious to the fact. Novello in reality would have dealt with the situation in exactly the same way, indeed he would have turned on a charm offensive and completely turned the tables. Many would have come to the end of their acquaintance and found themselves liking him in spite of themselves. For these qualities alone, Novello would have possibly made in reality a very good diplomat.

The downstairs servants who are also awash with, and mirror, the pretensions and hypocrisy seething above them, are less judgmental of Novello and practically swoon in his presence. For many of them he is the most exciting and fascinating of all the houseguests at *Gosford Park*. They are a true reflection of Novello's mass audience of the time, the very people who allowed him his fame by paying to watch his films and, for some, entering for the first time the unknown world of live theatre where he performs. As Novello's character entertains in the elegant drawing room surrounded by the shallow and insincere characters who sneer at him silently, the maids and house boys gather in little clusters hiding behind curtains and at the top of stair wells to hear him sing and play. As he does they lose themselves in the music and Novello and his true audience become as one. This very fact in reality ensured his future success and reflected the power he would again have over all those aunt Mabels - and to draw them by their thousands into the theatre and cinema once more.

During the time he is depicted in *Gosford Park*, Novello may have been experiencing a slack period but it wasn't to be for long. He had started to work on a scenario for a stage play in the final weeks he was in Hollywood, which revolved around a Russian aristocrat who managed to escape the revolution and eventually finds himself penniless and homeless in London. His inspiration to write a stage play based on a Russian émigré had no doubt been due to his experience with Chatterton in the flop *Once A Lady*. In that film her character had been the Russian émigré, but Novello decided he would create a leading character for himself who picked up that particular mantle. The awfulness of the script for that film, and MGM's inability to appreciate his talents as a writer, beyond the "Tarzan" script, made him determined to prove them wrong. The play was titled *I Lived With You* and would turn out to be very successful in the theatre, and then be made into a successful British film. But more of that later. Ruritania beckoned me along the road of discovery.

Glamorous Beginning

One evening I was approached by a London producer who wanted to attempt a revival of one of Novello's famous musicals from the 1930s. I was asked if I would be interested in rewriting the libretto of his musical play *Glamorous Night* to make it work for a contemporary audience. Of course I was interested, as much as I instinctively knew it would be challenging, if only because tastes had changed so dramatically, but decided to take time to mull it over and also to investigate the musicals in more detail.

From this point on I became more and more absorbed in the research I began on Novello, his life and career, What I discovered surprised me, the sheer scope of his body of work and his many talents amazed me. It puzzled me why he was such a forgotten figure after having achieved so much during his long career. There must, I reasoned, be an explanation for history erasing him from the public conscience. My appetite was voracious and I read everything I could get my hands on. The biographies written after his death seemed almost saccharine in their sentimentality, so I decided to see if there was anyone left alive who either worked with him or knew him on a personal level.

In the meantime I had also read the librettos of his various musicals including *Glamorous Night*, *The Dancing Years*, *Perchance To Dream* and *King's Rhapsody*. Instinctively I felt a connection to what Novello had communicated to his audiences through these musicals; putting them into context with their time and place and events in the world made me see the picture even clearer. I began to admire Novello and feel quite angry that, although he was very obviously an artist that time had rendered old fashioned, he deserved to be remembered positively in terms of theatre history.

A further meeting was arranged where I expressed my positive feelings towards a revival, but I felt it depended on the right show being chosen. *The Dancing Years* was suggested, but I felt perhaps it would be better to maybe look at *Glamorous Night*. This production had been his first musical play and, to my mind, if an attempt to revive any of his shows were undertaken, it should be this one. Besides, it had a great title, one that instantly captures the imagination. Besides, if Novello stood for anything it was glamour. If the public were to be reacquainted with Novello, it had to be glamorous to stand a chance. There was one other area that I felt quite strongly about, that it should be presented as a period piece firmly rooted in the 1930s. Any attempt to update the action to the present day would be ludicrous and would make any rewriting of dialogue difficult. The area where it could benefit from contemporary technique was in its staging; my idea to create a staging that would give it a flow-through feel using automated scenic changes and lighting, in fact similar techniques used in sung-through musicals such as Les Miserables and Phantom Of The Opera. To my surprise my suggestions were taken on board, so I set about the task with enthusiasm. But first I needed to undertake more detailed research.

During this early stage I would make the acquaintance of a Mr Nick Gaze, who ran the Novello Appreciation Society from his home in Gloucester. After making an initial contact by telephone, he invited me to visit him and discuss Novello to aid my research. From this initial meeting we became great friends and he freely allowed me to examine all the extensive records and details he had amassed on Novello and his career. He also kindly made arrangements for me to visit Red Roofs, Novello's country house near Maidenhead. I felt quite strongly that I needed to get a real feel of Novello's life, and where he lived and worked was paramount to my research in this area. Indeed, the ensuing months would see me becoming more and more absorbed into Novello's life and world.

Red Roofs was quite a famous house during Novello's lifetime and was often featured in magazine and newspaper articles. It's name derived from the numerous red tiled roofs adorning the buildings. Most of Novello's work in terms of writing and composing his musicals was undertaken at the house. It was also a venue for celebrity weekend parties and used as a holiday residence by many stars of the period. Set in the uppermost corner of Littlewick Green, it is a typical English country house. Those who were visitors to the house are numerous and include Laurence Olivier, Vivien Leigh, Tyrone Power, Joan Crawford, Douglas Fairbanks's Jnr, Greta Garbo, Noel Coward, Ramon Navarro, Mary Ellis, Olive Gilbert and just about everyone who was a famous name of the period between 1927 and 1951. It is certainly a house that could tell some intriguing stories if only its walls could speak. It is also a house that says much about Novello in terms of his taste and domestic aspirations considering his celebrity status.

Traveling to Maidenhead through the Berkshire countryside I found myself on the way to Red Roofs. I had seen pictures of the house and its interiors from old magazine articles, and read descriptions various from past articles and biographies. As a result of the months I had spent absorbing myself with Novello I had been struck by the sense of sadness, or perhaps melancholy would be a better word, which seemed to emanate from his past and his memory. There are times when photographs taken of him decades before seemed to reflect this sadness; especially in his eyes. I had by this time heard the stories of his ability to plunge into depression and also his bouts of insecurity, but it had seemed just a cold, lifeless fact about him. As I delved further into his past I began to sense that the melancholy remained almost tangible, but firmly attached to the memory of him. The journey progressed with all these thoughts in my mind, and the real sense of mystery that surrounded his career – and his achievements almost being erased from the public domain. True I felt that the loyalty of his friends had suffocated his memory by over protection, which had in time, and by accident I imagine, created a banality about him which reflected little of the courage and determination of the man. The views I could see of a very English countryside must have been very similar to the ones he had seen as he traveled from London to Littlewick Green. Taking the old back roads heightened this feeling and it was possible for a few seconds to imagine going back in time and trying to get answers for the questions from the man himself.

Turning into Littlewick Green, past the Church, an expanse of lush green assaults the eye and on the fringes surrounding the green itself are tasteful and quaint houses and cottages; with one or two dotted towards the center - a perfect English village. It is almost unchanged since Novello's time and one can immediately see its attraction and charm. During a warm summer day the cricket team play a lazy game whilst their audience sit outside the pub drinking equally warm beer. It is an idyllic spot and a place where it would be easy to lose any sense of the hustle and bustle of city life. Strolling along the little lanes that branch off here and there, they are still what could be accurately described as a real English Lane; similar to the one's described in so many songs and poems of the past. In a way it has a strange melancholy of its own, due to its seemingly adamant refusal to acknowledge the cynicism and ugliness of the 21st century, through the break in the protective trees that act as the entrance to this old fashioned place. It is also a place determined to ignore the urban sprawl beyond and gray motorways which have slowly spun their polluting web around it. Indeed, if you didn't know exactly where it was, you could pass it daily and be oblivious to its existence.

In the top left hand corner of the village are a spattering of tiny cottages which face onto the green itself. Looking around it would be impossible to distinguish which house could have belonged to such a high profile celebrity like Novello. There is nothing grand or imposing which you could associate as being the haunt of Hollywood legends. No mansions or pretentious overbearing houses. But next to that spattering of tiny cottages the gable of a house is visible along with a high garden wall with a doorway cut into its brickwork, with a plain wooden gate. On closer inspection there is a blue plaque attached to the white painted gable that indicates that this is indeed the house where Novello lived.

My thoughts as I approached Littlewick Green were a whirl. For some reason I had started to feel very uneasy as my destination became ever closer. Why this was I am not entirely sure; perhaps it was due to my absorption in the subject and too many late nights undertaking my research.

It was uncanny too, as I began to feel like I was about to visit a place, a place where I had been before. It seemed odd, as I knew I hadn't been there before, but turning into Littlewick Green and under the canopy of trees it all began to look somehow familiar. The thing that struck me was the atmosphere of the village itself. It had an aura of melancholy as if it was yearning to be part of a past where it had once been a happy thriving community. It seemed to have lost some purpose and bearing on reality. At one time it would have been a very different community with ordinary working people inhabiting its cottages and houses, people who were unaffected by rising house prices, globalisation and effects of modern living. Now, even the most humble of cottages would be beyond the means of more humble families and the working class. They had become desirable and hugely expensive residences for those with considerable means. However, it seemed as if the village itself had not forgotten and, although still beautiful and unspoilt, it was devoid of an ingredient that had once given it a soul. No more scruffy boys played noisily on the green or climbed the trees, reducing their clothes to tatters in the process, or chased the posh cars as they drove through the green to Novello's house. No more women gossiping and going about their daily business on wash day; sheets and clothes flapping and snapping in the wind. Even the pub at the top of the green, which commands a position of prominence, seems to be devoid of the men grumbling and discussing the weather, cricket, politics and how their wives nag them or love them. These very people were the soul of the place and the very people who were fiercely protective of their famous neighbour; people who respected his privacy and whom it would never have even occurred to sell a story to a newspaper about him. I am sure there is still a community spirit at Littlewick Green, but it will be very different to the one that existed then. Maybe the melancholy of the place is due to the impression it gives of being preserved in aspic or taking on the form of a film set which awaits the return of actors and crew from a long lunch break.

My unease at visiting Red Roofs increased to the point where I had to spend a few minutes on the green and steady myself with a few lungs of fresh air. It began to irritate me that I should feel this way, after all it was only a house and I was only going there because it once belonged to the man I was researching. I had never known him but I had begun to feel as if I had. When you absorb yourself in intense research the line can become blurred; and there were moments I felt as if I knew Novello as well as he knew himself, that somehow maybe I had been here before. It wouldn't have surprised me to see aunt Mabel come floating across the green towards me, like Coward's character Elvira from Blithe spirit, with chiffon dress and scarf fluttering in the breeze to once again hold my hand and lead me through the gate. Whatever, I wasn't going to allow my anxiety, an over active imagination, or any perceived atmosphere of melancholy, prevent me from walking through that wooden gate and into the grounds and the house itself.

Entering the gate and standing on the huge expanse of lawn brought to life all those faded black and white photographs I had seen of the house and its past occupants. The building seems slightly eccentric in its construction as there is nothing linear or square about it. It seems a jumble at first sight with bay windows and an arch canopy over the main doorway, then off round the corner to the far right is a set of stairs leading up to a first floor room and another bay window, its walls have white paint covering the original red brickwork. But its crowning glory and the feature from which it derives its name are the muddle of red tiled roofs that complete it and give the structure a sense of being whole. Standing there did nothing to diminish my real sense of unease and I felt an overwhelming sadness. It has changed hardly at all and even the windows and doors seem recognisable. There was a real sense of faded elegance about the place, as if it needed lashings of love and attention from the past.

Photographs of all those Hollywood stars and other celebrities who had stayed there suddenly came into view as I looked at the façade of the house. The picture of Joan Crawford and Douglas Fairbanks Jnr standing by the front door, dressed so elegantly, with a beaming Novello behind them brought to mind my conversation with Fairbanks and how after so many years he could vividly recall "many happy visits" to this house. The Englishness and humbleness of the house enthralled them along with so many others. Crawford liked being here but she didn't particularly like coming to England. She was like a fish out of water when away from the Hollywood, she lived only when on a film set and felt at home with the unreal reality around her in Hollywood. Garbo came here too, and one can imagine the shock for the cook who worked for Novello, who adored Garbo, when he was presented to his heroine as a surprise in the kitchen whilst frying chips. The house seems to have absorbed all this past, all that history; and perhaps elements of all those personalities which passed through it.

June Bloom, the owner at the time, appeared at the front door and extended a warm welcome. The hallway and drawing room are modest in size but full of character the famous wrought iron gates from David Garrick's house still in place. It struck me that nothing had changed much at all with the passing of years; a little faded perhaps but still recognisable and again filled with an atmosphere that was calm but melancholic. It was as far removed as one could get from the grandeur of *Gosford Park*, and it has to be said it is quite a modest residence for someone of Novello's standing at the time he lived here. June informed me that people who had been to the house believed they sensed Novello's presence still; I have to say this didn't surprise me in the least and can only say I was affected by the atmosphere myself. If I am honest all I wanted to do was get away from there as quickly as I could, as I couldn't make sense of the overwhelming feelings the house generated in me. She also told me a story concerning Novello's partner Bobbie Andrews, who she invited in one afternoon when she first bought the house in the early 1960s. At that time he was living in one of the cottages that had originally housed Novello's staff. On entering the house he instantly burst into tears, sat down and sobbed uncontrollably for an hour. It was, June said, too sad for him and he couldn't bear it. He never came into the house again. The story made the hairs on the back of my neck stand on end - to the point where it was almost possible to hear his sobbing somewhere in the house.

June also converted one of the cottages that is attached to the house into a little theatre, now accessible from the main house. Whenever she arranges a performance by her drama students, she informed me, she always leaves one particular seat empty for Novello. She seems to accept the fact that Novello is still "there" quite matter of factly. I have since spoken to other people who have had experiences whilst visiting the house. Doris Bentham, a delightful and charming lady I spoke to, recalled visiting the house with a friend, and was graciously shown around. Walking through one of the rooms she noticed an older man sitting in a chair. He didn't speak, just smiled as they passed. On enquiring who the gentleman was as they were leaving, the response was: "Oh, that will be Ivor. Some people see him and some people don't, it all depends what mood he's in." I tell it as it was told to me, but I have to say that my experience of visiting Red Roofs left me with a feeling of utter sadness which would make me think twice before going again.

Why Bobbie ended up living in one of the staff cottages is another mystery. Novello's will provided for him handsomely. He was left twenty thousand pounds in cash, a considerable amount in 1951, and the will stated he could live in Red Roofs for the rest of his life, with an annual upkeep allowance for the house from the estate, and on his death the house would then revert back to Novello's estate. But within a year of Novello's death the house was turned into an actors' retirement home that wasn't successful and eventually closed. Part of the grounds were sold off as a result, which means that the original music room and swimming pool are now part of another property; indeed the swimming pool is now a sunken garden for a house that was built on the land. June Bloom bought the main house and two attached cottages in the early 1960s. It does seem odd that all these things happened when Novello had made express wishes about what he wanted to happen after his death. Bobbie lived in the staff cottage until his death in the early 1970s.

The research continued after the experiences of Red Roofs and, if anything, became more intense and more mysterious. In his lifetime Novello was approaching 1935 and his first musical at the Theatre Royal, Drury Lane. This is the next leg of the journey, a journey which would help me to perhaps understand Novello's Ruritania, and ultimately lead me to *Gosford Park*.

Donald Macleod (Presenter Composer of the Week BBC Radio 3), David Slattery-Christy and Rosy Runciman (Archivist for Sir Cameron Mackintosh) in the Waldorf Bar of the West End's Novello Theatre. The images fom Glamorous Night in 1935 in this picture section were those donated by David Slattery-Christy to the theatre for display.

Elisabeth Welch at Cleo the stowaway in Glamorous Night, 1935

Elisabeth Welch sings The Girl I Knew as a curtain number in
Glamorous Night at the Theatre Royal, Drury Lane, 1935

The Gypsy Wedding scene in Glamorous Night at the Theatre Royal, Drury Lane, 1935. The cast total was over 120!

Mary Ellis makes her entrance as Militza

Mary Ellis as Militza & Barry Jones as King Stephan in Glamorous Night

Mary Ellis as Militza in Glamorous Night

Novello as Anthony Allen & Mary Ellis as the Gypsy Militza in Glamorous Night at the Theatre Royal, Drury Lane, 1935

Novello & Mary Ellis – Glamorous Night

The Ballroom Scene – Glamorous Night - 1935

The Opera Sequence – Glamorous Night - 1935

The Gypsy Wedding scene – Novello's character Anthony marries Militza with full cast of 120. Glamorous Night at the Theatre, Royal, Drury Lane, 1935

Rare image of the final 'vision' scene in Glamorous Night. With an eye to the new invention of television, Novello's character Anthony watches back in England as Militza marries King Stephan out of duty - in spite of her love for Anthony.

Rare image of the liner SS Silver Star that glided across the stage and then exploded and sank in view of the audience – utilizing all the Victorian stage machinery installed at Drury Lane. Novello and Mary Ellis can be seen looking out into the audience for this scene prior to the explosion. Glamorous Night, Theatre Royal, Drury Lane, 1935

Mary Ellis – Opera Sequence – Glamorous Night 1935

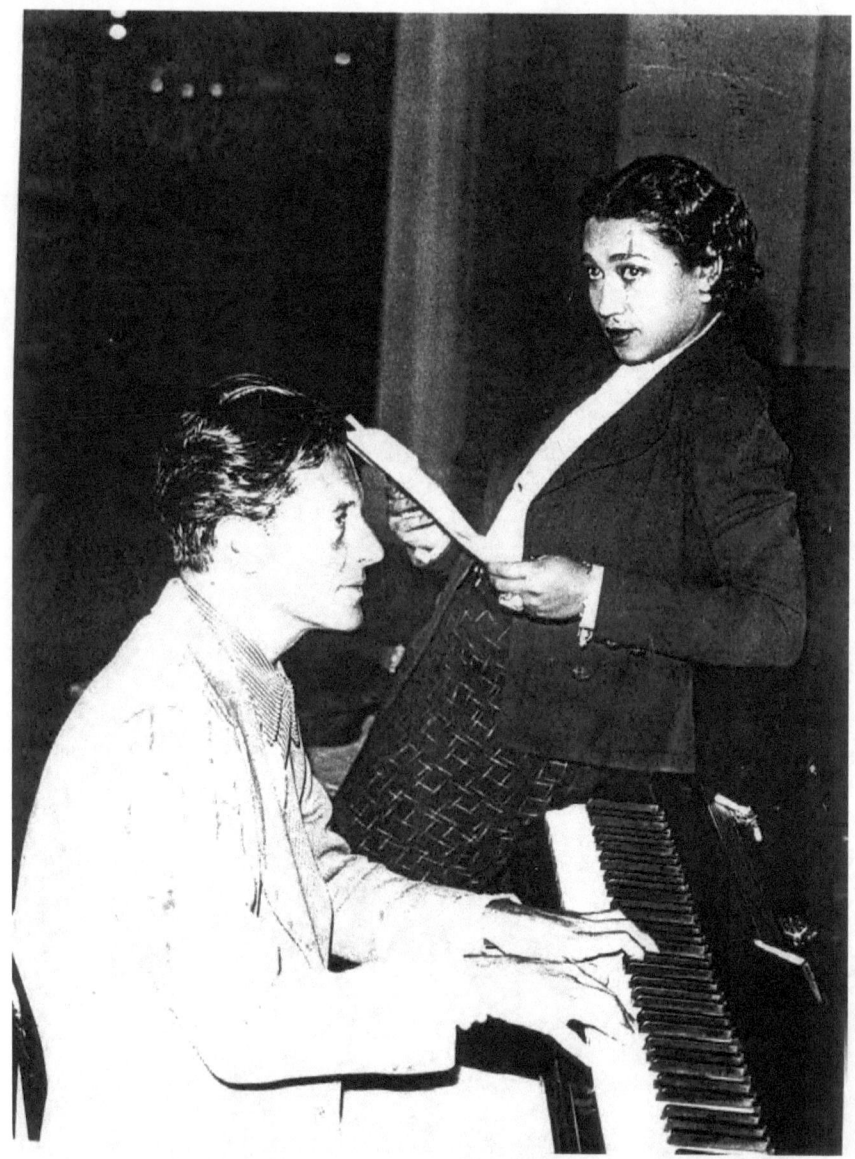

Another rare image that shows Novello rehearsing with Elisabeth Welch for Glamorous Night in the Grand Saloon at Drury Lane, 1935

Another rare image of Novello rehearsing with Elisabeth Welch for Glamorous Night in 1935

Although these images are not crisp I wanted to include them because they are so informal and joyous. It is apparent that Welch and Novello adored each other.

Oliver Messell who did the designs for Novello's spectacular musical Glamorous Night at Drury Lane, 1935

Poster design for the revival of Glamorous Night adapted by David Slattery-Christy. It would finally have its premiere at the Buxton Opera House in 2008

Trefor Jones as Lorenti in the original production of Glamorous Night

Richard Potts as Stephan - Glamorous Night – Buxton - 2008

Sarah Potts as Militza & David Walters as Anthony
Glamorous Night – Buxton - 2008

A RUSSIAN ÉMIGRÉ AND A GLAMOROUS FIGHT!

'My worry is you will never find an 'Ivor' personality!!'

Mary Ellis

Novello was tiring of films and by 1934 he had made the decision to abandon this element of his career for good. The official reason he gave was his desire to completely "dedicate his energy and time to the theatre", a theatre he undoubtedly loved. But there were other reasons, mainly his inability to compete at the top with screen actors who had successfully mastered the medium, and who were also much younger than Novello and more fitting to take on the mantle of romantic matinee idol. He had also just passed his fortieth birthday, and no doubt was perfectly aware he was no longer in the first flush of youth, although he did retain the good looks that had served him so well thus far. It is also fair to say that, as much as he had made the transition from silent to sound films, his voice was not wholly masculine when recorded for films and this would have made it difficult for him to play anything other than comic, slightly eccentric characters.

Shortly after his return from the disaster that had been Hollywood, he accepted, in 1932, an offer to film yet another version of *The Lodger*. A purely money making exercise for both Novello and the Twickenham Film Studios, where the plot was rehashed and Novello's character renamed Angeloff, who this time actually did commit the murder. It was not a commercial success and languished in dusty film cans quickly forgotten. That said, it did provide Novello with a handsome fee.

1933 saw him cast as Gaston in *The Sleeping Car* opposite Madelaine Carroll's character, Ann, an heiress. It attempted to be a farce and indeed it was, but not in the way it had been hoped at the outset. It had a ridiculous plot set in France, which involved Carroll's character attempting to marry a Frenchman, Gaston, to avoid being deported for driving her car recklessly. At the outset a business arrangement, but Carroll's character finds herself falling in love with Gaston and farcical complications ensue. Viewing this film is an almost a surreal experience and it does have its charms in spite of its nonsense. It is worth watching to see Novello flouncing around in silk pajamas being petulant and bitchy, and gives an eye opening insight to his camp behaviour; a behaviour which he held court nightly with during his own parties at Red Roofs or "the flat." *Film Weekly* opined that:

"It is a curious tale, because it starts off as a flirtatious comedy and reaches its climax somewhere in the more dubious by-ways of bedroom farce. But there are some bright moments between the light comedy beginning and the farcical finish…The film has comedy, if not wit, and piquant characters, if not real people…Ivor Novello does his best…"

With this kind of performance, which has to be said suited his ability and comic timing skills, he was never going to make film bosses take him seriously as an actor of drama or true *Waterloo Bridge* style romances. Indeed, this kind of comic performance ability was really his forte when it came to stage or screen. To watch these performances on screen is to understand Novello and his abilities and why he had them laughing in the aisles in the theatre. But, as I am sure Novello was aware, he could only get away with that kind of screen performance with youth on his side. The day would come when it would be perceived as ridiculous and probably embarrassing.

During the making of *Sleeping Car* he had been working in his stage play *I Lived With You*. It opened on March 2nd, 1932, at the Prince of Wales Theatre, and was an instant success playing to full houses for its entire run of several months. It launched Novello back into the West End and his fans were delighted, it also propelled him back into his number 1 Box Office position as actor-producer-playwright. Coward was as always baffled and could often be heard exclaiming "how does he do it!", but he would stand and join in the roar of applause on first nights with everyone else in spite of his misgivings on the merits of the script.

I Lived With You was made into a film in 1933 and enjoyed an equal success to that it achieved on the stage. Novello's portrayal of Prince Felix, an impoverished Russian émigré, was inspired and tapped into the mystery and romance of anything Russian at the time. It had not been that many years since the murder of the Tsar and his family had rocked the world and the isolating blanket of revolution and communism had extinguished the magic and grandeur associated with Imperial Russia. In the decade or so since that terrible fate the Romanovs had suffered, an influx of Russian émigrés appeared all over the world; they had been lucky enough to escape but had lost everything in the process, and not a few impostors took up the mantle to elicit comfort and financial gain from those sympathetic to their plight. The romance of a Russian Count or Countess, usually related in some way to the deceased Imperial family, was irresistible and thus guaranteed them being feted in social circles.

Novello's character is discovered in the maze at Hampton Court and charms the hapless girl into inviting him home. His tale of woe, and need for food, plus his grand stories of the Imperial court bewitch her. She takes him home and he promptly moves in with her family. Before long they are all dancing to his tune and, in spite of their moments of doubt as to his credibility, fall hook line and sinker for everything he chooses to say or demand - all the while he sits on the sofa munching chocolates and indulging himself in the game that amuses him thoroughly. The silk pajamas do make an appearance but he captivates with the glint of mischief in his eye and his admirable comic talents. His co stars were Ida Lupino, whose father Novello had worked with back in the early revue days in the 1920s, Isabel Jeans, a well know actress at the time, and Minnie Raynor, renowned as comedienne for playing course cockney maids; indeed she would have a part in all Novello's stage productions.

"In the midst of all the activities Mr Novello continuously glitters," declared *The Times*, "the prince has been over-romanticised by the author, who would have done better to ride his emotions more lightly, but the actor in Mr Novello knows how to control his mount and to give it the appearance, if not of a thoroughbred, at any rate of a winner in amusing company."

During the writing of this book I received a charming letter from the actor Ian Richardson, by way of replying to a letter I had written to him regarding Novello. He had never seen Novello on the stage but stated:

"I did see, and hugely enjoy, the film *I Lived With You* where his depiction of an émigré Russian was beautifully observed and very funny," adding that, "It is a source of regret that he played so little comedy, as this film shows conclusively that he had a masterly comic touch. I know quite a lot of émigré Russians and the portrait was also extremely accurate!"

Novello would be delighted to know that sincere praise would come from such a respected and admired actor of our time. Novello did play more comedy, but only on the stage, and those performances are gone, as is the way of any live performance. But it does give the best example of the kind of skill Novello had in terms of timing and appeal. Ian's wife, Maroussia, also had some information which was extremely useful to my compiling this book. Her mother, Elizabeth Frank, worked in London as a journalist in the late 1940s and had interviewed Novello for a biography article she had been commissioned to undertake for a magazine; the content of which aided my research for this book.

Novello's final film would be shot in 1934 and was a predictable love story set in the Austrian Tyrol. His co-star was Fay Compton, another well known actress at the time, who was also starring opposite Novello in another of his plays running in the West End titled *Murder In Mayfair*. *Autumn Crocus* told the story of an English spinster tourist who falls in love with a handsome Austrian man, played by Novello. It had moments of comedy, in which Novello and Compton excelled, and moments of emotional intensity required for such a story. In these emotional scenes Novello seems to have struggled; perhaps this was another difficulty he recognised in himself. On the silent screen he could play emotional and romantic scenes with ease, but when sound was involved it was harder to make these scenes work without the inner and vocal masculinity. Male film stars were becoming rugged and possessed a masculine voice to match their appearance - the likes of Douglas Fairbanks Jnr and Clark Gable were making real headway into global stardom by this time. There were other problems in as much as they could not travel to shoot location shots in Austria, as both Novello and Compton were working in the theatre together at night. This fact also created problems for the film. Basil Dean, producing the film, remarked that:

"With the applause of the previous evening still ringing in their ears, it was difficult to hold the full attention of Fay and Ivor to their parts; by four o'clock in the afternoon their thoughts were turning to their approaching night's work."

Novello's heart wasn't really in it anymore, and it showed despite his professionalism. On the whole the film was a moderate success and served its purpose in satisfying Novello's loyal fans living in the far-flung provinces. But it didn't set the world on fire, and it would, he had decided, be the last film he would make. And it was. He was now poised to embark on the next stage of his career, one that would see him astound his critics and enable him to utilise his talents as a composer. The year was 1935, fate and opportunity would bring Novello to the Theatre Royal, Drury Lane, where his first musical play *Glamorous Night* would be performed.

Sixty years later I was still determined that *Glamorous Night* held more possibilities for a revival than any of Novello's other musicals. Undertaking a revival had its risks and after analyzing the libretto I soon realised the reality involved in restructuring and rewriting was going to be a challenge. In terms of dialogue, it was dated and old fashioned. That said, I was still determined it should be kept in period, as this would allow for the glamour of the time and the fashions to shine through. This alone offered many positive possibilities in terms of overall design and style for the production. The art deco period was full of rich possibilities and perfect as a way to compliment any production. But I still felt I wanted to understand Novello more, to imagine what made him tick and what he was trying to achieve with the production in 1935. I would find myself reading anything and everything I could about him, and would wander around the West End visiting places he had frequented and walking along streets he would have strolled along. All the while I tried to see the West End as he would have seen it. It amazed me how you can walk along a street a thousand times and never really notice what is there in the fabric and structure of the buildings, the period they reflected. I would start to look above the ground floor windows of shops and see for the first time the history that is clearly visible and how these buildings have evolved and changed. Hints to their past are there if you choose to look. I began to see a whole new side to London architecture, one that had been smothered by so called modernisation; at ground level the eye is met with plate glass and stainless steel - look above and it is astounding what is revealed. Would that forgotten world of the 1930s be understood in the cynical age we live in? Money and consumerism, mass media, pseudo celebrity worships? Maybe the radical changes in the postmodern age had indeed rendered Novello, and everything he stood for, redundant and forever to be lost in the mists of time. But the one thing that time had not affected was human emotions, they affect people now as they affected them then. Love and romance is eternal, and maybe that vital ingredient would make a contemporary connection.

Studying the libretto of *Glamorous Night* I started to adapt and restructure but keep true to the spirit of the original. It was an interesting plot, one which involved Novello's character arriving by ship in a Ruritanian country. Ruritania is a mythical land invented by Novello - a place where anything was possible. In *Glamorous Night* it was ruled by a King who has a gypsy mistress, Militza, who gave up the man she loved, Novello's character Anthony Allen, to marry the King to prevent him abdicating. She put her country first, as doing one's duty was heart-wrenching but expected of someone in that position. Duty first, matters of the heart a definite second. Considering the year Novello wrote this story, and the high profile friends he had in Whitehall via Edward Marsh, he must have been aware of the affair between the Prince of Wales and the nearly twice divorced American Mrs. Simpson - that was causing such concern within government circles and the Royal Family. At the time nothing had appeared in the British newspapers about the affair, largely by way of a gentleman's agreement between Whitehall and Fleet Street's press Barons; a situation that would be unheard of today. Indeed the British publics were oblivious to the ensuing constitutional crisis until the very end, when Edward VIII abdicated in December 1936. It has also been suggested that the story was also partially inspired by King Carroll of Romania and his mistress Madame Lupescu, whom he blatantly flaunted in the clubs and restaurants of the West End, shocking polite society; who nevertheless enjoyed the ensuing gossip with relish.

Whatever the inspiration for the story, it was very close to what was actually happening at the time in our own Royal family. The story also reflected the invention of television, and how the radio moguls were fearful of the damage it could do to their industry. Novello's character, Anthony Allen, being the inventor, was banished by Lord Radio and sent abroad to Ruritania. This was in effect a sub plot to the main romantic love story, and as such could easily be eradicated to allow the focus to remain on the love story between Anthony, Militza, and the Ruritanian King. In 1935 the development of television was a fascinating one for the public and it is easy to see why Novello would include it, indeed the final scene involved Novello's character watching the Royal wedding in Ruritania via his television invention in England.

I then discovered that Mary Ellis, Novello's co-star in *Glamorous Night*, was alive and well and living in London. In 1995 she was 96 years old. I sent a letter to her Eaton Square home and waited for a response. Hopefully she would be able to give me answers to so many questions.

For the first time in many years Novello began to compose music. He set about creating a score for *Glamorous Night* but needed someone to write the lyrics. Interestingly I discovered, through a manuscript book that had belonged to Novello, he had written by hand the music for a song he gave the title *Glamorous Night* sometime during the 1920s. But then he had a habit of writing down melodies and even giving them a title whenever the mood took him. Mostly with no thought he might actually use them. But now he needed a lyricist, and he thought a young friend he had met just might be the answer to his problem. Novello first encountered a young Christopher Hassall two years previously whilst on tour.

During 1933 Novello, on tour with his play *Proscenium*, was visiting Oxford with Edward Marsh, and staying at the Randolph Hotel. It is worth noting that *Proscenium* had been written with Novello's self-indulgent characteristics fully to the fore. Conceived as a vehicle for himself and Zena Dare, a well known actress and firm friend of Novello, it was primarily about theatre people and their on and off stage exploits. Funny to those involved in the profession but, as had happened with his previous attempt to write a play in the same vein *Party*, it was confusing to those not privy to the machinations of back stage antics. That said, *Proscenium* did involve a universal love story at its core, which allowed those unfamiliar with theatrical life an opportunity relate to the characters to some degree. In the West End they did hardly any business, but Novello managed to recoup the losses, or at least some of them, by taking the productions on provincial tours; where Novello's fans would care little as long as they could gaze at him adoringly. It is also interesting to note that Novello had a skill of writing parts for specific actors and actresses whom he admired; much as he was so adept at writing parts for himself perfectly tailored to his talents. Zena Dare indicated this trait when she recalled:

"He wrote the part so beautifully for the personality of someone who amused him, and it came off so successfully that, although nobody's indispensable, you were indispensable to Ivor, and if somebody else - your understudy - played it, it wasn't quite the same. I can't tell you why."

During their sojourn in Oxford, Marsh arrived in the bar to meet Novello at a pre arranged time and, after waiting for over an hour growing ever impatient, he returned to his room rather furious that Novello hadn't arrived and had not even contacted him or sent apologies. He was, it has to be said, also slightly concerned, as he knew it was out of character for his friend to be so discourteous. He eventually went to bed and attempted to sleep, but was awoken at midnight by a frantic knocking at his door. Novello offered his apologies and told Marsh to come down to the dining room at once as he wanted him to meet someone.

Novello had decided on the spur of the moment to go to a late performance presented by OUDS at the Oxford Playhouse, situated practically next door to the Randolph Hotel, and had been smitten with a young actor playing the part of Romeo in an excerpt from Shakespeare's play. He had gone back stage and introduced himself to Christopher Hassall. Hassall, aged 22, was several years Novello's junior and was an undergraduate at the University. He was handsome, shy, and Novello was instantly smitten. They chatted and Novello asked him back to the hotel, where he suddenly remembered Marsh and their missed appointment. Novello arranged for a cold supper to be served for the three of them, and

Marsh remembered how absurd he felt eating cold meats and limp lettuce at that ungodly hour of the morning; whilst Novello apologised profusely to him and flirted outrageously with Hassall. Marsh left them and retired to bed, but not before Novello informed him enthusiastically that Hassall was also a poet and arranged for him to see Marsh the next day so he could assess some of his poetic efforts.

Novello and Hassall became firm friends from that meeting, and Hassall was seduced completely by Novello. Marsh found himself struggling to like the young man, but put aside any thoughts of Hassall and instead concentrated on his primary reason for meeting Novello in Oxford. Once again they had to sit and untangle the shambolic state of his mother's finances. Novello's mother would prove to be uncontrollable and ever frustrating in the management of her financial obligations. It would always result in Novello having to pay off numerous debtors, then the whole process would start over again. Marsh wanted Novello to be stricter with his mother and allow her to "sink or swim" - perhaps not bailing her out would teach her a valuable lesson and thus prevent her reckless behaviour in the future. But all to no avail - Novello would always give in and clean up the financial mess. Marsh was right in assuming that Clara knew her son would do just that. It was a delicate balancing act betwixt Marsh, Novello and Clara, one where Marsh instinctively knew he would come off the loser if he forced Novello to choose between them. Amidst this frustration, Marsh had not immediately hit it off with Hassall, no doubt seeing him as just another of Novello's pretty young conquests to be seduced and then perhaps forgotten when the next one came along. Marsh found him "irritatingly diffident" but persevered due to Novello's insistence and this he did by "asking the youth to dinner in a weeks time" from whence a friendship was affirmed which would last a lifetime. Marsh was impressed by Hassall's poems and was in turn seduced but only in a literary sense.

Marsh, and it has to be said, Bobbie Andrews, were both of the opinion that Novello should perhaps start composing music again. It was a skill he possessed which was greatly underused since his obsession with conquering the theatre as an actor and playwright. He had achieved both of these ambitions and perhaps it would be prudent to once again allow his musical talents to come to the fore. By this time his success composing for revue shows was but a faded memory. Bobbie was instrumental in keeping

Novello on track and also pointing out he would not always be able to rely on his looks to keep his star in the ascendant. Novello's relationship with Bobbie was still on solid ground although they both enjoyed the charms of handsome young men without the inconvenience of undue jealousy. In fact their open relationship seemingly added to the strength of their bond and affection for each other. Not doubt their attitude towards their partnership was viewed quite differently than it would be today. There was no real thought that such partnerships between homosexual men bore any similarity to a heterosexual marriage; or the pressures of monogamy imposed on the latter. Their friendship was based on mutual respect and affection and neither of them would have thought for a moment to insist the other remained sexually faithful. It just didn't come into the way of thinking. After all, their sexual relationship was in fact illegal, and as such it was an aspect of their lives that was suppressed and hidden away from anyone other than close friends and associates. Within the confines of their homes, they were relaxed and easy going and all those they trusted were fully aware. The evolution of homosexual relationships to take on the form and disciplines of their heterosexual counterparts would take several decades and a complete change in public attitudes and the law.

1934 would present Novello with an opportunity to once again exercise his composing skills and ultimately transform his career once again. Legend has it, propagated by the ever effective public relations skill of Novello's associates, that his arrival at Drury Lane with *Glamorous Night* had been borne out of chance and practically created overnight. No doubt there are snippets of truth to the events that brought about the musical but obviously embellished and romanticised for publicity purposes.

Harry Tennent was the then manager of Drury Lane and in the habit, as was Novello, of lunching at London's Ivy Restaurant. Much as it is used today, in the 1930s the Ivy was the haunt of celebrities of the time, where they would pass a few hours in the middle of the day enveloped in gossip and rumour, which fortified them as much as any of the exotic dishes on offer, prior to their nightly appearances on the stages various of the famous London theatres. On one particular day, Novello was having Lunch with Tennent who, after the normal niceties, began to explain the plight of Drury Lane. The theatre was not doing too well and it was in danger of experiencing a complete financial disaster; indeed bankruptcy was a distinct possibility. Novello was instantly interested and thought perhaps he could take advantage of the situation. He had hankered after a chance to perform at Drury Lane for several years, and had also been inspired by the fact his friend Noel Coward had managed to present his offering of *Cavalcade* at that very theatre in 1930. Listening to Tennent he decided to leap in with a suggestion, the suggestion being that he had a musical play that would be ideal for Drury Lane. Whether he had or not has always been fiercely debated, but Tennent was sufficiently interested to ask Novello if he would come to the theatre the next day with a synopsis and some of the music to play to the board of trustees. Novello agreed and made arrangements for the following day. As Tennent left, he asked what the title of the musical play was. Novello, it is alleged, promptly replied *Glamorous Night*. It is more likely that Novello had been thinking of writing a musical play for some time and had even started sketching out ideas for the same. The last two years had seen Marsh and Bobbie prompting him to start composing music again, and there is the first draft of the song *Glamorous Night* in his early workbook as proof. There is no doubt that Novello was adept at creating a good title for his plays, and the title of his first musical would prove to be just as good. *Glamorous Night* was intriguing and conjured up images of glamour and romance in the mind of the reader - his name attached to such a show would add to this marketing dream.

Novello returned home and, according to the legend, sat down and wrote the story and some of the music for *Glamorous Night*. Working all night in "the flat" high above the Strand Theatre he managed to pull all the elements together in preparation for the consideration of the Drury Lane trustees the next day. That he did go through a procedure such as this is without doubt. But it is more likely he had already composed some music and had drafted out a synopsis. He had also been to see the American singer Mary Ellis perform at His Majesty's Theatre in a production called *Music In The Air* and had been captivated by her voice in a way that had not touched him since he had seen Lily Elsie perform *The Merry Widow* . It fired his imagination and set him on the road to *Glamorous Night* and Drury Lane. Fate as ever, was lending a helping hand to Novello, a hand that always had, and always would, be there for him when he needed it most.

Novello duly arrived at Drury Lane the following day and sold his idea to the trustees. They accepted his production and agreed it would have an opening date of early May, 1935. Once these formalities were over, he had to set about the real task of constructing a production which would not only work for the difficult demands of Dury Lane, but would also utilise all the Victorian stage machinery available at that theatre. His plans were on a colossal scale, but he had nothing to lose but to try.

Mary Ellis, he discovered, had starred on Broadway as the original *Rose Marie*, but had been banished from the New York theatre due to a dispute over her contract when she walked out after nearly a year of the run - which resulted in a feud which would have long lasting implications. Her reasons were numerous but her main worry was the effect the role was having on her voice with eight strenuous performances per week. Ellis was trained at the Metropolitan Opera House in New York, and had sung with Caruso, so she was used to the respect that opera singers have for their vocal chords. They would never contemplate singing eight times a week for a year in an opera; even eight times a month would be excessive in opera terms. Her fear was that the strain would destroy her voice, or at the very least damage it, and thus her career would suffer. Coming from an opera background it must have been difficult to then be expected to approach musical theatre in a different way with a different discipline. She struggled on but after nearly a year had passed, she had had enough. Refused a release from her contract, she walked out, which effectively destroyed her Broadway career for ever, indeed she never graced a Broadway stage again. It is remarkable that managements at the time exerted such power and control over artistes, it also clearly defines the fact that artistes had very little, if any, power when faced with ruthless managements and producers. This is no doubt the reason that Ellis was an active campaigner and founding member of the British Actors' Equity association. But Broadway's loss would turn out to be Novello's gain.

Ellis remembered her first encounter with Novello and recalled that she noticed "a very handsome man almost leaning out of the stage box he occupied" whilst she performed in *Music In The Air*. "I was intrigued and flattered and then somebody informed me he was called Ivor Novello. He sent me a huge box of Lilies and I agreed to meet him." Ellis had, she claimed, very little knowledge of Novello, apart from his plays, but did remember his song *Keep The Home Fires Burning*, and was amazed to discover Novello remembered her performance at the Met in New York all those years before in Puccini's opera. There is no doubt that Novello was captivated by Ellis and was determined she would star alongside him in *Glamorous Night*. Indeed for Novello, there could be no *Glamorous Night* without Mary Ellis. After several meetings, and playing her some of the music he had composed during a visit she made to "the flat", Ellis agreed to star in the show alongside Novello. There was one slight problem. Ellis was contracted to make a film in Hollywood and had to leave immediately to fulfil the obligation. Undeterred, Novello arranged to send her the script and recordings of the music, cut onto wax disks, so she could learn them prior to her return in time for the rehearsals. This agreed, Ellis set off for Hollywood and Novello began to work on the show in earnest.

Ellis was at this time trying to make a career for herself in Hollywood, and was determined the moguls of Broadway were not going to destroy her career as an actress and singer. She may be unable to play on Broadway, but that didn't stop her from undertaking a contract with Novello to appear on the West End stage. Her dreams of Hollywood film stardom would soon be dashed. She had been signed to appear in a film titled *All The King's Horses*, which as it turned out was a complete flop and ended her Hollywood dream forever. It would seem that Ellis and Novello were destined to come together, as much as their respective attempts to break into Hollywood film stardom were equally destined to fail.

Ellis's contract with Novello gave her equal billing alongside Novello and included some pretty generous terms. She would receive three hundred and fifty pounds per-week or 5% of the gross box-office, whichever was the greater. Even the agreed weekly fee was a huge amount of money in 1935, and considering Ellis' profile was not at that stage a high one, it does reflect how determined Novello was to secure her services. As always he was pretty shrewd when it came to assessing the talents of others and he knew that Ellis would be perfect for her vocal abilities and her acting skills. These two elements are not always present in equal measures - there are actors who can sing adequately and fantastic singers who can act with varying degrees of success. But only rarely does an actress come along who can sing to a grand opera standard and act superbly. Ellis was the exception, and Novello knew it.

Ellis seemed to go through her career scaling the heights and then, just as she reached a pinnacle of achievement, would tire of it and walk away. This was not helped by her volatile temperament, and she did cause many of the problems she encountered as a result of her own actions. Whilst at the Metropolitan Opera in New York, the 1918/19 season was her last, she had been given every opportunity to develop her considerable soprano skills, even being chosen to sing a juvenile lead role with Caruso, who at that time was a huge international opera star. She recalled a performance where, whilst waiting in the wings, Caruso handed her a handkerchief and asked that if he gestured her in such a way as they sang the duet she should hand it to him. As they were singing she noticed a trickle of blood running down his chin and he gestured for the handkerchief. She duly handed it to him and he wiped the blood away and continued as if nothing had happened. Obviously she was in awe of Caruso and, many years later, would say that "no recording could ever do justice to the magnificence of his voice." A week after she sang the duet with him he was dead. The internal bleeding as a result of his failing respitory system and his years of drug addition. In fact she was the last person to sing with him prior to his unexpected death. Tired of waiting for acclaim, and a realisation that perhaps she was not considered remarkable enough for the world of grand opera, she astounded everyone by walking out and refusing an offer to renew her contract.

Ellis had also been keen to develop her skills as an actress and auditioned for the famous Broadway impresario David Belasco. Belasco was a ruthless and demanding producer who left a trail of broken egos and dreams. His relationship with Ellis would fair little better, but she managed to gain valuable experience in terms of acting in classical drama. Belasco cast her in a Broadway company performing Shakespeare's *Taming Of The Shrew* and she received favourable notices for her performance. It was a modern dress adaptation, and it is fascinating to see the production photographs that reflect the 1920s fashions. Inevitably they quarreled and the relationship fell apart, but Ellis had got what she wanted and moved on in spite of Belasco's fury.

She was then asked to audition for Arthur Hammerstein's musical comedy titled *Rose Marie,* which included music and lyric contributions by Hammerstein's nephew Oscar, who would form a partnership with Richard Rodgers in years to come, and she was cast in the leading part for the

Broadway production. For anyone else this would have been the pinnacle of their dream, and considering the profile, and very positive reviews Ellis and the show received, she unbelievably began to tire of the demands of the show on her voice and wanted out. Hammerstein Snr refused to release her from her contract, understandable considering it was a smash hit and was raking in the money, but Ellis continued to fight and plead for her release. Once she realised that Hammerstein was going to hold her to the contract that was 'indefinite', therefore obliging her to stay with the production however long it ran, she walked out and refused to perform the role again. Hammerstein was furious and, understandably some might say, vowed to make sure she would never work on Broadway again. The extent of his fury and bitterness towards Ellis is demonstrated by the fact that even the passage of time, allowing tempers to cool and harsh words to be forgotten, he never forgave her for deserting the production and breaking her contract. Once again, Ellis had thrown away what many would perceive to be a golden opportunity, one that could have established her as an enduring Broadway star in the future. It would also have resulted in her appearance at Drury Lane in the title role of *Rose Marie* some ten years before she actually appeared there in *Glamorous Night*. *Rose Marie* would eventually find longevity via Hollywood, where the famous partnership of Nelson Eddy and Jeanette Macdonald would immortalise the roles.

After being ostracised from Broadway, Ellis eventually traveled to England determined to establish herself and further her career. She took small roles in West End plays but didn't set the world on fire, this in spite of positive comments in various reviews. Eventually she was asked to appear as a singer and actress in the revue *Music In The Air* that eventually led to her path crossing that of Novello's. Her volatile temperament would cause problems, but Ellis had met her match with Novello and he could more than equal her outbursts. As Bette Davies famously said: "Fasten your seatbelts, it's going to be a bumpy ride!" And it was.

Ellis's departure for Hollywood allowed Novello to undertake some serious work on the score for *Glamorous Night*. He needed a lyricist and, prompted by Bobbie's suggestion, sent for Christopher Hassall. Hassall had by this time moved to London and was working by taking small acting roles in various West End productions. He had become friends with some of the most prominent homosexual men of the theatre including John Gielgud, the infamous impresario Binkie Beaumont and, of course, Ivor Novello. Hassall had been contracted to play a small part in Novello's production of *Murder In Mayfair*, a predictable drawing room murder mystery of the period, and had a reputation for being less than reliable and very disorganised. Arriving late one day, he was informed at the stage door that Novello wanted to see him immediately. Fearing a telling off for his less than perfect timekeeping, he duly went to Novello's dressing room. Novello asked him to attempt to write some lyrics for the piece of music he had given the title *Glamorous Night* - no doubt the same section I have seen in a workbook of Novello's dating from the late 1920s. Hassall returned his suggested lyrics to Novello the next day, so good were they, that from that point on wrote nearly all the lyrics for Novello's musicals.

Probably just as well Novello unearthed this latent talent in Hassall, as he was far from effective as an actor and only really managed to get parts because of his blond hair and youthful looks. Novello recalled Hassall's employment as understudy for a production of *Romeo & Juliet* at the Queen's Theatre. Hassall had performed an excerpt of the play as Romeo in an Oxford University Dramatic Society production, indeed the production that brought him to the attention of Novello. Hassall figured that as the understudy the chances were he would never go on, so he didn't bother to learn his lines. It came to haunt him when he was informed he would have to go on and perform the part due to illness. He panicked, but eventually confessed he didn't know it - and was promptly sacked. Novello had decided that Hassall was not cut out for acting and, once his position as lyricist for Novello was agreed, he never played on stage again.

Hassall's association and friendship with Novello, Binkie and Giulgud would set tongues wagging about his own sexuality . Hassall's eventual marriage would serve to silence such comments, but then he wouldn't have been the first homosexual man to get married in the hope that it would camouflage this part of his nature. It is fairly certain that Novello was captivated by his youth and good looks, and Hassall would have been flattered by the attention of such a charismatic and famous man. That Novello seduced him is without doubt, and no doubt his association with Gielgud also had an initial physical element.

After having conversations with his son, Nicholas Hassall, almost sixty years later, it became clear that there was still an element of unhappiness that had permeated down to the present day. Nicholas is a charming and eccentric character who agreed to speak to me about his father. He has no fixed abode and lives a nomadic existence traveling all over Europe in a camper van. Luckily for me he usually spends the autumn on a campsite in Hertfordshire - at which time he is able to have contact with his late father's estate and collect any royalties which have accrued, as well as deal with any other business he needs to conduct.

Kindly meeting me at the train station, in what can only be described as a battered and aged wreck of a car, he greeted me with a warm smile and a firm handshake. He was bubbly and full of charm and was fascinated why I had such an interest in his father and his work with Novello, and was, as it turned out, not suspicious or defensive in any way. Having seen photographs of his father, it was easy to see the similarities beneath the rather unkempt demeanour he exhibited to the world; and it soon became apparent he had inherited his father's less than organised approach to life. His smile was also not unlike his father's, and he had striking intelligent eyes that reflected an honesty, charm, and sincerity that was disarming.

On asking him why he chose to lead such a nomadic life he replied directly that he hated being tied down, and didn't want anything to do with the materialistic so called normalities of life. He liked to travel, to be on the move and found it exciting that you could find yourself in a different place every day. He told me quite matter of factly that he had never discussed his father and Novello with anyone before; indeed he had been approached several times in years past but had always declined. On asking why he had agreed to talk to me, his answer was abrupt but honest. "I'm not sure, something instinctively made me say yes, then when I spoke to you on the telephone I knew I had made the right decision."

His childhood memories were filled with Edward Marsh, who he remembered as a slightly frightening old man, Novello, and of course his relationship with his mother and his sister, Imogen. Novello was his godfather, and he remembered quite clearly his kindness on visits to "the flat" or Red Roofs. "My father adored Novello," he recalled, "much to the utter frustration of my mother."

His mother quickly discovered that her husband's life revolved around Novello. She resented his constant demands on Hassall's time and attention and, remarkably, decided that he was more firmly married to Novello than he was to her. She resented the fact that Novello would "snap his fingers" and Hassall would immediately drop everything, including her, and go to him without question or complaint.

She was left with the task of caring for the children and for much of the time she never saw her husband. It was the beginning of an unhappy marriage where Hassall's wife would slip into depressions so severe it would eventually affect her mental health considerably. Sadly for her, and his children, they were no match for the fascination and loyalty Hassall afforded to Novello.

Nicholas, although a child, was aware of the friction between his parents, caused by Novello. He was forthright when I asked him whether he thought his father had a sexual relationship with Novello. "My father was not a homosexual in the accepted sense, but I certainly think there was a strange element to his relationship with Novello, which caused my mother much distress and unhappiness." On the subject of his father's possible sexual relationship with Novello he was thoughtful and then explained that on reflection he " felt there was perhaps an initial sexual liaison between my father and Novello, but it developed into a deep friendship and working relationship." He went on to say he felt that if anything had developed between them, then Novello had been his father's only homosexual relationship. But he wasn't aware of his father's friendship with John Gieulgud. The affect this had on his parents' marriage was a sad one as it was, he said, "gradually destroyed, crumbling into bitterness on my mother's part simply because my father was dominated by Novello," who had his father at his beck and call and he "would always go running to him when summoned."

His father was, it seems, somewhat of a mystery even to his son, and there were elements of his father's character that remained closed to him. After Novello's death, it seems his father began to try and sustain his career by distancing himself from Novello and the work they had done together. His work as librettist for the opera Troilus & Cressida along with William Walton achieved some success, and he wrote biographies on Edward Marsh and Rupert Brooke that consumed his time and energy. He also wrote lyrics and a new libretto for Lehar's *The Merry Widow*, one of Novello's favourite operettas, which was produced at Sadler's Wells in 1958. But he never again received the prominence that he had whilst working with Novello. His death in 1964 was eerily reminiscent of Novello's a decade or so before. Hassall was only 52 years-old and died of a similar heart disease as that Novello had succumbed to.

Hassall's daughter, Imogen, carved a successful career for herself as both a screen and stage actress and appeared in many films and plays during the 1960s and 1970s. She succumbed to her deteriorating mental health and, after several failed attempts at suicide, she succeeded in 1980 at the age of 36. Nicholas then, has experienced more than his share of personal tragedy and survived. It gives an insight as to why he lives life for the moment and refuses to conform to societies expectations and demands. I can't say I blame him. It was fascinating to meet him, and I appreciated his candor.

Novello's plans for *Glamorous Night* were taking shape and form and, inspired by the melodramas he had seen at Drury Lane years before, and recognising the elegance he witnessed with productions like *The Merry Widow*, he set about contriving a spectacle which would prove to be very expensive - twenty seven thousand pounds, a huge amount of money in 1935 - and include a full scale ocean liner, opulent palace ballrooms, and a cast of over 120, and the might of the full scale Drury Lane orchestra. Tennent was nervous at the money being spent and was further alarmed to discover that Novello wanted real ermine to edge the massive flats to be constructed for the ballroom scene, a scene which utilised the full depth of the Drury Lane stage; which is rarely used in its entirety. He balked at this extravagance and after discussion Novello agreed to scrap the idea. It does however give a clue as to the lavishness that Novello was determined to achieve with the production. Novello compiled a team to service the production which included Leotine Sagan, a German who would direct the production, indeed the first woman to direct a West End musical; a young designer trying to establish his career, Oliver Messel, along with Ralph Reader as the dance master and choreographer.

Among those who successfully auditioned for the production included Olive Gilbert, who would appear in all Novello's musicals from this point, and become a firm friend, and a young Black singer called Elisabeth Welch. Welch had come to prominence for her performances in cabaret clubs and originated from New York. Her father was a strict man and had forbade her to become a singer or make any attempt to become a stage actress. She left New York and, as her mother was Scottish, she came to England to try her luck here. She came to the attention of Novello and thus secured a place in the cast of *Glamorous Night*; although it was an odd and slightly disjointed experience for her, it managed to set her on the road to stardom.

During my research I was allowed access to the archive at Drury Lane, an archive that houses a considerable amount of photographs and documents relating to Novello and his time at Drury Lane. This in itself was fascinating, but events surrounding my visits there would prove to be just as intriguing. The archive is usually closed and, it has to be said, very few people realise it is even there. An average sized room situated off a corridor on the first floor, it is accessible via the stage door entrance to the theatre. True to form with back stage areas of any theatre, one could imagine it hasn't changed much in the last hundred years; indeed I would go as far as saying I doubt the corridors had been decorated since Novello wandered around them in the 1930s. Back stage at Drury Lane has an atmosphere all of its own, giving one the impression that it has absorbed all the history and personalities it has been exposed to for decades. The archive itself is packed full of endless documents and photographs which have gathered dust over many years. Some of the documents probably haven't been looked at for a hundred years. Sitting alone in that room, with the barely adequate daylight that struggled in through the small sash window, was like being in a different world - and time. Archives, by their very nature, hold secrets and hints of the past for which they act as guardian, this one was like a time capsule

A few days after I had been paying daily visits to the archive, I arrived to find myself stopped by the stage door keeper. He then told me that someone had been apprehended trying to leave the building with Novello documents from the archive On being challenged, he fled the building dropping what he had on the floor. It was recovered and returned to the archive. As a result the security was tightened. The incident puzzled me because I couldn't imagine how anyone knew that I had been given access to the archive, but more intriguing, what had they feared I might find? This kind of paranoia surrounding Novello's memory was disturbing to say the least, if not unusual, to the point where I found myself looking nervously over my shoulder as I left the theatre each day.

I never found anything remotely scandalous in the archive, but did find some interesting documents and Leotine Sagan's working script with her hand written notes scrawled over the pages. Mary Ellis's contract was among the documents, along with a script which showed that Elisabeth Welch's character, the stowaway, and Minnie Rainer's maid, had originally been one character. By coincidence I had decided in the rewrite that these two characters should become one, as it made more sense and allowed a development of the character within the story. No wonder Elisabeth Welch declared herself to be at odds with the production "appearing as a stowaway to sing *Shanty Town*" and then declaring "no one knew where I came from and then, after singing this one song, I disappeared never to be seen again!" She did however sing a "curtain" song titled *The Girl I Knew* which had no bearing on the plot or storyline, just a nice little cabaret song to sing in front of the curtain because time was needed to undertake a big scene change. Welch's songs in the show did demonstrate Novello's ability to compose songs with an ear to Berlin or Porter, but he was firmly rooted in Ruritania, via his excursion to the land of *The Merry Widow*, to be interested at all in anything but grand operetta.

The Girl I Knew was a great song and I decided to adjust the lyrics slightly and turn it into a duet. Welch's original character, Cleo, became the maid in the rewrite, and this song would fit perfectly as a duet for Cleo and Militza. The revised script would also allow for the development of Lorenti, the opera tenor, who has a past history with Cleo, to progress through the story instead of appearing for the opera scene and then disappearing. In many ways, these changes actually reverted back to some of the elements of the script that were cut during the original rehearsals to reduce the running time. I suspect that Welch's character was cut in two to accommodate Minnie Raynor's need for a part, as the maid, which was a shame, but then Welch would probably have balked at playing "the maid" anyway.

The other discovery was an initial draft of a song called *Someday My Heart Will Awake* intended for the show. Again due to some pretty serious cuts to the script, as it ran for over four hours, this was abandoned. It would reappear years later in Novello's final show *King's Rhapsody*. Based on that information the decision was made to reinstate it in *Glamorous Night* where it fitted like a glove in terms of Militza's story and character development.

Amidst all this frenzied activity at Drury Lane, Novello was embroiled in rehearsals and ensuring Ellis, who was still in Hollywood, received the script up-dates and the music he was recording on wax disks and sending to her. By the time rehearsals started in mid March, there was still no sign of Ellis; indeed the film she was contracted to make had also been delayed, but assurances were wired across the Atlantic that she would be there eventually. Ellis herself recalled that it was a frustrating time and one where she was panicking in case she couldn't get back. There was even a point where Novello resigned himself to possibly recasting; which would have been an almost impossible task at such a late stage.

Whilst in America Ellis was receiving the script and music and learning her lines and songs. They included the title song *Glamorous Night*; *Fold Your Wings*, a duet with Trefor Jones; *Shine Through My Dreams*, *When The Gypsy Played* all accompanied by a full opera sequence. She was delighted with the songs and felt they had been perfectly tailored for her voice, and relayed her delight to Novello via telegram, also assuring him she had learnt everything and, although delayed, she would be there eventually.

For Novello is was a trying time, and Tennent was also putting on the pressure due to the considerable financial investment thus far expended on the production. Should Ellis withdraw, for reasons beyond her control, then it would be financial ruin for Drury Lane, and one suspects Novello's reputation along with his own. Tennent was fraught and flew into more than one rage of disbelief. Novello, never one to rise to anyone's bait, and who hated any kind of confrontation, calmed and assured him. Although he admitted after the event that Bobbie consoled him privately at "the flat", and kept him focused and firmly on track.

Ellis finally sent a telegram to say she was sailing from New York and would be in London in a few days. Such was the lateness of her arrival for rehearsals, she was met off the train at Waterloo and whisked straight to

Drury Lane by car. She first swept in to a press conference, and then went straight into lengthy rehearsals with hardly time to draw breath. To Novello's, and everyone else's relief, she was word perfect and knew all the songs, which aided her integration into the production at a rapid speed. She recalled "working very long hours and well into the night" as they had only a couple of weeks until opening night.

Ellis was a complex character and had a reputation for being difficult and standoffish with other members of the cast. She would rarely socialise or exchange small talk with them and many found her overbearing. At times the atmosphere when she had quarreled with Novello was also unbearable, but even on these occasions they went on stage and no one would have guessed, such was their professionalism. Novello was quoted as saying, "we fought, we quarreled, but we loved!" Which just about sums it up.

Meeting a 96 year-old Ellis so many years later and, it has to be said, long after her fame had died along with her contemporaries, I could still sense the willful and volatile character she had once been. She was charming and delightful but could withdraw into herself for no apparent reason. Her elegant apartment in Eaton Square was almost of that other world she belonged, one where she was a star of the British musical theatre stage. In the apartment below on the ground floor was where her once neighbour and friend Vivien Leigh had lived and died. Their mutual friend was Novello; indeed Novello had championed the early talent of Vivien Hartley, and advised her to change her name to Vivien Leigh, much as he had championed the talent of Mary Ellis.

My respect for her was genuine and I found her comments regarding the proposed revival of *Glamorous Night* heartening, stating how she "so appreciated my vibrant approach and all its possibilities," adding sincerely, "how she wished she were younger to help in any way" with the production. As much as she was complimentary she had her reservations in one area. Her constant worry, which she voiced more than once, was how could we possibly find "an Ivor personality." She knew quite correctly that Novello was the heart of any production he appeared in and it catered for his unique personality so effectively as to render it almost impossible for anyone to step into his shoes. She knew him and worked with him and she understood better than any other living person his characteristics;

impossible for those like myself who had only books and films with which to asses him and attempt to bring him to life.

I also sensed an element of resentment with regard to her own career. She was quick to point out in no uncertain terms that she had done much more than just work with Novello. Indeed this was true and she could recall her time at the Metropolitan Opera in New York and her association with Caruso; indeed at the time I met her she was the last person alive who had sang with Caruso. She had also worked in theatre, films and a Coward musical called *After The Ball* - all long after her association with Novello. Her experiences with Coward were not good and they quarreled and fell out in a spectacular way. It was the last time she sang on a West End stage, and I would have wished for her a better experience for her last performance in a musical. But, sad as it is, nothing ever really gave her the prominence she had enjoyed whilst working in Novello's shows. There was also an odd connection between us and it involved a Granada production of Sherlock Holmes, which starred Jeremy Brett, which was the last film work Ellis undertook in her career. I also appeared in the episode as an army captain who was required to Polka with fury in a crowded ballroom dressed in full military regalia. Ellis played an elderly aristocratic lady. At the time of filming, I had no idea she was involved, or I would have made the effort to speak to her several years before I did.

My impression of Ellis was wholly positive and, after that first meeting I did make the effort the deliver a bunch of Roses on her birthday each year. She did seem much younger than her years but then she did start to decline and died in 2004 aged 105. For me her label as being difficult and overbearing, and her ability to quarrel and fall out with people, was I feel down to an inner sense of insecurity. It was an insecurity borne out of the honesty with which she looked upon her own talents and abilities, and because she suffered her share of setback and was unfairly treated at the hands of others who were ruthless in wielding their power and influence. Indeed she did become frustrated at "only being associated with Ivor's musicals", however in spite of this, she did retain a deep affection and respect for the man who changed her fortunes in this country.

As rehearsals progressed tempers and fears began to diminish. Ellis' professionalism and fierce energy soon ensured her integration into the production. She then worked tirelessly to develop her character and performance to a high standard, which resulted in everyone including Novello feeling happy but exhausted. As opening night approached, the usual cuts and fine tuning carried on long into the night until eventually everything was ready. The backstage staff had struggled with the enormity of the sets and found the full scale port side of the ocean liner, named the SS Silver Star, which filled the proscenium opening to be the biggest challenge; especially when it had to explode and sink in view of the audience. The massive hydraulic lifts beneath the Drury Lane stage had never had to achieve such a huge feat, but somehow they managed the impossible. The gypsy encampment and the lavish ballroom scene, which used to entire depth of the stage, along with the exterior of the Opera House scene with horse drawn carriages, all had as much rehearsal as the cast. Setting and striking such elaborate and complex scenes quickly and safely, ensuring they didn't hold up the production, were undertaken with military precision. The whole show had a seamless flow, and involved over two hundred people with cast and crew.

These extraordinary sets, and the sheer scale of them, were vividly brought to life in a black and white way for me - in a way by Novello himself. I was contacted by Nick Gaze from the Novello Society in Gloucester, and he informed me that Olive Gilbert's nieces would like to meet me. Gilbert had been cast in *Glamorous Night* and had then become a close friend of Novello's until his death. She had also lived in the flat below Novello's at 11 Aldwych. Her nieces, Betty and Lily, were most gracious and kind and Betty especially bore a striking resemblance to her late aunt. They lived in a small Gloustershire village and were eager to talk about their memories of the past. They had both met Novello and had liked him enormously, and had enjoyed visiting "the flat" and Red Roofs with their aunt on many occasions. Betty was a real Welsh lady and, whilst chain smoking cigarettes, regaled me with stories her aunt had passed on to her. The story concerning Mary Ellis and Novello quarrelling and falling out were amongst the tales, but they also added that Ellis did not endear herself to other members of the company by cutting them dead and refusing to socialise. She apparently played the 'star' routine to its zenith and no exception was made to any fans who might decide to stand at the stage door for her departure. She would, they informed me, invariably slip out via the front of house to avoid them. Their aunt had little time for her in a personal way, but they enjoyed a professional relationship as far as the shows were concerned. Their aunt had been amazed that she had been lucky enough to be cast by Novello, and thanked her good fortune. She enjoyed a close relationship with Novello, but in many ways she mothered him and looked after him completely as time progressed. She ultimately became responsible for ensuring his staff had prepared everything he needed, whenever he needed it, as well as performing in his latest musical.

During the course of their friendship, Gilbert had begun to purchase small Jade objects, which Novello had a particular liking for, and presenting them to him as presents on Birthdays and Christmas - even opening nights. Although Gilbert was left these in Novello's will, many disappeared and were never seen again. Another intriguing story involved a painting by Picasso of Novello. It had been given to him as a gift from the artist, and had been hung at Red Roofs. After Novello's death it vanished and has never been seen since, and in spite of their aunt's attempts to discover its whereabouts, it has to this day never come to light. Again, perhaps it is languishing in a dusty attic somewhere waiting to be discovered?

As it turned out I paid Lily and Betty several visits and, in spite of the good rapport we had, I always felt they knew far more than they ever told me. On occasions I would ask about Novello's homosexuality or his prison sentence and they would clam up. They also had a habit of looking at each other knowingly, as if seeking reassurance they weren't saying too much or giving anything away. In spite of this they one day produced a few articles that they said had belonged to Novello and had been passed on to their aunt when he died. Betty had them stored away in the garage, and feared that if anything happened to her they would just be destroyed or thrown in a skip. One of these items was a huge album of nearly 60 photographs from *Glamorous Night*, which not only reflected the cast but also the sets by Oliver Messell. I realised immediately that this was a valuable item in terms of theatre history and humbled that they wanted me to have it for use and safe keeping. The photographs themselves were excellent in terms of condition and quality. They also brought to life the enormity of the production and especially the liner SS Silver Star that cruised into position whilst Novello and Ellis played out a scene from its promenade deck.

Glamorous Night opened on the 6th May, 1935, and catapulted both Novello's and Ellis's career to new heights. The first night reviews were generally very good, with only a few jaded dissenters, and the first ticket issue sold out very quickly. Despite all the "knockers", a term for those who gossip negatively about the show's chances prior to opening, Novello had pulled it off in spite of these detractors. Many had forgotten his ability to compose music and were astonished, mainly because he had neglected this element of his abilities to develop as a writer and actor. His part in the production was non-singing, but it didn't matter, as Ellis and others provided that element in what was a fantastical story set in an imaginary Ruritanian Kingdom; with a seemingly nonchalant Novello wandering through the proceedings in which everything happened around him, as if he was meeting these fascinating characters for the first time. Sandy Wilson, then an eager young boy sitting in the gods of Drury Lane, later wrote:

"Musicals as a rule, have three credits below the title: Book by..., Lyrics by..., Music by... A Novello show had one legend only: Devised, Written and Composed by Ivor Novello. And of these three functions, the 'devising' was the one that singled out a Novello Show from any other, because, starting with the theatre itself - the Theatre Royal, Drury Lane - he did in truth physically devise an experience for his audience which would exploit for their benefit the full resources of one of the most impressive and elaborately equipped stages in the world, in a way that they have never remotely been exploited since."

The press had a field day and were on the whole favourable, but one can sense their utter bewilderment. *The Daily Telegraph* declared:

"In contriving this show Mr Novello has brought off the biggest achievement of his career. It is not an easy task, now that the 'talkies' have been brought to technical perfection, to invent a big-scale stage entertainment that will rival them in popular appeal. Only a superb theatrical craftsman could bring it off - and that is exactly what Mr Novello is... Superior persons will no doubt scoff at the show, and dismiss it as a lot of nonsense...if it is nonsense, it is glamorous nonsense, and for those who are ready to be entertained, it is the best show of its kind Drury Lane has had for years."

Ivor Brown, from the *Observer*, was a little more forthright in his opinion: "I lift my hat to Mr Novello. He can wade through tosh with the straightest face: the tongue never visibly touches the cheek. Both as actor and as author he can pursue adventures too preposterous even for the films and do it with that solemn fixity of purpose which romantic melodrama inexorably demands."

Ultimately it didn't matter what the critics said, such was Novello's popularity his fans would flock to see the show whatever their opinion. Sheridan Morley once said that Novello was, like Andrew Lloyd Webber is today, virtually critic proof. This was true indeed for Novello - and he would continue to confound his critics, as he had always done. McQueen Pope, Novello's publicist, was in the audience on the first night, 2nd May, 1935, and described the experience:

"I stood in my usual place, just inside the right hand entrance of the Grand Circle. I saw that curtain ascend. And what followed was history…When the curtain fell again, there was such a scene as the old walls around us had hardly witnessed. That night is a piece of treasured memory. One recalls the mass excitement of it, the welcome Ivor received, the applause for them all and the roar for Mary Ellis. But transcending all that was the amazing roar which followed her singing. Mary Ellis, that night, touched the heights. She is not a tall or a big woman, but she dominates. She is a force and energy personified…she was a revelation. She tore the house into roars of enthusiasm. Seldom has such a performance been seen or heard as hers in *Glamorous Night*"

Listening to the music from *Glamorous Night* so many decades after the event it is hard to imagine the experience of hearing it live. That said, there is something within its structure that reflects the innate melancholy that Novello possessed as part of his being. There is a tangible sadness lurking within which still has the ability to emerge and touch the listener, touch you in such a way that it is hard to ever forget those melodies. Hassall's lyrics are at times poetic and then a little too sweet. Ian Richardson remarked in his letter to me that Novello's music was perhaps let down by the "banality of the lyrics", which is perhaps a little harsh and not an opinion I entirely agree with. However, they do at times seem to be cloying in their sentiment; but in their time they worked perfectly and sold thousands of records.

Today Novello's music seems to ache for a return to a world where life was simpler and it was okay to believe in romance and make believe worlds such as Ruritania. Maybe also a time when imaginations were not slaves to the domination of external mass media bombardment, where people's imaginations could provide them with an unhindered ability to be stimulated by their own thoughts and creations aided by what they witnessed in the theatre. Should it be possible to go back in time for one night, I feel I would choose that first night of *Glamorous Night*.

Continuing with my own task of restructuring the script had thus far gone quite well. Still determined to remain with the true spirit of the original, I began to experiment with an idea to interweave Novello's experiences of creating the show into the revised script - to replace the original prologue that depicted the invention of television and the radio barons. Having attained the professional rights for the show through the Novello Estate and Samuel French Ltd, where my main point of contact was an agent who worked for the publishers, Lynn Nortcliff. Lynn was at first a little cautious of me, but mainly because of my frantic enthusiasm. However my proposals and ideas for the revised script had not caused any objections thus far with the Novello Estate. Lynn has since become a great friend and revealed that when first meeting me she suspected I had been "plugged into a socket" such was my wired up enthusiasm and voracious appetite in terms of my research and task. Of all the people I encountered on this journey, Lynn has been the one who turned out to be the most sincere and the most loyal; and the one I respect enormously for her help and knowledge surrounding the mine field of professional performing rights issues.

My own experiences then, had begun to take on a surreal quality - such was my immersion in this lost world I began to feel more at home there than I did in my own time. It became all-consuming and the more questions I had answered, it seemed that more questions appeared unanswered. This journey *In Search of Ruritania* was exhausting, but I made the decision to carry on.

Ivor Novello

END OF AN ERA

"I've been completely ignored. No one cares about me anymore, and I was Ivor's last lover."

Gordon Duttson

As the 1930s progressed, Novello was working furiously on establishing his career in the new medium of musicals. After the success of *Glamorous Night* it wasn't all plain sailing. He was invited to follow up the success by submitting his new show *Careless Rapture* to the Drury Lane trustees, which they promptly turned down flat. Understandably he was angry and was at a loss as to what he could do. As it turned out he need not have feared, the show they had accepted, *Rise & Shine*, flopped spectacularly and they called him and asked if he would consider producing *Careless Rapture* after all. He did, but on much better terms than he was originally considered. The two shows that followed *Glamorous Night* were *Careless Rapture* (1936) and *Crest Of The Wave* (1937), and both of them are examples of a man who fully exercised his new found position of power, but who also fully indulged himself in storylines which were so threadbare as to be non existent. But the music and songs and spectacle more than made up for this deficiency. They were fantastical and involved all kinds of stage effects from earthquakes to train crashes, and of course the obligatory romantic glamour, all with a cast of 150! Extraordinary, and something that would not be possible today under any circumstances, prompting one critic to liken the experience to "being enveloped in an over sweet pink blancmange!" To me these two shows are Novello enjoying himself, along with his leading lady Dorothy Dickson; one suspects that Mary Ellis wouldn't have been associated with either of these productions with a velvet covered barge pole! Rather than a serious attempt to create anything remotely enduring, they really were from the critics point of view "tosh" in every sense of the word, and Novello knew it, but for the time, they were breathtaking in an MGM musical meets Busby Berkely and Novello at Drury Lane kind of way.

By 1937 there was also the consequences of the ever gathering storm clouds that had begun to spread from their place of origin: Hitler's Germany. People were becoming aware of the ever increasing threat posed by his Nazi regime and were becoming distinctly jittery. The abdication of Edward VIII in December 1936 had shocked everybody, and real feelings of dissent and disillusion were on the streets. Many people didn't want to lose such a popular King and the ensuing mess had created a worrying divide in public opinion. Although the ex King had left the country, and his brother George VI firmly placed on the vacant throne in his place, there was still a bad aftertaste in many people's mouths over the whole affair. The government and the Royal family hoped that the impending Coronation in 1937 would unify the people behind their new King.

Amidst this real life drama and romanticism of a real King abdicating for the sake of "the woman I love", and a German Dictator stomping around Europe saber rattling, Novello was living his own fantastical adventures upon the stage of Drury Lane with his tongue, one suspects, firmly in his cheek. But it was a fantastic diversion and perfect escapism for the public, a place where the realities of life could be forgotten for a couple of hours at least. As perfect as this kind of entertainment was for the troubled times in which they occurred, no one could have foreseen his next move.

Amidst this atmosphere of uncertainty and genuine fear, Novello would hatch a plot that would see him perform at Drury Lane in a Shakespeare classic. To say that those who knew him were aghast at what they perceived to be folly is an understatement, but he was spurred on by Marsh's intellectual aspirations and encouragement. One can only wonder what Bobbie must have thought, but he went along with it anyway in spite of genuine misgivings. When it was announced that Novello and Dorothy

Dickson would be cast in Shakespeare's *Henry V*, with Novello playing the King, there were audible gasps of disbelief echoing around the West End. Novello was many things, but a classical actor he was not. It was a disaster by all accounts, although some who witnessed it were impressed at how he handled particular moments in certain speeches. But all were of the opinion that it was way beyond his capabilities as an actor. One has to admire the sheer courage of the man, and in spite of everything, he really did give it his best. Amidst all this was his genuine concern about events in the world, and being wholly patriotic saw it as a way to contribute something meaningful and serious. As misguided as this decision might have been, in many ways it proves beyond a shadow of a doubt that his past insecurities and fears had been well and truly conquered, and that he was willing to take a chance on appearing in something so far removed from his own comfort zone, or what his audiences wanted from him, simply because he wanted to satisfy a personal ambition. In that respect he succeeded. Once again fate managed to come to his rescue and allow him to bow out of this particular disaster with grace. Chamberlain's continued policy of appeasement and the ensuing Munich crisis was blamed for the diminishing audiences and Henry V closed with quiet dignity. No doubt a collective sigh of relief from his true friends could be heard gently rippling through the West End.

It wasn't until Novello turned his attention to his next show *The Dancing Years* that he really developed and evolved what he had started with *Glamorous Night*. *The Dancing Years* was in many ways remarkable as it was created into a musical theatre form which is nearer to what we can recognise today. It was also remarkable in as much as Novello abandoned all the spectacular effects his previous three Drury Lane shows used as integral elements. It would instead rely much more on a solid story line as its foundations, one that reflected events happening in the world at the time. In that way alone, it became a first in terms of a musical reflecting world events actually happening in the moment of its conception; as opposed to the hindsight the passing of years allows. Sadly for Novello, it would prove impossible to present in the form he wished at its creation. This was a result of opposition from the Lord Chamberlain's office that, at the time, acted as censor for all proposed theatre productions. This government office had the power to insist on the removal of what it considered to be unsuitable dialogue and/or situations in any proposed production. Once satisfied, a license would be issued for the production to go ahead. All theatrical productions were required to gain this consent, and be subjected to what amounted to government censorship. This unpopular system would remain in place until the 1960s when it was finally abolished.

Novello's main theme for *The Dancing Years* was a reaction to the news that all Jewish composers in Vienna and Germany had been ostracized by the Nazi authorities. Their work was banned and much of their existing published works were burned on public bonfires. Novello was aghast that this kind of brutality was allowed to exist and the seeds for the show were sown from that information. That Novello should be so personally affected is obvious in that he too was a composer and putting himself in the position of those so harshly repressed made him angry. It made him consider his own reaction and feelings if he too were to suffer a similar fate.

Central to the plot would be a composer, Rudi Kleber, who finds fame by composing music for the Vienna Opera House, it marks his progress prior to his oppression, during his time when his music is banned, and life after his fate at the hands of a brutal regime like the Nazis. Interwoven into this would also be a love story swathed in Novello's romantic ideals. By means of a prologue and epilogue, it referred directly to the Nazis, in all their brutality, and the incarceration and death sentence imposed on the composer. The three Masque scenes would depict Vienna at each stage of its journey from a gay carefree city full of music to its decline and oppression by the Nazis. The complete version of this would never be seen by the public because the Lord Chamberlain's office refused to give a license for the script unless all references to the Nazis were removed and elements of the composer's fate were re-written to be less directly associated with what was happening in Germany, and thus be less inflammatory. It is hard to understand today why they insisted upon this, but at the time there was still an effort to appease Hitler, and the Prime Minister, Neville Chamberlain, had been waving his "peace in our time" agreement between the British Government and Hitler. The thinking was that depicting the Nazis as the barbarians they were, and referring to them directly, would be seen as a form of hostility, and they were also fearful of the effect it would have on the audiences; and its possible ability to create anti German feelings and exacerbate the problem. On top of this, the general public, although aware of the Nazis and Hitler, were fairly ignorant of the more brutal side of their nature that had as yet not seeped into the public domain.

Novello was frustrated and furious, and probably more so because of his association with Marsh who was still at this point privy to information in Whitehall about the Nazis and their prejudices; especially against Jews, but also homosexuals, gypsies, and those afflicted with mental or physical deformities, and of course political opponents generally. Novello would have recoiled in horror, realising that he would himself be a target for persecution had he lived across the channel. Churchill, Marsh's boss, was it must be remembered a friend of Novello's and, along with many others, including Coward, were totally against the government's policy of appeasing Hitler. Their protests were voiced privately, and only eventually would Neville Chamberlain be forced to resign when it became clear Hitler had no intention of adhering to any agreement in pursuit of his world domination plans. In fact the "peace in our time" agreement Hitler had signed with Prime Minister Chamberlain was exposed as nothing but a sham. Coward had also shocked Novello by having a blazing row with him over remarks he made at the time Chamberlain's appeasement policy had duped so many. Novello innocently remarked that he was delighted it was peace and not war, and was horrified at Coward's response. That said, Coward made him think and he eventually realised his friend had been right to admonish him. In truth Novello, like so many who had lived through the First World War, preferred not to think about the harsh possibilities of another. He hated cruelty and violence in any shape or form, and couldn't bear to face it initially. Like so many, the hope that he and others clung to was that somehow it could be averted and peace would reign.

Eventually Novello's script for *The Dancing Years* was passed by the censors, but it had been so heavily cut that what remained was workable but far less direct and powerful as a result. However, the music and songs were some of Novello's best and included *My Dearest Dear, Waltz Of My Heart, My Life Belongs To You, Wings Of Sleep* to name but a few. He had no hesitation in asking Mary Ellis to play the lead opposite him, opera star Maria Ziegler, indeed she had no hesitation in agreeing. This show would also be personal for both of them. Ellis was in fact German, and was appalled at the events sweeping across Europe and Hitler's dictatorial regime. There were those who also suspected she was of Jewish descent, but this is an area that she always refused to discuss. Novello would also, whilst performing in this musical, face, like the character he played, his own experience of being incarcerated in a prison cell. Life really did imitate art for both of them.

It says a great deal about Novello, and his distinct lack of ego, that after all the trials, tribulations, quarrels and arguments he had experienced with Ellis during *Glamorous Night* he knew instinctively that only she could possibly create the role of Maria Ziegler in *The Dancing Years*. Indeed it also shows that he understood Ellis far more than she understood herself, and that her volatile temperament was as a result of her deep insecurities, which she managed to hide so well beneath a veneer of tough professionalism. Ellis herself was also initially frustrated because of Novello's homosexuality, and perhaps had hoped, as her parents had on meeting him and seeing them together in *Glamorous Night*, that there was a real attraction between them. Indeed, when her parents asked her if she was going to marry Novello, she recalled years later that she "had to explain to them why it was not possible."

Novello worked furiously on the book and music for *The Dancing Years* and, as usual, Bobbie and Marsh were his loyal sounding boards who he could bounce ideas off to progress the script and also console him over the wrangling with the Lord Chamberlain's office. Life and art were perfect bed partners during the conception of this show as the hot topic on everyone's lips at the start of 1939 was the escalating crisis and the inevitability of another war.

It is perhaps hard for us to appreciate how horrified the people of this country were at the prospect of yet another war. No one wanted to go through what had been experienced during the First World War, as that had been in many people's minds the war to end all wars. Unfortunately, the seeds of another war were sown when the last one ended. The Treaty of Versailles had imposed crippling conditions on a defeated Germany and, to make matters worse in the opinion of many Germans, had also humiliated their country unnecessarily. Due to reparations the country had suffered crippling debts and massive inflation to the point where money was worthless and a suitcase of bank notes would just about purchase a loaf of bread. That's all supposing a loaf of bread could be found. Added to this, the fear of communism creeping into Germany from where it had gained a stronghold in Russia was a terrifying prospect. All these economic and political conditions became fertile ground for Hitler and his Nazi Party. At heart the German people were a proud nation and they felt they had been reduced to the gutter and been shorn of their self-respect. Everything conspired to assist Hitler at this crucial time and, instead of seeing the warning signs early on, Britain, like many other countries, were more concerned with their own economies which had taken a battering due to world depression on the stock markets. By the latter part of the 1930s it was in fact too late, and would only be a matter of time.

Perhaps the fact that everyone, including Novello, were forced to see the harsh realities and the terrible consequences which were increasingly possible, made him take stock and really approach his next musical for Drury Lane from a more serious point of view. He wanted this show to have a real message and a gravity to the sub text which certainly hadn't been evident in his previous works; certainly not to the extent it would be apparent in *The Dancing Years*. Psychologically he was definitely in another place. Not only personally but also professionally. Musically the show had a beautiful score that reflected not only his usual melancholy but also elements of hope, but a hope that comes out of initial despair. Listening to this music today, gives a clue to his state of mind and how he was perhaps thinking at the time. It has a sentimental romanticism at its edges, but beyond that is a despair and an unhappiness borne out of uncertainty. The show also had very simple staging and no spectacular effects whatsoever. It didn't need them, because it stood alone as a solid story with solid characters facing adversity with courage. Of course it had its lighter and more lavish moments, it wouldn't have been a Novello show without them, but at its core, its heart, it was giving a serious message. The regret is that the prologue and epilogue were cut by the censors, although by the time it came back into the West End in 1941 he was allowed to reinstate some of the banned scenes and use Nazi uniforms for the guards. It could have been an even better show without the censor's interference and moved firmly into the realms of serious drama. Novello had, one senses, suddenly found maturity in his approach to his work by the seriousness he and everyone in the country found themselves in.

Leotine Sagan was again the Director and, being a German, it must have been a very difficult task for her. Mary Ellis was, as mentioned, also of

German descent, but not many were aware of it. But Novello stood by his decision, and his two very temperamental divas, because they were his friends, he respected them, and they thought as he did and were appalled at events happening in Germany. It is also interesting to note that, in spite of so many of his close friends who found Ellis unbearable and stand-offish to work with, Novello still never hesitated in casting her as his leading lady. More surprising considering he disliked any kind of bad atmospheres or confrontational situations, but ultimately his decision was entirely for the good of the production and he knew there was no one better to create the role of Maria Ziegler in *The Dancing Years*.

Another of Novello's close associates echoed the difficulties many experienced working with Ellis. Gordon Duttson agreed to meet me for the first time in 1997 and, as he was still living in London, we met initially at the Mountbatten Hotel in Covent Garden. Arriving early I sat in the lounge of the hotel and waited the arrival of Duttson. It occurred to me that this man was not just a link to Novello in terms of his career but also in a personal way. Whereas with the few others I had met, who had worked with Novello, I had not yet encountered anyone who enjoyed a close personal relationship with him. Duttson would, I hoped, be that exception.

On his arrival I was taken aback with the initial hostility of Duttson. His attitude was extremely defensive and confrontational in equal measures. It instantly made me feel as if I were an enemy in the eyes of this man. He was obviously advanced in years and, having seen photographs of him in his youth, it was evident the years had not been kind to him. He was slouched and unkempt and extremely scruffy in his appearance, but in spite of that one could sense a restrained energy lurking beneath the surface; almost like an angry animal who could pounce unexpectedly at any moment. It was then, quite difficult to relax in the company of this man, and as a result proved to be an exhausting encounter. It soon became apparent why he was so angry.

His initial remarks were all a result of a deep suspicion about my motives towards his friend, and he was of the opinion that no one had the right to question or do anything but revere Novello's memory. Having explained my task of rewriting *Glamorous Night's* libretto and my sincere intention to ensure the spirit of the original remained; indeed my hope to incorporate

Novello as a character in the production, did little to alleviate a tense situation. At this he fixed his steely eyes on me, eyes which were almost black as I recall, and they seemed to be searching inside and behind my own eyes for answers to something I was oblivious to. On the subject of Mary Ellis, he laughed darkly, then with a good dash of sarcasm, informed me that indeed she had been difficult and had been disliked by some of those involved, but it was all, as a result of jealousy. Not just professional but personally. Anyone to whom Novello was close became a target for bitchy remarks because those who hadn't achieved entry to his intimate circle were jealous.

It suddenly dawned on me that this man was shrouded in sadness, and as the meeting progressed I realised why that sadness had manifested in him. He was very bitter at the way some had treated him after Novello's death and his opinion of Bobbie was especially venomous. In his opinion Bobbie had just been there for what he could get, at least in the final years. He had, Duttson informed me, been involved with many men and had only thought about himself. This surprised me and I countered it by saying that Novello and Bobbie had remained firm and loyal to the last. He acknowledged that there was a bond between them and of course Bobbie never left because he had nowhere to go; and that he wasn't going to relinquish his lifestyle by walking out. Duttson then spurted out angrily: "I've been completely ignored. No one cares about me anymore, and I was Ivor's last lover."

This really was the root of the problem and the resulting anger and bitterness that had eaten away at this man for decades. I suddenly felt very sad for him. As the conversation progressed I began to see him in a new light. In his mind Novello was still this huge celebrity who had been the centre of his world. He was at the time, a young man infatuated with the man who not only employed him but who also became his lover. Fresh in his mind was that position of influence and power it had given him whilst Novello lived, but it was also the very thing that caused him to be out-cast by others, and as a result began his own decline into a world where, in his imagination, that world still existed somewhere.

He was angry with a world that had long forgotten his famous lover, because he perceived that as the world ignoring him and not recognising his place in Novello's fame. As much as his suspicion and hostility abated slightly, he was I soon discovered happy that someone had recognised him and was interested in what he had to say. As a result he then, to my complete surprise, invited me to his flat in Victoria.

Nothing, and I mean nothing, could have prepared me for that visit. His flat was tiny, cramped and dingy. He lived in complete squalor. This only added to my sense of sadness for the man, and it was so claustrophobic it seemed to lack not only daylight but also enough air to actually breath. He seemed oblivious to the chaos and dust that surrounded him and began to show me photograph albums that contained faded black and white photographs of himself and Novello in happier times. They were intimate and personal photographs, and showed that he had traveled the world with his famous lover, from New York, to Novello's houses in Jamaica and South Africa and of course at "the flat" and Red Roofs. A very young Duttson sat in these photographs next to Novello and smiled out. He was a handsome man in his early twenties and, as much as it was obvious the man standing next to me was an older version, it was hard to equate the happy youth and the bitter old man being the same person. From Hollywood Stars to eminent British Stars, they appeared in these photographs and at the time treated Duttson as an equal, but once Novello was dead, they no longer had to afford him that respect. Therein lay the tragedy for Duttson.

After Novello's death he had initially been close to Ellis for reasons that were disturbing to them at the time. In the months following Novello's death some of his personal belongings and intimate photograph albums began to appear in collector's shops in the West End. Other things would mysteriously appear for sale in newspaper adverts. Ellis had first noticed this when passing a dealer's shop and was shocked to see a personal photograph album of Novello's displayed in the window for sale. She engaged Duttson to purchase as much of these things as they could find, and also to try and find out where they had come from and who had sold them. It transpired, according to Duttson, that Bobbie and his sister Maidie were selling these private articles to the highest bidder. They managed to retrieve nearly everything that had been put up for sale, but as a result they never forgave Bobbie or his sister for what they perceived to be the betrayal of Novello's memory.

Duttson had then found that, once this had been accomplished, Ellis cooled towards him and in effect cut off the lines of communication. This only added to his bitterness. During the time they were buying up all the personal belongings, Duttson had managed to purchase and keep some of the private albums. The very ones he was allowing me to see. He had decided, after visiting June Bloom, who now owns Red Roofs, that when he died he was leaving his collection to the house. I can only assume that is what happened.

I was glad I met Duttson and wished him well. It had allowed me a peak into the other world of Novello that included the jealousy and behaviour of those vying for a position and status in his life. And, as is so often the case where human emotions are concerned, an insight into what some perceived as betrayal after his death. Could this in-fighting and squabbling among his close friends have been the cause of so many closing ranks and ultimately suffocating Novello's legacy? It was a real possibility, and if nothing else was certainly a vital ingredient in the eventual outcome. One of the last things I discussed with Duttson was regarding Novello's feelings for *The Dancing Years*. He said it remained a favourite of all his shows in spite of the censorship imposed on it by the Lord Chamberlain's office, and Novello had hoped it would one day be able to have a production that included all his original intentions.

Back in 1939 Novello was about to embark on rehearsals for *The Dancing Years* and had cast an unknown actress, Roma Beaumont, to play the character of Greta, the rival love interest between his own character, Rudi Kleber, and Ellis's Maria. It was in fact a foil, as the young Greta was just infatuated and no serious rival to the relationship between Rudi and Maria. Due to a misunderstanding, Rudi and Maria miss the opportunity to cement their relationship completely; with a pregnant Maria running away and leaving behind the man she loves in the mistaken belief he is about to marry Greta. The conversation she overhears between Rudi and Greta is in fact just a childish game. It is not until years later that the mistake comes to light, and Maria discovers that Rudi has been imprisoned by the Nazis. She manages to visit him through the influence of her husband, Prince Metterling. She persuades him to exert his power to halt Rudi's execution and secure his release from prison. It is at this time Rudi discovers that he is the father of Maria's son - and she assures him their son is untainted by the Nazis. Interwoven with this love story is the decline of Vienna from a once free and creative city into a cowed and brutalised place controlled by the Nazis.

From the outset Novello was determined to reflect the evils of Nazism, even if he couldn't refer to them by name, and also highlight the persecution of the Jews. By making his own character Jewish, and creating the prologue and epilogue, showing him as an aged Jewish man about to be executed by the Nazis after repressing and destroying his music, it was a potent and brave cocktail which reflected accurately exactly what was happening at the time in Germany. That the censors slashed chunks of this and imposed other restrictions is very unfortunate. In the end he did manage to get the message across and managed to retain enough to make the show powerful and compelling for the audiences who saw it. Sadly, most of the productions since, and their have been few, always failed to reinstate the prologue and epilogue with the result being a watered down version which fails to reflect Novello's original intentions. *The Dancing Years* opened on 23rd March, 1939, at Drury Lane, and astounded and delighted with its simplicity and captivating story. London's *Evening Standard* reported on the opening night thus:

"He knows his audience so well indeed that, although we may quibble over details, we are forced to admit that in *The Dancing Years* he has given it a most vivid and glamorous entertainment - perhaps the most vivid and glamorous he has ever accomplished. Mr Novello, as Rudi strikes romantic poses, plays the piano better than he conducts and shows himself the incomparable stage architect in every scene. Miss Mary Ellis has never been better: a tender, passionate and utterly lovely performance. And Miss Roma Beaumont, as Grete, captured our hearts from the moment she took the stage."

The spirit of the production, and that its message was heard loud and clear, was summed up in *The News Chronicle* review:

"And when in the last scene of all, in the captured Vienna of 1938, Mr Novello, now artistically decrepit, defies the conquerors and brings the house down - why, this is only to show that Mr Novello is astute enough to make the best of both worlds, the tinkles of 1911 and the tragedies of our own day."

Novello's own feelings on the world situation at the time were clearly identified in some of the dialogue and this extract is from a speech his character makes; a speech which is still capable of resonating in today's troubled world:

"We shall see great changes and feel it here - times of unrest and anger and hatred in the world - and these things are strong. We shall almost forget to laugh and make music, but we shan't quite forget, and some day we'll wake up, as from an evil dream, and the world will smile again and forget hate, and the sweetness of music and friendliness will once more be important…"

Fate, for the first time, dealt Novello a nasty blow, a blow that would strike everyone. When war was declared in September 1939, *The Dancing Years* was closed along with all theatrical productions on orders of the government. Drury Lane was taken over and commandeered for the war effort. The country was stunned that once again Germany had created a war, there was an atmosphere of utter disbelief. A gloom descended on the nation and everyone waited for the first assault. For Novello it was the end of his Drury Lane years. He would never again play in that theatre, and like so many, he must have wondered if he would survive the war. Along with other prominent Jews, homosexuals, politicians and Nazi opponents, they were perfectly aware they would be the first to be arrested if the Germans successfully invaded Great Britain.

As the war progressed and London was subjected to the worst air attacks in its history. The Blitz, as it became known, would see many parts of London, especially the East End and docklands area completely destroyed. In fact the Blitz changed the face of London forever. Novello's life was dramatically changed as well, and everyone endured the hardships imposed, and the distinct lack of supplies resulted in a strict rationing system for not only food but also clothes and petrol. Eventually the closure orders imposed on theatres and cinemas around the country were relaxed and Novello was able to organise a tour of *The Dancing Years* to the provinces.

Being too old for war duty in the services, Novello felt that it was a way of bringing some kind of solace and cheer to all those around the country who were suffering terrible hardships.

However, the production suffered as it crawled around the country in almost slow motion. Novello and his company had to rely on the rail network to transport them, and all the scenery and costumes. During the war the rail system was slow and often it would take an interminable amount of hours to travel relatively short distances on dark, cold trains with little in the way of comfort for those involved. Once arriving at their destination, further complications would occur due to the compulsory blackouts imposed to protect towns and cities from enemy aircraft. As a result, those arriving in an unfamiliar place would often be lost in the dark and unable to find their lodgings or even the theatre where they were playing. Lodgings also became a distinctly welcome luxury, as at times the entire company would have to sleep rough in the theatres in which they were performing. Much to the dismay of most, they also found that many theatres had no stage crews because they had all been called up for war duty. On such occasions Home Guard recruits would be rallied and asked for assistance in setting and striking the scenery and taking on the job of stage crew for the duration of the production.

In spite of these difficulties and the frustrations involved, not to mention the humour and camaraderie that inevitably arose, due to the imposed disorganisation and lack of skills possessed by some, Novello managed to keep the whole thing going and delighted audiences all over the country with a rather disheveled and less than glamorous looking production. Ultimately it didn't matter, for the audiences the only thing that mattered was the fact that Novello was there, and as a result they could forget the war that was raging outside. However, there were many occasions when reality and fantasy suddenly became one. During air raids the audiences were usually kept in the theatre, sometimes until the early hours of the morning, and on a couple of occasions all night. When this happened Novello and his cast would cheerfully entertain them in a relaxed, informal way. This usually took the form of Novello playing the piano and organising a sing-along session with audience and cast. It was grueling and tiring but to his credit, Novello never allowed the difficulties and hardships to dint his spirits, at least publicly.

By 1941 the West End theatres had, to all intents and purposes, and as far as they were able, returned to a fairly "business as usual" state of play. The government had quickly realised that stars such as Novello had an important role to play in keeping up morale among those still at home and also the service men and women returning on leave. *The Dancing Years* would prove to be a hugely popular musical and, in spite of the cuts imposed by the censor, proved to be enduring because the message that lay hidden beneath the plot was easily revealed to audiences and in a way was stronger for it. All this buoyed Novello and, after the success of the tour of the provinces with the show, in spite of the grueling hardships endured by everyone in the cast, he jumped at the opportunity to stage the show once again in the West End. Drury Lane was out of the question because it had been commandeered by ENSA, and thus the production moved into the Adelphi Theatre and enjoyed a considerable run. Mary Ellis was by this time engaged in war work in Scotland and another actress, Muriel Baron, who had replaced her for the tour, now played the role of Maria Ziegler in what was a West End revival of the production. Novello was pleased to be back in London, in spite of the continuing air raids, and relieved he could live at "the flat", and be near enough to visit Red Roofs at the weekends.

The atmosphere in London at the time was tense and frightening but the war had brought people together in a way that had never happened before. The Blitz was the first time that those left at home during any conflict had been subjected to the horrors of air raids and the death and destruction it wrought. The spirit among people, however devastating the experience, was positive indeed. The exact opposite to what Hitler had hoped, as he was convinced his orders to destroy swathes of the city would break morale among the public and ensure him the early surrender of England. He was to be proved very wrong, and if anything it strengthened the resolve of everyone. That said, people truly believed that Hitler intended to invade Britain, and Churchill was also aware that it was a real possibility. In 1941 England stood alone after all of the continent had fallen under the control of Hitler's regime.

Novello would have experienced first hand the terror of the Blitz at "the flat" as the City is but a stones throw away. The force of the blasts and the trembling of the buildings was very distressing for those involved and the use of incendiary bombs added to the fear. In addition there were the fairly strategic buildings situated not that far away including a BBC Radio building which broadcast to the world, and the newspaper industry of Fleet Street, which were both prime targets for the bombers. There must have been times when it felt as if the world would come to an end; and for many it did, the smell of death permeated the air after particularly ferocious night raids.

Happy to be doing his bit and, in spite of feeling he had been playing Rudi in *The Dancing Years* forever, Novello still enjoyed performing the show. He had got to the point where he nicknamed the show among his friends as either "The Advancing Years" or "The Prancing Queers" depending on the mood he was in. Whatever his personal feelings he did well to stem his natural boredom threshold, resigned to the fact that extraordinary times required extraordinary measures from everyone - even himself. But as with life and human nature there are measures and measures, depending on how one chooses to look at them.

Rationing was imposed on everything from food to clothes to petrol. Petrol rationing was very strict because, as would seem logical, the fuel was needed for service vehicles and below that only for essential transport services. This situation was first brought to light in Novello's world when he found the Petrol Board, a government department set up to issue permits to the public to obtain petrol, baulked at his request for coupons to use for his Rolls Royce. The ensuing argument Novello based on his need to return to Red Roofs for weekends after performing in eight shows at the Adelphi Theatre. As Red Roofs is situated near Maidenhead in Berkshire, Novello reasoned, he would need the Rolls to drive him there on a Saturday evening after the performance, then return him to London in time for the Monday evening performance. The officials at the Petrol Board would discuss and debate this and let him know. Initially infuriated that he hadn't received approval instantly, he resigned himself to wait and see what happened. In the meantime, he vented his frustration to his friends and colleagues, who listened and smiled, though they perhaps should have said that maybe there was a case for his request not being "essential." But then Novello was a man who had everything he wanted, and wasn't used to being refused anything. In his mind he was doing a vital service for the war effort and he couldn't understand why anyone would not consider his need to rest and relax at Red Roofs as essential. For now, the debate and arguing betwixt

Novello and the Petrol Board rumbled on.

The war would also bring a tragedy to Novello which was very personal. In 1942 his mother died. Psychologically this was a far greater blow to Novello than many realised and, not unlike the reaction to his father's death, brought into sharp focus how she had always been a central figure in his life; despite her eccentricities and the financial disasters she had wrought upon him, her demise was a shattering blow. Clara had always, practically up to the every end, been a vital and energetic woman who for all intents and purposes seemed immortal to her son. That she was no longer there in a way made him feel as is he had somehow been cut adrift. Many had found her overbearing and at times a frightening woman, a woman who seemed selfish and certainly spoiled by her famous son. For his part he remained completely loyal to her and never complained about the costs of bailing her out of countless financial troubles; indeed, even making sure that these lapses in her life never became public knowledge during her lifetime. Without her he felt he would never have achieved what he had, and certainly she was the one who initially made him face up to life and grasp every opportunity as quickly as he could, who had bullied him out of his laziness and demanded he make use of his talents constructively, talents she had seen in him long before he had ever been aware he possessed them. He was also sad that she should die amidst the terrible war, and that she went to her grave not knowing whether the England she loved passionately would overcome and be victorious in the end. To him, her death had robbed her of so much he had wanted her to be there for. But it must have also crossed his mind that perhaps she was lucky , seeing her country fall under the control of Hitler would have killed her quicker than any cancer; indeed the fate that was awaiting her son a little further along the road would also have possibly killed her spirit if not her body.

Ivor Novello

LET'S FACE THE MUSIC!

"He is trying to put all the blame on me. That is grossly unfair. He was willing to do anything crooked so long as he had the use of the car."

Dora Constable.

War raged on in Europe whilst Novello continued to entertain the public in *The Dancing Years* in the West End, whilst his production of *Glamorous Night* embarked on a tour with a secondary cast. Novello had inevitably began to tire of the repetition involved with, for the time, a very long run of his musical, and set about creating a show to once again star Mary Ellis and Elisabeth Welch. He would not this time have a role in the production because he was committed to continue performing in *The Dancing Years*, but it served its purpose in enabling him to create something new and thus alleviate his boredom. He had, with his usual charm, persuaded Mary Ellis to return to London and work. His argument being that she could do far more good by entertaining than she ever could by nursing in Scotland. She was duly persuaded and returned for rehearsals of *Arc De Triomphe*. The show was a mixture of song and dance and had an opera sequence in the final act which depicted Joan of Arc; and also catered for Ellis' and Novello's grand opera aspirations. Looking at the piece today, it is easy to see the propagandist element to the production and the message of hope that it contained. It proceeded with its run at the Phoenix Theatre and did steady if not fantastic business; which could be counter balanced financially by Novello because *The Dancing Years* was playing to full houses daily.

As 1942 progressed into 1943, Novello still found himself embroiled in arguments with the Petrol Board over using his Rolls Royce at weekends, and their final decision to not allow him petrol coupons for the vehicle because it was neither deemed a "priority" nor in their view "essential" infuriated him. With this final decision from the Petrol Board, Novello flew into a petulant rage and smashed up his dressing room at the Adelphi Theatre. Bobbie was horrified by this outburst and seriously worried that the stress and pressure were affecting his lover to a degree where his health would eventually suffer. His concerns were also justified because of the depth of the dark depressions Novello seemed to sink into, more noticeable since his mother's death, and the amount of time it would take for him to emerge from these bouts of despair. Bobbie was, much to Novello's relief, always on hand to support and soothe his anger and frustration. Casting Bobbie in small parts in his shows had its benefits for both of them, but more so for Novello.

My task a few decades later was to try and reflect the spirit of the shows that Novello produced at Drury Lane – and it was no mean feat. Having staged events at Drury Lane on three occasions, twice in the Grand Saloon and once on the main stage, I realised from the start that they had to be presented with a full understanding of the originals and, if possible, contain more than a glimmer of the glamour and style for which they were rightly famous sixty years before. Compared to the original budgets for these productions, and in spite of the fact that they were on a miniscule scale by comparison, I had very limited resources indeed which, if not used wisely, would have resulted in productions which did the material and music an injustice. Just about the last thing I wanted to happen after so much work and effort to understand Novello and what he was trying to do in his time. As is obvious, my research on Novello went far beyond my original intention with the script work I was undertaking on *Glamorous Night*, carrying on to the end of his life and far beyond. Initially I had started out with a desire to understand the early stages of his life and the road that led Novello to *Glamorous Night*, but such was the intensity of my experience and the journey I found myself embarked upon it was impossible to not continue past 1935 and complete the picture. But I considered it necessary and worthwhile, hoping the long road leading to an understanding of his Ruritania would be worth it in the end.

The experience of listening to the music Novello composed for his musicals is at times a confusing one. The music purist might say that they were a frothy and inconsequential as the productions they were composed for. But it is clear that the structure of the music, even looking at it from a layman's point of view, is compelling in its depth. Underneath the melodies lay hidden elements that have the power to render most of them unforgettable; in a way which is quite difficult to ascertain. Deep below the surface of what seem to be simple melodies there are elements of the sadness and melancholy which was an innate part of Novello's psychological make up. At times they can seem desperate and cloying in their sentimental values, but it is more than that, and one suspects even the self admitted laziness of Novello can be traced in his music. At times it can feel like the lush, romanticised melancholy is overdone to a point where only so much can be listened to in one sitting. But it becomes compelling once this initial reaction has worn off. Many of the melodies are like a maggot that enters your brain, sets up home, and refuses to let you forget it is there.

The lyrics by Christopher Hassall are often criticised for being too florid, or over sentimental and even for destroying the impact of the composed melodies. Ian Richardson, in his letter to me, said that in his opinion the reason why Novello's music is mostly forgotten is due to "the banality of the lyrics." At first it seems rather a brutal opinion of Hassall and his ability as a lyricist, but then one has to consider the times when these were written and the productions they were intended for. In today's fast paced and cynical world it is easy to see how these lyrics have become thus perceived. But in their time, a time that was less frenetic and certainly less cynical, it is easy to see how they fitted so perfectly. Experiencing a theatre musical was to experience a world that was larger than life and not necessarily a true reflection of life itself. In that larger world it was okay for heroes and heroines to express their love and desire for each other through songs which were full of "glamorous, rapturous nights" where the characters "spirits longed for" each other. Even today we happily suspend our disbelief when entering the world of musical theatre, so too did audiences all those decades ago. It is just the way we, and those then, perceive the world which is around us. And even today we still love the drama of love and romance and unrequited love - because they are all ingredients which mirror our own experiences of life. Sir Cameron Mackintosh & Lord Lloyd Webber's musical *The Phantom Of The Opera* is in many ways cast straight from Novello's mould. It has the same melodramatic flavour, interwoven around a romanticised and glamorized operetta style story that runs the gamut of human emotions. To date it is also one of the world's longest running and one of the most popular musicals of all time, proving there is an audience of billions out there who need and want to embrace all those ingredients.

It also has to be remembered that Novello, through his musicals, recaptured an era that many of his audience members would recall first hand, or was in the recent past vividly enough to still be clearly appreciated by others. The Edwardian era and *The Merry Widow* can be seen clearly as a major influence on Novello in terms of the structure and compositions within his musicals. From the glamour of a leading lady, to whom for a few hours each night he could be in love with, and thus a heterosexual man to the eyes of the audience, to the quality of the sets and ridiculousness of the situations; all done with total sincerity, which is perhaps also part of the reason they were embraced. Sheridan Morley once said that Novello was old-fashioned even in his time – something that is absolutely correct. But he got away with it because it was and Ivor Novello show. Women in their multitudes made their way to the theatre to see him above all else.

All his shows reflected that Edwardian era and were held in such nostalgic esteem above any other and, because of the skill of Novello in terms of his performance, he could place himself in these shows in a non-singing role and it didn't appear at odds with the overall production. His ability to make them laugh and to move his audiences with the power of his melodies is without question. As has been noted, Novello has been the only man who has devised, written, composed and starred in his own musicals on such a scale in the West End. The nearest contemporary comparison that can be made is to one woman. She has also devised, written, composed and starred in *Acorn Antiques The Musical*. Admittedly she shared the lead role with Julie Walters, but she did star on alternate nights. Experiencing the now late Victoria Wood's musical also brought to mind the days when going to the theatre meant seeing a "star" live and in action. In today's West End, especially musical theatre, there are no stars as the shows have become the star, the performers singing machines rather than personalities. Wood or Walter's first entrance was greeted with thunderous applause that they graciously acknowledged, then got on with the job in hand. This was exactly the kind of reaction Novello always received on his first entrance in either play or musical. It was part of the excitement of going to the theatre, and rarely occurs in today's theatre.

The late Victoria Wood was not someone you would instantly compare to Novello, but in fact they had much in common. Novello was also a master at writing and playing comedy, and could render his audiences helpless with laughter. Had there been the technology of television in Novello's time, no doubt he would also have been a natural for that medium too. Novello and Wood were both known for their satirical and witty songs. Novello's contribution in this area is still in evidence but the jokes and references are left sterile and meaningless out of their time. In the years leading up to the 1920s and into that decade he was in great demand to write these witty numbers for West End revue shows. Perhaps in a hundred years from now Wood's songs with lyrics such as "beat me on the bottom with a Woman's Weekly" will leave the listener confused instead of amused. No doubt Novello, had he still been around, would have laughed heartily and enjoyed the experience of being exposed to Victoria Wood and her talents. Wood's West End musical, like Novello's in his time, cost a great deal of money. Investors have to be fairly sure of at least a chance of getting a return on their money before they decide to hand it over.

Staging an investors showcase production in the Grand Saloon at Drury Lane was an idea that I put forward to try and garner interest in the revival of *Glamorous Night* and all its possibilities. Although it would be fairly basic in what could be achieved, I was determined to at least create some of the atmosphere of the original; albeit in reduced circumstances. The Grand Saloon at Drury Lane is situated on the first floor and serves as the bar area for the Grand Circle of the auditorium, and to me it seemed the only place to hold such an event considering the history behind *Glamorous Night*, and that it was originally produced in, and therefore part of that theatre's history. The Saloon itself is a large and ornate room with marble pillars and several large chandeliers; at the far end is an ante-room which has large French polished double doors that lead into the main Saloon. All this, I quickly decided, would serve perfectly as a set for the event, and properly utilised would add the required glamour and opulence to the occasion.

The choice of artists for the production was a little more complex, mainly because Novello's music, although seemingly simple, is in fact terribly difficult to sing technically. Many a time I had sat through concerts where the singers were inexperienced and thus the songs murdered. Vital then that the showcase had singers who were trained for the demands of the music; bearing in mind Novello composed songs that required an operatic technique. Eventually I had a cast in place. Soprano Fiona O'Neil, and Tenor Richard Braebrook were veterans of English National Opera and were cast as Miltza and Lorenti. Gia Frances, who at the time was working in *Buddy* at The Strand Theatre [now the Novello Theatre], was perfect to pick up the mantle of Elizabeth Welch and sing Shanty Town as Cleo. The chorus was gathered from the Royal Academy of Music with the assistance of the ever-helpful Mary Hammond.

With limited rehearsal time, as is always the way with such things, we set about creating a concert which to all intents and purposes was a mini version of the show. I had decided early on, after having been exposed to events where artists just sing and make no connection with character or situation, that I wanted them all to develop their characters and understand the show as much as possible. Peter McDermot, who had appeared in the lead role in the London production of my play *The Post Card*, was cast as the narrator to link the story and songs together, so the audience could at least have a sense of the narrative. I answered numerous questions and in the process realised how much knowledge I had acquired. They were all delighted to hear that the performance would be fully costumed, directed and choreographed. In the limited time we had we achieved a lot, and eventually it all came together.

The invited audience consisted of many recognisable names in the theatre world and representatives of those who had expressed an interest in possibly investing in the production. Some other well-known names from the industry included David Jacobs, Michael Codron, Nika Burns, David Kinsey, Duncan Weldon and Sandy Wilson. The memorable sections for me, although everyone performed superbly on the day, was the opening where the narrator set the scene and then to the strains of the *Glamorous Night* waltz the huge double doors slowly opened to reveal couples waltzing in full evening dress. It was magical - my intention was to create a window to the past slowly revealing its inhabitants. The idea, although simple, had worked and grabbed the audience's attention. The chorus then began to sing the *Glamorous Night* waltz and move into the main body of the room. From this point the narrator provided the links and the songs were interwoven to create a fluid story. Gia Frances and I had discussed the song *Shanty Town* and experimented performing it as a sexy cabaret number, and move away from the down trodden way Welch had performed it in the original as a black stowaway aboard the SS Silver Star. Her performance that day was sexy, exciting and stopped the show.

Overall the day was a success and considering everything it was received in a very positive and enthusiastic way. Sandy Wilson was introduced to me that day and I found him to be a charming and delightful man. He had as a youth seen the original production of *Glamorous Night* and had, he said, been inspired by Novello to try and break into the theatre and write a musical. He managed both and is recognised the world over as the creator and composer of *The Boyfriend*. I was delighted to then receive an invitation to his flat for a cup of tea and a chat. He was intrigued as to why I should be interested in Novello, even more so because I was fairly young and could never have seen him in his shows. I explained then that it was a long story, and if he reads this book he will understand why, but I felt strongly then that it was a shame the world had forgotten about Novello's achievements, regardless of whether one likes or dislikes his style. In the scheme of things and for the sake of theatre history he merited recognition. I also truly believed that a Novello show such as *Glamorous Night* really could find an audience if produced in the right way, and was approached with sincerity, realism and, it has to be said, no hint of sentimentality attached. Sandy also kindly informed me that he had spoken to Mary Ellis on the telephone and told her how good the showcase was, and she asked him to pass on to me her delight that it had gone so well. It was a compliment given with sincerity and, considering the two people from whence it came, made me feel I had achieved something positive, and was very much appreciated.

Shortly after the showcase I met the choreographer Gillian Gregory, who subsequently agreed to come on board at this stage of the project. I had great respect for Gillian and her achievements and she was a joy to work with. Between us we embarked on a plan to present a small extract of

Glamorous Night on the main stage of Drury Lane for an event that publicised up coming West End productions. Having secured the services of soprano Tiffany Edwards, and Tenor Graham Bruce, we set about constructing a small segment that would, in our opinion, reflect to its best advantage three songs from the score. We chose the title song *Glamorous Night*, *Shine Through My Dreams* and *Fold Your Wings*, which were arranged for the event into a medley. Sheridan Morley was acting as master of ceremonies and I therefore had to write an introduction and explanation for him to use in his address to the audience prior to the segment being performed. During rehearsals he remarked that he couldn't believe there had never been a serious revival of the show in the years following Novello's death in 1951, but indeed there hadn't.

On the day of the performance we had a rehearsal and sound check in haste, as is the nature of these kind of events, and all went as well as could be expected. As the audience entered Gillian and I sat at the back of the Grand Circle and watched the show with much trepidation, awaiting the turn of our *Glamorous Night* segment. It was finally introduced and performed without a hitch, and the audience reacted in a positive and heartening manner. The only moment we felt was over milked was the bows taken by the performers - and in their defense they had been taken aback by the reception they received and were enjoying the moment. I always believe less is more, and I knew Gillian agreed with that philosophy, and would have preferred them to exit, dare I say glamorously, but swiftly. The greatest pleasure for me was the fact that, if only for a moment, I had managed to engineer the return of Novello's music and songs to the stage where they had first been heard.

As things transpired the revival of *Glamorous Night* was not meant to be. The costs of staging the show would prove to be beyond what anyone was prepared to invest, and the initial investors had for reasons various backed out or proved to be insincere in their initial intentions. It was very sad and, in spite of this, I still feel the new libretto and staging I developed would have worked. Perhaps my biggest regret was not being able to continue working with Gillian on the project. But perhaps time will maybe present us with another opportunity. Nothing is impossible.

For Novello back in 1943, he was about to face the music but in a way that even he couldn't have imagined in his wildest Ruritanian dreams. His dispute with the Petrol Board had finally come to its conclusion and he was not permitted to use his Rolls Royce. But an alternative presented itself that, rather unwisely, Novello decided to take advantage of. He had been introduced to a young woman named Grace Walton who had become what we would call today an obsessive fan. She attended so many performances of *The Dancing Years*, sitting in the same seat in the stalls whilst it was on tour and then at the Adelphi once it returned to the West End, that she had come to the attention of most of the cast. Walton initially struck up a friendship with Minnie Raynor who eventually mentioned her to Novello. On one particular day, as Novello left "the flat", she was standing outside the doorway at 11 Aldwych. He was on his way to the theatre and asked if she would like to walk with him and chat; something we was known to do with fans he recognised when in the right mood. Walton jumped at the offer, and what transpired from that initial meeting and subsequent conversations would have an unexpected and traumatic effect on Novello's life.

Novello was in many ways living a life that was beyond the comprehension of most ordinary people. He had for so many years been surrounded by people who operated the machinery of his life so smoothly that he became oblivious to reality. He was used to having everything he wanted whenever he wanted and never by demand. Those around him just made sure it was there and he never thought about it or beyond it. Possibly the only thing that didn't just appear as if by magic was petrol for his Rolls Royce, and in wartime conditions it was a commodity even his staff and friends, and all the money in the world, couldn't procure. He became aware of it and was angry.

An example of Novello's more self-centred temperament is described by W McQueen Pope in his 1950 biography on Novello. Pope was a man that had been at Novello's side since the early 1930s, he managed all the press and publicity Novello received and, after such a long relationship, considered himself to be a friend. He recalled one occasion when he called into the theatre to speak to Novello on some business, and instantly felt an atmosphere so thick it could be cut with a knife as he entered his dressing room. Bobbie and Olive Gilbert and others close to Novello were all sitting in an uncomfortable silence. It transpired that Pope saw laid before him every luxury food item one could imagine, but Novello was sulking because there were no boiled eggs. In spite of all the food in evidence, eggs were what he wanted, and there weren't any. Pope was understandably incredulous, as most of the food he saw laid out had not been seen in war ravaged England for a few years; indeed he even states he had not seen an egg "since before the war." The most surprising element to this account is Pope's statement that he was never asked if he wanted anything to eat. He took no offence at his exclusion.

It does give an insight into not only Novello's ability to be petulant and spoiled, but also his seeming ignorance of how fortunate he was to have such things at his disposal, and that those around Novello revered him to the point of worship. Any normal friend, especially in wartime, would have been asked to enjoy something of the feast that was laid out. But none was offered, none received, and no question of criticising such selfish behaviour entered Pope's mind; indeed he went as far as to say "Novello deserved all those things" for all the pleasure he brought to so many people. The fact is when an individual has achieved such fame and prominence in the world, not to mention wealth, those around them behave in a different way than they would with other mere mortals. This is especially the case when their very existence and employment rely on the reflected glory emanating from the celebrity. For Novello, this was normal and he would have never conceived that it could be seen as selfish or extraordinary behaviour. This was exactly the reason why Grace Walton, in contriving a situation to ingratiate herself, out of blind adulation, was able to send him fool him and send him hurtling back to reality with an almighty thud!

Walton had succeeded in maneuvering herself into the periphery of Novello's world, and subsequently became a regular visitor to his dressing room at the Adlephi Theatre. Through those visits she became aware of his problem regarding the refusal of the Petrol Board to allow him fuel for his Rolls Royce. Seizing the opportunity, she made a suggestion that perhaps would help to solve the problem. Walton worked for an Insurance company, which had offices in London and Reading, and in the vicinity of Red Roofs. She proposed that her company could make use of the car for business purposes by way of transporting documents between offices, and thus provide the petrol. She could see no reason why it would not be possible for Novello to use the car to drive him to Littlewick Green and back at the weekends, as it would be part of its official business journey. Novello eagerly agreed to her proposition - and for once didn't mention the arrangement to anyone, even Bobbie, which would prove to be a fatal error.

During October of 1943 he received a telephone call from the Director of Electric and General Trusts Ltd, the firm Walton worked for, to inform him the situation regarding his car and the petrol use had come to their attention. They had no knowledge of, or had ever agreed to such an arrangement. Grace Walton was in fact a false name, and it transpired her real name was Dora Constable. Neither did she hold a senior position at the company, which she had claimed when making the arrangement with Novello, indeed the opposite was in fact the case. She was actually a mere clerk. This evidence alone suggests that Constable was a fantasist and was so infatuated with Novello she would have done anything to be part of his life. Novello was far from blameless because he had seen a way of getting something for which he had been refused official permission - the use of his Rolls Royce. The fact he failed to mention the arrangement to anyone in his intimate circle, suggests that perhaps he knew they would question the arrangement; or at least make sure he contacted her employer to confirm it was genuine and above board. In a way Novello was as much a fantasist as Constable. He wanted his car to use at weekends and he had managed to achieve this against the odds. That is all that concerned him.

Once the situation came to light in all its unpleasant details, on the advice of his close friends, he immediately informed the Petrol Board of the situation. As a result of this Novello was issued with a summons, along with Constable, accused of conspiring to commit an offence against the Motor Vehicles Order of 1942. They both appeared at Bow Street Magistrates Court in early 1944 and pleaded not guilty. Constable was fined fifty pounds and released. Novello was sentenced to two months in prison, against which he appealed, and received bail until a further hearing was arranged. No importance seemed to have been attached to the fact that Constable had used a false name - certainly the court seemed not to hold this against her, which seems odd. However, Novello had firmly stated he

was innocent and, unwisely considering his position in the world against that of Constable, placed the blame firmly at her door. Perhaps had he not done this and instead recognised his own naivety and stupidity, and accepted some responsibility for his actions, then the outcome would have been different.

"He is trying to put all the blame on me," Constable told the Daily Mirror, " That is grossly unfair. He was willing to do anything crooked so long as he had the use of the car." She also claimed that she felt "if she could not do anything to assist Mr. Novello it would go far towards losing his friendship which I so deeply value."

Apart from the statements made by Novello and Constable, and his opinion that she was "an inveterate liar", the Magistrates were of the opinion that even if the company for which Miss Constable worked had agreed to the proposal, it would still be a flagrant flouting of the petrol laws and therefore still an offence.

Novello's appeal was set for the 16th May, 1944, at Newington Butts. The hope was that the sentence of eight weeks would be reduced to a fine and costs. In fact the Judge, after hearing the evidence, reduced the sentence to four weeks in prison. Novello was taken from the court and transported to Wormwood Scrubs to serve his sentence. The Daily Sketch reported thus:

"Dark-haired smartly tailored Ivor Novello turned to the public benches, almost entirely filled by actors and actresses, at London Sessions yesterday, and in almost a whisper said: "Good-bye." He had just heard that his appeal against sentence of eight weeks' imprisonment imposed at Bow-street, for conspiring to commit an offence against a motor vehicles control Order, had been dismissed - but the prison sentence was reduced from eight to four weeks."

Edward Marsh was aghast at the outcome and publicly declared that "It's the most monstrous miscarriage of justice," adding sadly, "till it actually happened I could never believe that it would…It was an incredible shock." Shocking as it was, it has to be said that Novello was foolish in the extreme and in many ways it highlighted his detachment from reality. He had been told he couldn't have something he wanted, probably for the first time in decades, and he didn't like it. The price for his actions would be even less palatable.

The public and personal humiliation Novello felt must have been much worse than the actual prison sentence. His arrival at Wormwood Scrubs would have involved the complete loss of his dignity. Stripped naked and then examined by the Prison Doctor, he would have showered and put on rough prison clothes before being taken to his cell and locked in. Cut off and isolated from all those around him, and those who made sure his every desire and comfort was catered for, would have been a shattering experience and the psychological effects immense. Indeed, among his friends there was the opinion that it altered him completely. Zena Dare declared that "he was never a strong man after going to prison" and the general feeling was it was the start of the ill health that would kill him.

It was also speculated that it prevented Novello receiving the Knighthood he would surely have been honoured with once the war was over, indeed McQueen Pope alludes to this in his biography on Novello. The fact is it would have been most unlikely he would have received such an honour because he was a homosexual. This fact alone would have stood in the way of such recognition at the time. Coward, his friend and contemporary, had to wait until 1970 to receive his Knighthood when attitudes towards homosexuality had changed significantly. By that time Novello had been long dead.

A knock on effect of him going to prison was the closure of *Arc De Triomphe* that had struggled to keep going anyway, despite the presence of Mary Ellis and Elisabeth Welch. *The Dancing Years* survived and on his release Novello went straight back into the show. The fear that it would destroy his career was unfounded and, much to Novello's relief, he found that the vast majority of the public were in fact sympathetic to his ordeal. Indeed many felt that he had been used for the publicity his sentence would generate; thus acting as a deterrent to others who considered flouting the petrol rationing laws. Winston Churchill had, according to Edward Marsh, also raged at the sentence imposed on Novello and declared that a "fine would have been more appropriate." It was said that Churchill wanted to intervene and get the prison sentence revoked – but Novello would not hear of it and refused the offer.

Much to his credit, I feel. Among the many people I have spoken to who were alive at the time, most have spoken in whispered horror and always say "he went to prison you know".

With the experience behind him, and with his usual fortitude, Novello threw himself back into work and even managed to organise a trip to France. Agreeing to perform in a play via ENSA to entertain the troops. Flying bombs had closed the London Theatres and *The Dancing Years* went on tour again. Its final performance with Novello in the lead role was performed at Blackpool Opera House in 1945. Whilst on this tour Novello began to write and compose what would be his next musical. *Perchance To Dream*.

Novello moved in to what would be the last few years of his life with creative zeal. His experiences of prison behind him, he never discussed the event and seemed to try and erase it from his personal history completely. Even his staff were instructed by Bobbie never to mention or discuss the affair amongst themselves, or anyone else. It was firmly a taboo subject and would forever remain so.

Perchance To Dream, opened at the Hippodrome Theatre, 1945, and is an interesting musical for Novello to have embarked upon, and his only musical where Hassall had no involvement with the lyrics. Although, his son Nicholas, did indicate that his father had been involved with the lyrics, but as he was officially still serving in the military, his name was not allowed to be credited. Whatever the truth of that, Novello is credited for both music and lyrics. The most famous song to emerge from the score and be a popular hit was *We'll Gather Lilacs*; indeed it is a song still included in the repertoire of classical singers, and recorded by Leslie Garrett among others in recent years. Even Frank Sinatra recorded a version of the song – although his pronunciation of Li-larks is unfortunate.

The storyline for the show was intriguing because it is quite spiritual and the main protagonists are reincarnated for three lifetimes until they manage to find a happy ending for themselves. The first act is set in the Regency period, the characters are then reborn into the 1920s, and then again in the present day. The main focus is on two people who are in love and want to be together but life conspires against them, until finally they are united in the present day. Novello played the romantic hero, Graham Rodney, a Highwayman. The plot it has to be said was a little disjointed and confusing for some but made up for this with the usual lavish décor and music. The critical reaction was mixed to say the least, but by this time the critics, where Novello was concerned, were resigned to their bemusement, if not entirely happy with it. James Agate, of *The Sunday Times*, in an obvious state of rapturous confusion attempted to make sense of what he had seen:

"Perchance I dreamed at the first night of Mr Novello's new Hippodrome show. Anyhow the following is what the lighter stage's most popular magician induced me to believe I saw. A Regency buck, who is also a highwayman. A cad who will wager $5,000 that he will seduce an unknown cousin within twenty-four hours of her stay under his roof, doubled with a verray parfit gentil knight prepared to lay wager and a hundred thousand pound pearl necklace at the feet of Purity Unsullied. A cut-purse who dies babbling of reincarnation. Did I spend the rest of the Dream-time watching what gross and vulgar spirits would call subsequent developments? Yes. Was time punctuated by aeons and aeons of Ballet? Yes. Was there a very, very great deal of lush romantic music, scored principally for harp after the manner of that popular composer, Herr Mittel Europa? Yes. Or so these things seemed; I vouch for none of them…Is the foregoing a trifle grudging, even bordering on the ungenerous? I think it may be, and I hasten to say that the curtain, when it went up, took with it the entire audience, which remained in seventh heaven until, after three hours and a half, the curtain descended and automatically brought the audience down with it."

It was a magnificent attempt on the part of Agate to somehow put into words his perception of the show, but his bewilderment shines through. Others were just as mystified, and indeed even the audiences had their moments of confusion, but it mattered not a jot. Novello hypnotised them and carried them along in spite of themselves.

"Miss Olive Gilbert is the principal singer," opined *The Times*, "and her prettiest song would seem to be *We'll Gather Lilacs*, but the songs gain much from the rapture with which Mr Novello listens to them…" Also in the cast as a chorus dancer was Gordon Duttson, who became Novello's secretary and lover.

Fascinating then that Novello should embark on a production where the emphasis is on reincarnation and spiritual matters, where characters who make a mistake in one life are allowed to return to put those matters right and move on. The years preceding this production Novello had experienced not only the death of his mother, but also his friends Minnie Raynor and Viola Tree. Perhaps these events made him open to the possibility that maybe we don't have just one lifetime; indeed that our spirit is able to be born again. It is also possible he had recognised his own mistake which had resulted in prison, and explored the idea that maybe one could come back reincarnated and have another chance to do things right. Most of the ingredients and situations in the show regarding spiritual and reincarnation are firmly held beliefs among many people. The Second World War created a renewed interest in all things spiritual, much as it had during the First World War, because of the inevitable loss and death that happens during such times. Novello's friends had also been concerned because he had remarked on occasions that he saw visions of his dead mother, who came to talk to him. It had also been noted that his depressions and dark moods had increased and lasted much longer.

Once the war was over and *Perchance To Dream* had finished its London run, Novello decided to take the production on tour to South Africa. The intention behind this was two fold. He had a real desire to take the show, and all the London cast, to South Africa, as it would be like a group holiday. He also wanted to leave behind, at least for a while, the cold grimness of Great Britain, and enjoy some tropical weather. The opportunity to travel was curtailed during the war, once it was over, there was nothing to stand in their way.

After a successful tour of South Africa, Novello traveled on to New York with Bobbie, Olive Gilbert and Gordon Duttson. From there they visited Jamaica where Noel Coward had bought a house. Novello fell in love with the island and built his own house there, a house he would visit every year until his death; indeed he spent his last holiday there in 1951.

By 1947 Novello's health and general well being began to be a cause for concern among those closest to him. His old heart problems had returned and had been triggered by a bout of bronchial pneumonia he had suffered at the outset of the war. He began to look very frail at times, but didn't allow this to impede his ever-creative drives. Little was known at the time about the genetic inheritance of heart complaints, and that his father had passed on the condition to him being a real possibility. At that time there was very little in the way of treatment, and the pioneering surgical procedures for heart bypass operations were yet to be refined. Had they been, it is almost certain he would have undergone such a procedure and his life increased by many years.

In spite of his health problems he began to work on another musical that would also be the last he would star in. In many ways this show would continue the development of his musical form that started with *Glamorous Night*, evolved further with the creation of *The Dancing Years*, and would evolve again to an even greater extent with *King's Rhapsody*. All the musicals in-between had been very entertaining and lavish with beautiful songs, but had not really been serious attempts to further develop his style in terms of his musical theatre genre. But then Novello knew he had to face the music, and that the music in question was the competition already crossing the Atlantic ready to do battle.

In August of 1949 *King's Rhapsody* opened at the Palace Theatre in London's West End and again delighted Novello fans but, as usual, completely baffled the critics. Also with a foothold in the West End was Rodgers & Hammerstein's *Oklahoma!* and Lerner and Lowe's *Brigadoon*, which one would assume were pretty stiff competition in terms of box-office draw. The truth was that Novello's *King's Rhapsody* beat them all - his was the only show where people waited for hours in the hope of "returns." The production had cost forty seven thousand pounds to stage, which compared to the cost of staging *Glamorous Night* at Drury Lane in 1935, a mere twenty seven thousand pounds, gives an indication of the level of inflation and spiraling costs as a result of the war. Still, it has to be said, eye watering sums for the time.

The plot for *King's Rhapsody* was pure Ruritania and Novello played an aged King Nikki who is in love with his mistress of many years but, out of duty to the crown and his country, is forced to marry a young suitable girl, Cristina, to be his queen, who bears his son and heir. After much intrigue and court gossip and inevitable heartbreak for all concerned, he remains loyal to his mistress and abdicates in favour of his young son. As his son is crowned, the ex King watches the coronation from the shadows of the Cathedral. Interwoven through the story are the inevitable revolting peasants and a scheming Prime Minster, played by Bobbie Andrews, who plots against the King to establish his own position of power. The cast also included Olive Gilbert, Phylis and Zena Dare, and a young soprano making her debut in the production Vanessa Lee. If some of the story seems eerily familiar, it's because it has elements of the intrigue and tragedy surrounding the Prince of Wales, Diana and Camilla in recent years. The *Observer* reported thus:

"Mr Novello, author, composer and actor, can with his tranquility stand up to all the bounding Oklahomans and Brigadooners in the world. He is far the biggest box-office attraction of our native stage and he has earned his victories by honest service of the public's appetite. Sweet tooth is sweetly served, and, what is more, abundantly. He hands out no trivial fable but lashings of plot with plentiful changes of scene. His tunes and Christopher Hassall's lyrics, at once simple and dulcet, make no pretence. When Olive Gilbert sings Fly Home Little heart, a myriad homes will be emptied by little hearts flying out to hear her. It is the kind of thing, I suppose, that New Yorkers would not endure, but our greater tolerance can give the Gun-getting Annie and her kind a three-year run and yet will now award Mr Novello and his colleagues a four or five years' term for this very different confection. Ivor himself sadly rules and gladly deserts Maurania, looking half Hamlet, half-Anthony, and wholly the darling of the public."

The Sunday Times were a little more sarcastic in their opinion: "A romantic confection which employs every imaginable stand-by of the light musical stage and which ends with Mr Novello kneeling alone upon the altar steps might be supposed to embody the ultimate in saccharine banality. Perhaps it does, but the result is an uncommonly pleasant evening in the theatre."

But it made no difference to the success of the show, and Novello's fans were not shy of hitting back at what they perceived to be unfair criticism. Milton Shulman, from the *Evening Standard*, opined the production "drips with cloying sentiment" and that "its situations are contrived and ludicrous" added insult to injury for many. Punctuating this attack with accusations that the script was "practically empty of wit" raised the blood pressure of the public who complained in their droves:

"After reading Milton Shulman's attack on *King's Rhapsody*, my family and I have determined not to buy the *Evening Standard* while he is on your staff."

This kind of backlash was unprecedented, and caused more than a few jitters at the Evening Standard's offices, but more than that it does give a clue as to the complete loyalty given to Novello by his fans.

It is interesting to consider the opinion that, in his time, these musical shows would have been a disaster had they gone to Broadway. Had he lived, it was his intention to take *King's Rhapsody* to America, much to the horror of those close to him who seemed to agree with the opinion they would not be a success. At that time, and considering the ever-growing dominance of the American musical, they were probably right. However, it would possibly be quite a different story today. As society has developed, and it has to be said the world become more cynical and less structured with the clouding of cultural identities, Novello's style would probably be embraced in a more positive way. Novello's depiction of dysfunctional Royal Families and court intrigues have in many ways mirrored our own Royal Family in recent years; indeed at times our Royal Family seem to belong to a world as strange as Novello's Ruritania, with their stoicism and ritualistic traditionalism. Indeed all the things the American's love so much about the eccentricities and pomp surrounding our Royal Family, which they see as almost belonging to another world, is exactly what Novello was depicting all those years ago. Indeed the Americans seem to be more fascinated by Novello in the present than the British.

During the run of *King's Rhapsody* in early 1950 Novello arranged to make a will. His health had not been good and, no doubt on the advice of his legal representatives, he decided to put his affairs in order and ensure those he loved and respected would benefit. He left sums of between 50 pounds and 1,000 pounds to all his domestic staff, and ensured that Bobbie received a cash lump sum of 20,000 pounds plus the use of Red Roofs and all its contents for the remainder of his life, with an annual maintenance payment from his estate for the upkeep and repair of the building. He also left a cash sum and personal effects to Olive Gilbert and other friends. He added a codicil to his will in the December of 1950, leaving the rights to *The Dancing*

Years to his manager, Tom Arnold, and Arnold's son; who was also Novello's Godson.

Novello had also begun to write his next show, which would star the famous comedienne Ciceley Courtneidge, and be called *Gay's The Word*. It would turn out to be a complete departure from Novello's Ruritanian style. Working with lyricist Alan Melville, they conspired to create songs which would not only move away from the lush romanticism, but also poke fun at Novello's own Ruritanian fantasy land. If nothing else it would prove to the world that Novello was quite capable of laughing at himself, and I suspect he began to realise he had to move on and evolve his style or the American musicals would sweep him into obscurity. 1951 would be the year that *Gay's The Word* opened in the West End. Novello would still be playing in *King's Rhapsody*, unaware he would soon be giving his last performance.

Gosford Park gave new life to Ivor Novello for the first time since his death in 1951. He once again came to the attention of millions and as a result no longer languished in obscurity - thanks to the determination and vision of Robert Altman.

Dame Kristin Scott Thomas & Robert Altman
on the set of Gosford Park

Jeremy Northam, Bob Balaban & Ryan Phillipe

Dame Maggie Smith – Constance Countess of Trentham

Dame Maggie Smith & Kelly MacDonald as Mary

Robert Altman & Dame Kristin Scott Thomas

Robert Altman had such an informal way of directing – he was happy to let his actors improvise in the moment. He created a collaborative atmosphere within which everyone thrived and could participate.

A favourite image of Jeremy Northam as Ivor Novello in Gosford Park

I remember watching the daily rushes during the filming of Jeremy's scenes and he completely immersed himself to give Novello's character a real authenticity. It was mazing to watch and to hear him sing some of those iconic songs composed by Novello. Something I shall never forget.

Bob Balaban, Jeremy Northam and Alan Bates – Gosford Park

Claudia Blakley as Mabel & Jeremy Northan as Novello – Gosford Park.

In this scene he is singing 'I Can Give You The Starlight' from The Dancing Years

Robert Altman on the set of Gosford Park

A truly remarkable and innovative director who was determined to have Ivor Novello as a character in Gosford Park. He had liked him since he had heard Keep The Home Fires Burning many years before.

Making a film of Novello's life was in his mind. Sadly he passed away before he could develop the idea further. What a film that would have been. He kindly gave me permission to use these images in the book from Gosford Park just prior to his death. I am very grateful to him for his kindness.

Robert Altman – Gosford Park

Ryan Phillipe & Dame Kristin Scott Thomas – Gosford Park

Michael Gambon & Geraldine Somerville – Gosford Park

Dame Kristin Scott Thomas – Gosford Park

Natasha Wightman – Gosford Park

Betty Paxton & Lily Moore with David Slattery-Christy. Olive Gilbert's nieces who gave me the Glamorous Night album that belonged to Novello. They would be thrilled to know the pictures are now in the Novello Theatre for everyone to enjoy.

West End's new Novello Theatre

Still of the film Gosford Park signed and given to me by Robert Altman. Shows John Atterbury, Dame Maggie Smith and Kelly Macdonald.

Donald Macleod (Presenter Composer of the Week BBC Radio 3) with Rosy Runciman (archivist for Sir Cameron Mackintosh), David Slattery-Christy (author & playwright) & William Differ (Operations Director for Sir Cameron Mackintosh) in the Waldorf Bar, Novello Theatre and Novello's old flat at 11 Aldwych in the music room

A DUO, A DRAG QUEEN AND A MOVIE

"It is time that some official recognition were shown of his achievement in keeping the British flag flying over Ruritania."

The Evening Standard

For my own part my journey thus far had been enlightening and by the late summer of 2000 was still progressing. Nick Gaze from the Novello Society contacted me around this time and asked me if I would be interested in staging and directing a concert to celebrate his life and work - on the 50th Anniversary of Novello's death on 6th March 2001. It was then decided that a service would also be held in the Actors' Church in Covent Garden, followed by a celebratory concert, which seemed a more suitable way to mark and market the occasion. I immediately suggested the Grand Saloon at Drury Lane as the first choice of venue suitable for such an event. And so it was agreed and plans were made.

After the disappointments faced with the revival of *Glamorous Night* being shelved, the opportunity to again present a concert at Drury Lane for this event, went some way to make all the effort and work worthwhile. As opposed to the previous concert I had devised and directed, this one would encompass all of Novello's music from his early revue days through to *Gay's The Word*. In itself a challenge, simply because of the volume of work involved, and not least being able to structure it in such a way as to be truly representative. With that thought in mind, I turned my attention to finding a good musical director.

Michael Topping was top of my list. I had become friendly with Michael and his professional partner Andy Simmons. Better known as Topping & Butch. They are a well respected and highly sought after cabaret duo, who had found fame initially on the Gay circuit for their parodies and comic renditions of musical theatre songs. Aside from this, Michael was a trained classical pianist and was very familiar with Novello's music; indeed he had great respect for Novello and was, I knew from past experience, passionate in his enthusiasm towards any project that inspired him. When I first suggested the possibility of him working as the musical director on the Novello concert his reaction was instantly enthusiastic. Having seen him performing with Andy, I also knew that they would be perfect to open the concert with one or two of the early revue songs Novello composed. Indeed, much to Andy's surprise and delight, I also wanted him to be the narrator in the concert to link everything together. Once this was organised, I turned my attention to another performer I had great respect for and wanted to be involved.

Colin Devereaux was also a superb live performer on the Gay cabaret circuit. Many times I had seen him perform as Dockyard Doris, and knew he was a brilliant comic with exceptional timing; and could hold an audience in the palm of his hand. He was also a greatly respected Pantomime Dame, booked up several years in advance. What also surprised me with Colin is how he could sing an emotional ballad and literally reduce his audience to tears such was the sincerity in his delivery of the lyrics. Colin was a big man, in fact his whole characterisation as Doris was based around the fact he was about 20 stone, dressed in a tent of a dress and had hair piled so high on his head he would have put Tesse O'Shea in the shade. I met him for the first time when I had been commissioned to write a newspaper feature article about him, and he agreed to be interviewed. I was amazed to discover that this larger than life performer who dominated the stage as Doris, was in fact a small, insecure and terribly shy man. As I got to know him, I knew that one day I wanted to work with him, and the opportunity arose. To my mind he was perfect to take on the Ciceley Courtneidge songs from *Gay's The Word*. I approached him and explained and he agreed. Much to my surprise he was excited at being able to perform at Drury Lane, simply because his grandmother, the famous music hall and pantomime star Marie Lloyd, had starred in many productions at the theatre. He was even more delighted when I pointed out that one of the songs I wanted him to perform was *Vitality*, which referred to his grandmother in the lyrics.

My other main worry was the day and timing of the concert. It was to be held on the afternoon of Tuesday 6th March, 2001. By coincidence it was the early hours of Tuesday 6th March, 1951, when Novello had died; so therefore the day of the week was the same at each end of the fifty years that had passed. The concert had to be held in the afternoon due to the main show being staged in the evening at Drury Lane. Also, my other concern was actually being able to entice an audience on what could be a cold or wet Tuesday afternoon. Most people are working during the week and it would limit what, if any audience, we could hope for. In the initial discussion about where and when the concert should be held, everyone felt it had to be that day to coincide with the church service. The main reasons then, why a larger auditorium was discounted.

The fact that I had successfully managed to secure the services of Michael, Andy and Colin reassured me in as much as I knew they all had a very big following among the cabaret community and it would help secure a decent audience. Once again I had contacted the ever helpful and delightful Mary Hammond at the Royal College of Music and she agreed to help me cast a small chorus of exceptional young singers who could do justice to the demands of Novello's music. Gia Frances, who had so brilliantly performed Elizabeth Welch's songs in the showcase, also agreed to reprise her performance in the celebration concert. After discussion with Nick Gaze from the Novello Society, I arranged for soprano Sandra Watkins and contralto Marie Sinnett to participate in the production. I had in the past heard both of them sing and I had been impressed how they connected with and performed such difficult songs. They were also from Novello's native Wales, so it seemed wholly appropriate that this aspect of his life should be represented.

So with cast and venue in place, I set about the task of constructing and selecting songs from Novello's musicals. *Glamorous Night* would be represented with the title song *Glamorous Night*, *Shine Through My Dreams* and *Shanty Town*; *Crest Of The Wave* with *Why Isn't It You*; *The Dancing Years* segment included: *My Life Belongs To You*, *My Dearest Dear*, *Wings Of Sleep* and *Waltz Of My Heart*. *Perchance To Dream* represented by *We'll Gather Lilacs* and *King's Rhapsody* with *Someday My Heart Will Awake*, *The Violin Began To Play* and *Gates Of Paradise*. The finale section would be from Gay's The Word with *Ruritania*, *Vitality* and *If Only He'd Looked My Way*. The only song included from Novello's revue days was *And Her Mother Came Too!*; not because of lack of choice, but the sheer volume of work from this period that an hour long concert could not possibly accommodate.

Rehearsal schedules were negotiated and agreed and rehearsal space was organised at the Royal Academy of Music and my old alma mater City University. Because of existing commitments at Drury Lane, the cast would only have one run through and one dress rehearsal in the actual venue; both of which would take place on the morning of the concert. Therefore the timing and sequencing required was assisted by marking out the rehearsal rooms appropriate to the venue and performance area we would be using. Considering that some of the cast would not meet until the day before for a full run through in the Great Hall at City University, it required almost military precision in terms of organisation. Much as before, my intention was to use the grand surroundings of the venue as the set for the concert. In addition to this I had arranged for white tie and tails for the men in the cast, and suitable gowns for the ladies, as it was important the event had the obligatory glamour to bring it to life.

Only once all these vital ingredients were in place and initial rehearsals taking place, did I turn my attention fully to the appropriate marketing for the event. Drury Lane and the Actors' Church had expressed a concern that there would be very few people wanting to attend. This was mainly due to the fact that Novello was hardly a household name anymore, and thus assumptions were made that it was all a bit pointless because nobody would turn up. In spite of this negativity, I felt confident that even with a small inconsequential audience, it could and would still be a positive experience and at least mark the occasion appropriately. Nick Gaze and I had agreed a poster and flyer design that had been sent out to the members of the society; so from therein we would probably rake in the majority of the audience. The Church service had been organised and actor Simon Williams, from Upstairs & Downstairs fame, Novello's Godson, had agreed to attend and help in any way he could. It occurred to me that Christopher Hassall's speech at Novello's memorial service in 1951 might be suitable for Simon to read at the church service. After reading the original I felt there were elements which were inappropriate after the passing of fifty years, so decided to re write it but keep to the spirit of the original as much as possible. This I did, and after passing it on to Simon for his thoughts, he offered his approval to the re write and delivered it superbly during the service.

My next move involved Radio 2 presenter Desmond Carrington. After listening to his Sunday show for many years, I had often heard him play songs from Novello's musicals, and relate his memories of the times he had seen Novello in action. I contacted him and explained what we were undertaking to mark the 50th anniversary, and expressed a hope that he might like to attend. In fact he did much more than that. He announced on his show the event was taking place with all the details and the appropriate telephone numbers for tickets to the Drury Lane Concert. It is something I shall be forever grateful to him for. Within minutes of his announcement the telephones began to ring and they never stopped. Within a matter of an hour we had sold all the seats for the concert, and realising very quickly that we could just about manage two performances back to back, I quickly contacting all the artists involved, and Drury Lane, explained the situation, and they all agreed without quibble that another performance should be sold. So we began to sell tickets for the second performance and within hours they too had sold out. The tragedy was that the telephones kept ringing and we could have filled the main auditorium of Drury Lane by the time the day arrived four weeks later. We even sold, with the agreement of Drury Lane management, a few extra "standing only" tickets. If nothing else it made me realise that far from nobody remembering Novello, there were countless people out there who did. Desmond Carrington, after I contacted him to explain the sell out situation, helped alleviate the problem by announcing that no more tickets were available. On the day, we turned away so many who had just turned up in the hope that a seat might be available by way of "returns." I was glad that Novello's return to Drury Lane, albeit the Grand Saloon, was a sell out and standing room only - just as it had been all those decades before when he presented his shows in the main auditorium. It was also satisfying to see the faces of those who had been so cynical when they realised how many were turned away and that we could have filled the main auditorium of the theatre that day. So much for nobody remembering Novello.

It did cross my mind to perhaps consider arranging the use of the main auditorium, but with so little time left to the day, and the fact that my cast were small and would have been lost on the main stage, plus the added technical requirements and expense required, it was impractical at such a late stage. Having to present the concert on a barren stage would, in my mind, have created a problem in terms of reflecting the glamour and elegance inherent in Novello's shows. Therefore, I stuck with the Grand Saloon that could provide a suitably ornate backdrop to the concert.

Rehearsals progressed and Michael Topping proved a helpful and enthusiastic musical director, one which all the cast appreciated and respected. My idea for staging the event to tell the story through the narration finally began to fall into place, and inevitably involved much discussion and writing additional narration. Everyone concerned seemed to suddenly understand what I was trying to achieve, and pulled out all the stops to make it work. Ultimately it was a team effort and everybody contributed suggestions and ideas along the way.

The day arrived and after a run through and then a dress rehearsal, some members of the cast had to leave and walk the short distance to be at the Actor's Church as they were performing songs not included in the concert as part of the service. The church was also packed to the rafters with people who had come to remember Novello, many of them unable to get tickets to the concert, but who still packed into the Church. It shocked everyone but delighted at the same time. Simon Williams was charming and thrilled to be part of the occasion, and spent time afterwards meeting people and discussing Novello. Sadly the announcement was made during the service that Roma Beaumont and Gordon Duttson had both died the previous day. Beaumont found fame in *The Dancing Years* playing Greta, and had been in a home for many years. Gordon Duttson, Novello's last lover and secretary, had been in the chorus of *Perchance To Dream* and *King's Rhapsody*, died in hospital. It was ironic they should both die practically fifty years to the day, and right they were acknowledged in the service.

Back at the theatre I was taking a short break before everyone returned in preparation for the first performance. My mind was totally focused on the job at hand and I was hoping that I had managed to create something that would do justice to Novello and his music. Absorbed in my own thoughts, I noticed Colin walking towards me with the theatre manager. The manager then said that Robert Altman's office had been on the telephone and wanted to speak to me - could I ring them back? Because my mind was preoccupied, and there had been heated discussions in the foyer by people who wanted tickets, I assumed that someone was trying to twist my arm for tickets. I muttered something curtly to that effect, and Colin stopped dead in his tracks so abruptly his wig nearly fell off and said words to the effect of "You can't say that to Robert Altman!" Only then did the name register. Of course I knew of Robert Altman and admired his work immensely, and was flabbergasted as to why he wanted to speak to me. The theatre manager gave me the telephone number he'd left, and I called him back. Having explained the ticket situation, and that no seats were left, I took a chance and offered two standing tickets. I was then asked if I would be prepared to consider working on a film they were shooting in England, a film called *Gosford Park* where one of the characters was Ivor Novello. I said yes, I was interested, and made arrangements to call David Levy, one of the Producers of the film, the next day. I then left the standing tickets with an usher at the main entrance, and turned my attention back to the performances.

The audiences started to arrive and it was a memorable day for many reasons. People were so excited and had traveled from all parts of the country, many of the older people recalling times they had seen Novello onstage and how delighted they were to be there on that day. One couple were both in their late eighties and had traveled from Scotland, in spite of their ailing health, making the long journey for the first time in years, determined they would be there on that day to again enjoy the music which had enthralled them when they first heard it at that very theatre. The loyalty still shown to Novello is always surprising, and even after all the years that have passed since his death, his power over his fans has not diminished. If I doubted it before that day, I would never doubt it again. Indeed, it is hard not to be drawn into the sentimental when listening to people speak of the affect he had on them by way of his persona and music. The fact they could still talk about him as if it was only yesterday they had last been to one of his shows, and how they felt they knew him as a friend; even though they had never met him. It is quite uncanny, and does to some degree bring into sharp focus how jaded and cynical the world has become, in that such loyalty has been so enduring but rare in today's world.

The performances were received enthusiastically and everyone involved were delighted at the response. The highlights for me were Sandra's performance and her delivery of those difficult songs, with her clear soprano voice and *My Dearest Dear* from *The Dancing Years* was her best; Gia's performance of Elisabeth Welch's *Shanty Town* from *Glamorous Night* again stopped the show. Michael and Andy performed and accompanied brilliantly and all their comedy skills came to the fore in *And Her Mother Came Too*, with the added benefit of Andy telling the story by way of narrative links, and the help he had given with the choreography. Colin was very nervous prior to the performance but it didn't show in the end. During rehearsals he had been astounded at the fantastic voices of all the singers, and was worried he would stand out like a sore thumb and how the audience would react to a drag queen in their midst. I assured him that wouldn't problem and soothed his nerves as best I could.

I shall never forget the sound of innumerable jaws thudding on the floor as he emerged in full drag to deliver *Vitality* from *Gay's The Word*, underpinned by the choreographed routine he did with the chorus as they accompanied him. It was very, very funny and many couldn't believe that this huge drag queen was among them and performing his false boobs off! He then sang the wistful *If Only He Looked My Way*, also from *Gay's The Word* , and with his skill as a performer abated their laughter and drew their tears. He delivered the song with such sincerity and pathos that it was impossible not to be moved. On his first entrance the audience were unsure of this huge drag queen bounding towards them with *Vitality*, but by the time he had sang the last note of his final song, he turned and slowly began to exit, and for a second or two there was utter silence, my heart was in my mouth as it flashed across my mind the audience hadn't liked him, then they roared their approval and it was deafening. I had taken a gamble with Colin, but it paid off handsomely, and I was glad as I knew he could deliver those songs, and because I thought it only appropriate that the concert should reflect personalities from the gay world. After all, Novello was an open homosexual among his friends, and would have no doubt enjoyed performers like Colin and Topping & Butch; and I am certain he would have approved.

Novello also approved of Ciceley Courtneidge's performance in *Gay's The Word* when he attended the first night at the Saville Theatre on February 16th, 1951. It had been many years since he had experienced a first night from "out front" and it turned out to be his last. Much to his delight the show was received enthusiastically by the press and public and sold out very quickly. By the time it opened in the West End it had already had a ten week season at Manchester's Palace Theatre, where it had been polished and undergone several rewrites, then embarked on a tour around the provinces.

The story revolved around an eccentric drama teacher called Gay, and the pupils who attended her acting school. In many ways it was tailored perfectly to fit Courtneidge's comic talents, but it also served another purpose. Novello was well aware of the development of the musical theatre genre in America, indeed he had seen musicals on Broadway before they ever crossed the Atlantic, and he knew they were going to be stiff competition. By writing *Gay's The Word* he was in fact experimenting and using it as a vehicle to develop a new style to make sure he could compete. He also in this show parodied and sent up his own style of Ruritanian romances and began to place them firmly in the past for his audiences. In a way he was acknowledging the fact his own musicals were of that past and therefore it was time to move on. The London *Evening Standard* said:

"Once more Ivor Novello proves that he is immortal without being divine. No Richard Rogers, Cole Porter or Irving Berlin can dethrone him…It is time that some official recognition were shown of his achievement in keeping the British flag flying over Ruritania."

It is interesting that his ability to be successful in the face of competition from the American composers, who have since become legends, was even then a source of bewilderment to many in the press and indeed the theatre industry. It was almost as if Novello had become an immoveable force, a force which was sustained by an incredible loyalty from a fan base that was unshakeable.

"Ivor Novello has done it again," opined *The Daily Herald*, "but this time it is different. He has turned his back on Ivornovania, where Rhapsodic Kings spent their Glamorous Nights in Careless Rapture…But if he is not careful, he will be putting his satirists out of work, for - whisper it - Novello has started guying himself."

Had he lived longer, it would have been interesting to see how far he would have taken this. He was it seems starting to once again reinvent himself and his style; something he had done many times since he first found fame with *Keep The Home Fires Burning* in 1915. Speculation will never provide answers to that question because by the beginning of March 1951, his time was fast running out.

On Saturday 3rd March 1951 Novello played his role of Nikki in *King's Rhapsody* at the matinee and evening performance. Morgan was waiting with the Rolls Royce at the Stage Door and, accompanied my Bobbie, they settled back for the drive to Red Roofs. The journey was a little under two hours as the traffic would be negligible at that late hour. Novello was tired after two performances but his conversation was about the holiday at his house in Jamaica, and his desire to return as soon as he could. As he had become older, and had suffered ill health for the first time, he found the cold winters in England almost unbearable. He also had in mind an idea for a new show, one that he wanted to discuss with Alan Melville who would be a guest at Red Roofs over the weekend. Bobbie was aware that a fresh idea was nurturing in his mind, but said little and let Novello sleep for the best part of the journey. He knew that Olive Gilbert had telephoned Mabel at Red Roofs and asked her to make sure the house was warm and that a cold supper was available for them. Gilbert would follow on in a car with Melville and his friend Tom Gill.

During the course of the weekend Novello seemed his usual self and relaxed in the company of his close friends. He discussed their recent holiday and what good business both his shows were doing in the West End. The Saturday evening was quite normal in that they enjoyed a dinner prepared by the staff and then either played cards or tinkled on the piano. Novello at times seemed deep in thought, but then would suddenly demand they played Canasta. On the Sunday morning, after a leisurely breakfast, they enjoyed a walk in the garden in spite of the cold. Novello commented on the fact that Spring and the warmer weather would not be far away, and as always, expressed his delight at not having to wait too long before the Lilac bloomed again. During the afternoon after lunch, he complained of a pain in his chest and excused himself to go and rest for a while. A couple of hours passed and he sent for Melville, who went to Novello's bedroom and sat at the foot of the bed. Novello told him of an idea for a show, and that he wanted Melville to work on it with him. They would, Novello said, return to Jamaica, just the two of them, as soon as he could arrange it. He was determined and enthusiastic and Melville agreed.

Late on the Sunday afternoon Lady Juliet Duff arrived to join the house party. She would also be an overnight guest, and travel back to London the following day with Novello and his friends. They all enjoyed a relaxed evening playing cards and listening to music; indeed Novello played some of his earlier songs and then suggested Olive sing a new song he had written on the aeroplane returning from Jamaica. Christopher Hassall had, he told his friends, just completed the lyrics and he was delighted with the result. As Olive began to sing the song, which he had given the title *Pray For Me*, his friends listened in quiet contemplation. Olive was a little shaken because the lyrics were so wistful and sad, and also seemed to reflect the thoughts of someone who was no longer there. At the end of Olive's rendition the guests applauded, but couldn't help but look at each other with silent concern. Novello jumped up from the piano and insisted they play cards, his mood so happy that everyone relaxed and enjoyed the rest of the evening.

The next day, Monday 5th March, the guests enjoyed a usual hearty breakfast and began packing in readiness for their return to London. Novello was in good spirits and as they assembled in the garden awaiting the cars, Lady Duff Gordon suggested taking a photograph of Novello, Bobbie, Melville and his friend Tom. They struck a pose, arms around each other, and she looked through the viewfinder but oddly couldn't see Novello in the group, on lowering the camera she could see that Melville had his arm round Novello and asked him to "move in a little." On looking through the viewfinder again she could clearly see them all, and duly took the photograph. She wouldn't think about the strange feeling she experienced at not being able to see him until a couple of days later. The party then departed for London.

That night Novello left "the flat" to make the short journey to the Palace Theatre. He performed as Nikki in *King's Rhapsody*, then left the theatre with Tom Arnold, his business manager, and Morgan drove them back to "the flat." They enjoyed a cold supper and drank some Champagne. During the course of this meeting Novello said he felt unwell and wanted to retire to bed. Arnold, not unduly concerned, asked where Bobbie was. Novello told him he would be home shortly. Arnold then left and Novello went to bed. Bobbie returned home at around 1am to find him seriously ill, he immediately rang down to Olive Gilbert's flat, and she came up straight away. A Doctor was called and on arrival realised he was too late. With Bobbie and Olive at his side, he died of heart failure at 2.20am on Tuesday 6th March 1951. Bobbie and Olive heard him say "I think I've had it" a moment before his heart finally gave up. In a state of shock, they just sat and stared at him, not quite able to believe it had really happened.

Leaving Olive to attend to matters at "the flat", Bobbie summoned Morgan and said he needed to return to Red Roofs immediately. They sped away into the night, and expressed their disbelief at what had happened. Olive had telephoned Red Roofs to make sure Mabel informed the rest of the staff of Novello's death, and to expect Bobbie. On arrival at Red Roofs, Bobbie began to collect together documents, photographs, home film footage and other personal belongings. He then built a bonfire in the garden and started to burn everything. What he did burn on that bonfire we shall never know, but obviously there were some sensitive documents that they had agreed between them would be thus destroyed in the event of his death. Once the task was completed, Bobbie and Morgan returned to London and "the flat"

Lady Juliet on hearing the news of his death instantly recalled taking the photograph and how Novello had seemed to become invisible through the viewfinder. It seemed eerie and no doubt sent shivers up her spine. The photograph she did eventually have developed, turned out to be the last ever taken of Novello. The items that Bobbie was so anxious to destroy that night more than likely included items relating to their homosexual lifestyle, which could have proved highly sensitive at the time and would have tarnished Novello's reputation; not to mention his own and that of those involved. Indeed some home movie film did survive and has come to light in recent years that captured the naked pool parties indulged in by Novello and his male friends. These events are also mentioned in Terence Rattigan's biography, as recalled by his lover at the time, Peter Osborn:

"For his father's sake [Rattigan's], the disguise that he was a heterosexual young man about town was to be maintained at all costs. But once Rattigan was out of his sphere of influence, he would take Osborn to parties, including a memorable one thrown by Ivor Novello in which the host took great pleasure in taking home movies of his guests bathing in the nude...best of all was that Terry and I were given our own bedroom, with a deep delicious double bed."

No doubt there were many items of a sensitive nature Bobbie would have destroyed that night - mainly to ensure high profile reputations were not compromised.

Not everyone was contacted and some of his friends heard the news second hand. Zena Dare recalled that: "I knew at seven o'clock in the morning when I heard it over the radio. We didn't play that night [in *King's Rhapsody*] but we did the next, with somebody else in his clothes. It was ghastly."

For *King's Rhapsody* and *Gay's The Word* it was business as usual as far as Tom Arnold was concerned, because he knew that is what Novello would have wanted. It proved to be hard for so many of his friends involved, and an air of gloom and sadness inevitably descended over the productions. Without his presence in *King's Rhapsody* the show soon started to lose business and eventually closed. *Gay's The Word* managed to keep afloat but eventually that too closed. Indeed Novello's presence as a force in the West End died with him and his shows proved to be impossible to produce without him. Within a matter of a few years, it was as if he had never existed. The West End moved on, American musicals dominated, and he became just a distant memory, one that became enveloped in the mists of time until he was obscured from view to everyone but those who had known him and seen his shows.

Those who shared the limelight with him also faded from public view. They would never again enjoy the prominence that Novello afforded them. Many thought their star shone independently, but his death proved them wrong. Once deprived of his reflected glory, they too vanished into obscurity.

Novello's emergence from his own obscurity was to happen fifty years after his death. As a result of my involvement with the 50th Anniversary Concert, I found myself a player in events that would once again catapult Novello and his music back into the public eye, and give him a global audience of millions. After the initial contact from Robert Altman's office on the day of the concert and a subsequent conversation with producer David Levy, I was invited to an apartment in Kensington for a meeting regarding *Gosford Park*.

David Levy had filled me in with some details over the telephone and I was delighted to assist in any way I could. At this stage, I was unaware of the magnitude of the project and that *Gosford Park* would be a major Hollywood film. On arrival at the apartment I have to be honest and say that nothing could have prepared me for what I would find. The apartment was teaming with people and a script meeting was in progress in preparation for the location shooting which would take place in a few days time. David Levy greeted me and, as I had a warm rapport with him on the telephone, I was pleased he also proved to be a very charming and friendly man. He instantly made me welcome and put me at ease. As we walked through the apartment, which was very large and very luxurious, it immediately became clear to me that this was no ordinary film. The people I met, and who kindly greeted me, was a little overwhelming at first. I was introduced to Robert Altman, Dame Maggie Smith, Charles Dance and Julian Fellowes to name a few. It was immediately apparent that the calibre of actors involved was way above any film I had ever seen. And so it proved to be. If anything it was a little too rich, and there were so many actors I had admired cast in the film, meeting them for the first time in such a glut resulted in an overload on the senses.

There was much interest in the concert and I was delighted to find myself answering questions on Novello. As he was in fact the only factual character in the film, it was inevitable that everyone was curious to know more about him. It surprised me that, apart from Robert Altman, who remembered Novello for some of his music, that most people were oblivious to his tremendous achievements in not only musicals but also as a film star and playwright. It has to be said there is nothing nicer than being able to impart knowledge about a particular subject, particularly when those asking are so enthusiastic and eager for information. I had taken with me a music workbook and a photograph album that had once belonged to Novello, which also proved to be of great interest to everyone.

Jeremy Northam had been cast to play Novello and physically, in terms of his handsome looks, was perfect casting. I had compiled a list of Novello's traits that I felt might help him. Just personal things like his aversion to carrying anything and his chain smoking habit, even the brand of cigarettes he favoured, also his dislike of any physical exercise or sport; indeed his ability to be terribly lazy and melancholic. Also his dislike of parties other than his own, where he could control the environment. Considering the lapse in time, and that no one really remembered Novello anymore, maybe these things could be seen as irrelevant. However, I felt quite strongly that, in spite of the obscurity, it was still important to reflect his traits accurately. To do anything less was a disservice to his memory.

Ideas for the music to be included in the film were also outlined that day. The concert at Drury Lane had been filmed, and I suggested that maybe a viewing of the video might help to assess some possible inclusions. The date the film is set did cause some concern because Novello's best music was composed after 1935, and the action is set in 1932. This had been decided mainly because it was a time when in reality Novello had returned from his disastrous stint in Hollywood, and was experiencing an uncertain period as regards his future. My suggestion was to not worry too much about the dates because, as I had discovered, Novello did tend to write down melodies and give them a title long before he ever used them; this I knew to be the case with the melody of Glamorous Night, which he had composed in the 1920s, and the song Someday My Heart Will Awake, which was written in an early form 15 years before he used it in 1949 for *King's Rhapsody*. This was gladly taken on board, and from there I focused on my first task to find some original sheet music for the more obscure songs used in the film such as *The Land That Might Have Been*, with lyrics by Sir Edward Marsh, and several others.

As my suggestion to view the video of the concert was agreed, I left and immediately drove straight to Gloucester, because decisions had to be made by the end of the following day, time was of the essence. Nick Gaze from the Novello Society had arranged the filming and had the master copy at his home. On arrival they had kindly created a copy for me which, after thanking them, I headed straight back to London to drop it off at the Kensington apartment. From there, I headed home and made preparations to search appropriate music archives.

After a few days, and several disgruntled music archivists who had to wade through boxes of music manuscript in forgotten warehouses, I managed to pull all the music together and everything was in place. A few days later I was setting out to the location to attend the day's shooting. In the mean time, David Levy, had expressed an interest in the song *Why Isn't It You*, which was featured in the concert, saying that Robert Altman wanted to use it as the "murder song." The problem was finding a possible 78 record. It proved to be difficult, mainly because not all Novello's songs were actually produced onto record, and obtaining the sheet music was also a struggle. Eventually I managed to get the sheet music, but the record proved impossible as it had never been released - at least not without the lyrics. Therefore an alternative was found which worked out well in the end. During discussions around this subject David Levy was puzzled when I told him a singer called Olive Groves may have recorded a particular song in the 1920s. He looked at me with a baffled expression and asked if I was joking. He couldn't imagine a singer being called Olive Groves, especially coming from California where they really do have Olive Groves! Julian Fellowes thought I was referring to Olive Gilbert, but no, there really was a singer called Olive Groves in the 1920s. Novello didn't meet Olive Gilbert until she auditioned for *Glamorous Night* in 1935.

Finally I had managed to collect together the sheet music for the songs that Jeremy would play and sing at the piano during the filming of several scenes. He now had the task of learning these in preparation for the following week's shoot. The subject of Novello's lack of singing ability did come into the discussions at this point. After his voice had broken at sixteen he was never able to sing sufficiently well to perform in public again, however he did still accompany himself at the piano and sing, albeit badly, whilst entertaining at his private parties. It would therefore only be a short bending of the truth for Jeremy, as Novello, to accompany himself and sing to a better standard in the film. Ultimately it made little difference and served the film and Jeremy's characterisation better.

Driving to the location shoot the following week I considered how strange fate can be, and that after all the work and effort I had given to Novello and his past in recent years it had brought me to this point. It struck me that all the star names appearing in *Gosford Park* enjoyed the same status in the industry today that Novello had enjoyed during his lifetime. My employment in the film as the Novello Consultant had provided me with an opportunity to enter that world as an equal and also given me an opportunity to experience first hand the unique atmosphere within. Reflecting on the other times I had been involved with location shooting whilst at Granada; on the Sherlock Holmes Adventures and with Edward Woodward on In Suspicious Circumstances. As interesting and enjoyable as they had been, they in no way compared to the sheer scale of what I was now involved in.

The "upstairs" scenes were being filmed in a Stately Home just on the outskirts of London, and the owners of the house, David Levy informed me, had asked that it remained a secret as they didn't want any publicity. As I drew nearer I began to see the small signs attached to trees and hedgerows with 'Gsfd Pk' written on them, strategically placed to assist those traveling to the location. They would mean nothing to anyone unaware of their significance, but I always find they add an air of mystery and intrigue to such a journey.

Arriving at the base camp, I decided not to immediately seek out David Levy, and after informing his PA I had arrived, I decided to walk the mile or so to the House used for the interior shots. It was a bright fresh day and it enabled me to gather my thoughts and soak in the surroundings. The house itself was quite impressive from a distance, but on closer inspection it had an air of melancholy about it. There were parts of the house that were in a fairly good state of repair, but other areas where it had suffered to the point where a faded elegance struggled to shine through the disrepair. Overall it had an excellent atmosphere and its haughty grandeur would prove to be perfect for the film and its characters.

Walking back along the drive to the base camp, I looked forward to seeing the interior of the house and how it had weathered time, and also how it had been dressed and prepared for that afternoon's scenes. On arrival back at the base camp I was met by David Levy and given the opportunity to watch some of the morning's rushes in the screening room. Being led into a very dark trailer that served as the screening room, I immediately stood on someone's feet and nearly sat in their lap. I apologised, and to my horror realised I had nearly sat on Stephen Fry. Fortunately the humour of the situation prevailed and he was utterly charming. Turning my attention to the rushes, it became evident that the quality and attention to detail were of the highest standard; as was that of the performances I saw.

After lunch the crew were heading back to the house to prepare for the afternoon shoot. The scenes involved were those in which Jeremy, as Novello, would play the piano and sing in the drawing room whilst the other characters spun their webs of intrigue and bitchiness. Robert Altman asked if I would like to drive to the house with him, and on that short journey he expressed his appreciation of the work I had undertaken to enable Novello and his music to be portrayed as accurately as possible in the film. He explained what the afternoons scenes involved, and suggested that if I felt anything didn't ring true, to let him know.

What I now refer to as the "Green dress" afternoon turned into a fascinating and very enjoyable experience. The skill of Robert Altman is his ability to give actors a freedom with their performance that rarely happens with film. He encourages them to improvise and not feel constrained by any structure they perceive to be around them, even if that be the dictates of the script. If it feels right in the moment, do it. From this philosophy has been born the most memorable moments in many of his films. On that afternoon, Dame Maggie Smith, improvised the line, whilst playing bridge, and surveying the assembled characters with haughty disdain, that "Green has always been a difficult colour" in reference to one of the characters wearing a green dress with whom she had clashed - hence my meaning of the 'Green dress' afternoon. In the moment it was superb and very funny, reducing most of us behind camera to helpless laughter.

The attention to detail was applied to every aspect of the film from how the dining table was laid, to what the characters wore, to the roles undertaken by the staff in a country house at that period. The settings were dressed with a military precision in terms of the detail, and former butlers and cooks and house maids were on hand to give advice and to interject if anything was wrong or out of place. The costumes were given the same attention, even down to the under clothes worn. Literally no expense was spared and it showed in the final film.

Jeremy began his scenes and his portrayal of Novello was, in my mind, as near to perfect as was possible. His delivery of the songs, which he played and sang live on the set, impressed everyone concerned. Within his overall performance he did reflect Novello's personality in a wholly believable way; a way that allowed those watching to get a glimpse of Novello's character and traits. Novello was more than a little camp, and the obvious thing would be to portray that in an over the top way, what most impressed me about Jeremy's performance was how he subsumed that campness and never allowed it to dominate. Jeremy later said that some people would probably say his portrayal was "nothing like Novello" and that "only Novello could be Novello", I believe he came as near as anybody could in creating a performance which did Novello full justice.

Watching the rushes of that afternoon's shoot was a real experience. The screening room was packed and everyone watched Jeremy's performance as Novello with admiration. Indeed, they burst into applause on more than one occasion. Watching these rushes it gave me an overall impression of how beautiful the film would be in its final form. The atmosphere created and the characterisations created by some of the world's best known actors and actresses rendered it unique. Alan Bates, who I had met previously when he attended a performance of one of my own plays, was kind enough to remind me of that visit and was genuinely thrilled I had become involved in the film. It was through him I met Helen Mirren, another actress I greatly admired and found her utterly charming. Indeed I have to say that in spite of all the stars involved in *Gosford Park*, there was no evidence of clashing egos or other such disputes. Everyone respected everyone and appreciated their contribution on equal terms. It was a happy, positive environment that was highly charged and creative. It also created a feeling of excitement, as it seemed inevitable that it would be an unforgettable film.

David Levy at this point asked me if I could play the piano. Sadly I had to say I didn't, and it has always been one of my biggest regrets. The reason behind the question was the fact they wanted someone to play Novello's music for the underscoring of the film, and to overdub Jeremy's playing in the drawing room scenes. I was asked if I could think of someone appropriate to undertake the job. It occurred to me that Michael Topping was a classically trained pianist, and I could suggest that David spoke to him. But by the time I spoke to David again it had transpired that Jeremy's brother , Christopher Northam, also a classical pianist, had agreed to do the job. It was probably the best choice in the end, as Jeremy and his brother had a connection that no one could have replaced, which created a seamlessness in the finally dubbed scenes.

Sometimes life does offer up a unique experience that, because of the personalities involved, is irreplaceable and unrepeatable. *Gosford Park* turned out to be one of those experiences for me. That it would also give life to Novello once again, sending him out into a world that had forgotten him, was an added bonus. I was glad I had been able to be part of that process; indeed I learnt so much and relished every second. Robert Altman kindly sent me a signed still of the movie, which I appreciated very much, and in a way made me feel less humble in the company of such talented and respected colleagues.

Gosford Park didn't end for me once the film was in the can. As everyone concerned awaited the release of the film, I was once again contacted by David Levy regarding a documentary that BBC Wales were planning on Novello. They had contacted him in the hope that they could travel to California and interview Robert Altman for the documentary, but due to his schedule it wasn't possible. However, they suggested that perhaps I would be the best person for the job. David then passed on my contact details to them and it was duly arranged.

Being so involved with Novello over the preceding months, I was in all honesty beginning to feel like he was taking over my life a little too much. The documentary was planned to chart Novello's life from his school days to his death in 1951 and reflect his ability to evolve and change his career to suit the demands of the times and the industry. It occurred to me that perhaps this would be an opportunity to discuss Novello in a way that was honest and informative. At this time I had heard stories that, although odd and slightly bizarre, did seem to move away from the attempts to sanitise his memory; which to me made him seem a bit too perfect and hence uninteresting. My career path would once again cross that of Stephen Fry, as he had been engaged to narrate the documentary in his inimitable style.

One such story I decided to impart for the benefit of the documentary, I had been told in good faith by a resident of Littlewick Green, where Novello's home Red Roofs was situated. The story referred to Novello's obsession with death and how he would play dead in a glass coffin and enjoy hearing his friend's play act their grief at his loss. The story then goes that he would be left alone with a young man of his liking, who would bring him back to life as a form of sexual foreplay. It is indeed a bizarre story, but it made me think, and it also tied in with a song Novello had written in one of his early music books dating to the 1920s. The lyrics he wrote referred exactly to this subject, and his thoughts on how people would react at his death and who would weep for him.

The other story concerned Novello's liking for what we would today call 'rough trade'. He had, apparently, a particular liking for manual workers, or ditch diggers working in road gangs, and would, with the assistance of Bobbie, find suitable candidates for mutual sexual experiences. The story also goes that as a result of this behaviour Novello was subjected to the odd blackmail attempt; which at the time was prevalent and a real fear for homosexuals because of the illegal status of their sexuality. Thus it was said that Bobbie continued to pay sums of money to individuals right up until Novello's death.

Whenever one hears such stories it is always difficult to say they are true beyond a shadow of a doubt. With the passing of time, no doubt they have been embellished for dramatic effect. That said, they did come from a source that had a direct link to where Novello lived, and had been passed down by those living in the area at the time Novello was alive. For that reason I wasn't shy in relaying these stories for the benefit of the documentary. There were those who made me very aware of their displeasure, but mainly because I had put the stories into the public domain, and not because they were considered to be untrue.

The end result of the Documentary titled *The Handsomest Man In Britain* was I felt positive, and I was personally pleased with my own contribution. It was aired prior to the release of *Gosford Park*, which I felt was a mistake. Had it been broadcast to coincide with the attention *Gosford Park* received, perhaps it would have faired much better. That said, it is often repeated and has played in various parts of the world.

In many ways *Gosford Park* did serve Novello's memory well. It gave him a world profile and, especially in America, renewed interest in him and his music. My feelings that his music would inevitably be his lasting legacy, are perhaps correct. His musicals, if produced today, would prove impossible to create in the way they were originally conceived; more because of the sheer scale and costs of such a production. But then, nothing is impossible, and it might yet happen.

The eventual release of *Gosford Park* and the awards it garnered also opened up other possibilities for me. I contributed to an article for the *New York Times* and produced feature articles on Novello for other USA publications. The *New York Times* also contacted me for assistance when they were compiling Elisabeth Welch's obituary, and I provided a photograph of her from the *Glamorous Night* collection of photographs.

Whilst in the pre planning stages of this book I heard that Sir Cameron Mackintosh was considering renaming the Strand Theatre in the West End to the Novello Theatre. It seemed appropriate because Novello had lived and worked in "the flat" above that theatre from 1913 to his death in 1951, and pleased he was receiving such high profile recognition. It brought to mind the album of photographs of *Glamorous Night*, which had belonged to Novello, and started their journey into my safe keeping from "the flat", when Olive Gilbert inherited them from him. Betty Paxton, her niece, had given them to me, for fear they would be destroyed if anything happened to her. My reaction was they should go back, and be displayed perhaps so others could enjoy them.

With this thought in mind I contacted Sir Cameron and explained the situation. I was happy to let him have them, as long as he gave an assurance they would be permanently displayed in the new Novello Theatre, returning to the place from where they originally came. The gesture on my part was not ever about money. It would have been inappropriate to try and sell these unique and rare photographs, as they had been given to me on trust to take care of for the future. No doubt they could have been sold and possibly for a considerable amount, but life is not just about money, and my offer was in recognition to Novello for what he had made possible for me to experience. On receiving the album of photographs, Sir Cameron kindly sent me a letter, in which he said:

"How very kind of you to send me the album of photographs which belonged to Ivor Novello. I am delighted that you feel able to part with them but appreciate it must have been very sad for you to let them go. I promise they will be taken great care of and I am sure enjoyed by many people at the renamed Novello Theatre…Thank you very much for your enormously generous gesture."

Now they are framed and displayed in the Novello Theatre, in the Waldorf Bar, "the flat" and also backstage, and I am glad to say preserved for posterity, and can be seen by all those patrons, tourists and performers among others who attend performances at the theatre.

The renaming of the theatre had, I was also pleased to hear, been for wholly practical reasons and devoid of any sentiment. Sir Cameron explained in a letter to me that "In renaming the Strand Theatre I am honouring Ivor Novello's name," but it was also for a more practical reason, which he stressed by adding, " I am also ironing out an anomaly that has long existed in that the Strand Theatre is actually situated on the Aldwych and has consequently caused much confusion to tourists trying to find it." Novello would have wholly approved of such a reason, and no doubt would find it highly amusing that he was serving to eliminate such confusion among tourists.

Today those tourists are part of the lifeblood of the West End theatres and have provided for the evolution and stability of the theatre industry as a whole. Novello did much the same in his time. He drew thousands into the West End theatres who had never been there before, much to the dismay of traditionalists, because they wanted to see him perform live. He attracted a whole new audience and with them came much needed revenue. The West End has moved on and it has now found a new audience in the tourist trade, which enables it to thrive. Novello's philosophy above any other was his desire to "fill the plush" and draw in new audiences. That he has become part of the West End again is due to many things. His portrayal in *Gosford Park* certainly gave him a global profile, and his name became instantly recognisable again. No doubt all these things led to it being possible for the theatre to be named after him. In some way, I like to think I have aided that process and contributed effectively to ensuring his achievements are not forgotten. That has always been important to me.

Inevitably there were to be some sad events. Early 2003 brought the news that Mary Ellis had died at her home in London. She was just a few weeks short of her 105th Birthday. She had a long and remarkable life, and one where she was destined to out-live her fame and all her contemporaries by decades. Not long after, Elizabeth Welch, who for years had suffered from Alzheimer's Disease, passed away aged 99. Robert Altman and Douglas Fairbanks Jnr are also no longer with us, which means they will sadly not get the opportunity to read this book, as they had expressed a desire to do. The passing of Roma Beaumont and Gordon Duttson has also been noted. To me they were all a vital link to Novello and a theatre world that has long since vanished. Colin Deveraux also passed away a few months after the Celebration Concert. He had been suffering from cancer at the time, but chose not to tell anyone. They were all unique in their way, and I was glad to have met them and afforded the opportunity to hear them tell their stories. In many ways it made me realise that I have been fortunate, because I was able to speak to these people and get their stories first hand. No one will ever be able to do that again.

Ruritania is perhaps best summed up as a place that represents that part of us all that can create an ideal world with the power of our own imaginations. Novello's Ruritania was not just about over sentimentalised situations and characters, garnished with florid music. It was a place he created which enabled his audiences to escape from the real world and lose themselves in another one. One where in spite of disappointments and harsh realities, his characters would be allowed to find some peace and contentment; if only in the final vision scene where they were reunited in a way which expressed a "hope" for the future. Novello lived his life in a world that at times seemed to offer little in the way of hope. World wars and economic depressions may not have touched him as harshly as it touched others, but he felt it was his job to connect with those realities and offer his audiences another kind of hope, the one of his imagination. In that he succeeded. Difficult for those of us today to truly appreciate; you had to live in those times to fully understand Novello and his work, but that is not to say that elements of his work are beyond appreciation today. When I started this journey, few had heard of him, now he has finally been acknowledged and afforded recognition; the recognition the London *Evening Standard* claimed he deserved in 1951.

As far as I am concerned the journey continues. One thing I have learnt over the years is that Novello will inevitably come to the fore in the most unexpected places at the most unexpected times. His story is much clearer now than it was all those years ago when aunt Mabel first introduced him to me. My hope is that perhaps you will now have a better understanding of Novello, his career and his music, but devoid of any sentiment.

Ivor Novello (1893-1951)

Ivor Novello

Included in Reference section: Music, Revue Shows, Films, Plays, Musicals:

Music:

1910 - *Spring Of The Year* (music & lyrics Novello)

1911 – *Little One* (Lyrics Bailey & Music Novello)

Slumber Tree (Lyrics Bailey & Music Novello)

1912 - *The Little Damozel* (music Novello, lyrics Teschemaker); *Blue Eyes*; *If*; *I'm In The Clouds*; *Lament*; *Our Help In Ages Past*; *Up There*.

1913 - *Not Really* (music & lyrics Novello); *The Haven of Memory*; *Hindu Lulaby*; *The Valley*; *Why Hurry, Little River*.

1914 - *Carnival Time* (music & lyrics Novello)

Keep The Home Fires Burning (music Novello, lyrics Lena Gilbert Ford)

1915 - *Laddie In Khaki* (music & lyrics Novello)

When The Great Day Comes (music Novello, lyrics Teschemaker)

Just A Jack Or A Tommy (music Novello, lyrics Huggins)

Radiance Of Your Eyes (music & lyrics Novello)

1916 - *The garden Of England* (music Novello, lyrics Grey)

Revue Shows:

Theodore and Co (Revue)

Gaiety Theatre.

First Night: September 14th, 1916.

Music by: **Ivor Novello** and Jerome Kern

Isn't There A Crowd Everywhere

What A Duke Should Be

I'll Make Myself A Home

The Candy Girls

You'd Better Not Wait For Him

He's Going To Call On Baby Grand

We Are Theodore & Co

My Friend John

Every Little Girl Can Teach Me Something New

Any Old Where

Walk A Little

Lazy Dancing Man

Ivor Novello

See-Saw (Revue)

Comedy Theatre

First Night: December 14th, 1916.

Music by: Phillip Braham, **Ivor Novello** and Harold Montague.

Lyrics by: A.B. Mills and Arthur Weigall.

Risk It

On The Tiles

Rude Questions

Dream Boat

Arlette (Musical Comedy)

Shaftesbury Theatre.

First Night: September 6th, 1917.

Music by: Jane Vieu, Guy Le Feuvre and **Ivor Novello**

Lyrics by: Adrain Ross, Clifford Grey.

Hail, All Hail

On The Staff

A Man Of Forty

Cousinly Love

Didn't Know The Way To

Just A Memory

The People's King

In Search of Ruritania

Tabs (Revue)

Vaudeville Theatre.

First Night: May 15th, 1918.

Music by: **Ivor Novello**

Additional music by: Guy Le Feuvre, Bob Adams, Muriel Lillie, Herman Darewski, Wlater Donaldson, Pat Thayer.

Lyrics by: Ronald Jeans, Douglas Furber, Adrain Ross, Walter Donaldson, Hugh Wright.

Mr Pau-Puk-Keewis

Feed The Brute

Think Again

When I Said Goodbye To You

Something Doing Over The Way

I Hate To Give Trouble

Goblin Golliwog Trees

Have You Ever Noticed

Come Out, Little Boy!

Who's Hooper! (Musical Comedy)

Adelphi Theatre.

First Night: September 13th, 1919.

Music by: Howard Talbot and **Ivor Novello**.

Lyrics by: Clifford Grey

My London Town

Ivor Novello

There's An Angel Watching Over Me

Wonderful Love

Wedding Jazz

When No-Ones Looking

Come, Landlord Fill The Flowing Bowl

A Ladies Man

If You Were King In Babylon

Who's Hooper?

The Garden Of My Dreams

Each Day In Passing

A Southern Maid (Operette)

Daly's Theatre

First Night: May 15th, 1920

Music by Harold Fraser-Simpson

Additional music by **Ivor Novello**

Lyrics by Harry Graham

Every Bit Of Loving In The World

I Want The Sun And The Moon

The Golden Moth (Musical Play)

Adelphi Theatre

First Night: October 5th, 1921

Music by **Ivor Novello**

Lyrics by PG Wodehouse & Adrian Ross

We've Had A Busy Day

Fairy Prince

Romance Is Calling

Lonely Soldier

Round The Corner

Dartmoor Days

Dear Eyes That Shine

My Girl

Nuts In May

If I Ever Lost You

Song Of Welcome

At The Servants' Ball

The Island Of Never-Mind-Where

Give Me A Thought Now And Then

A to Z (Revue)

Prince Of Wales Theatre

First Night October 21st, 1921

Music by **Ivor Novello** and Philip Braham

Lyrics by Ronal Jeans, Dion Titheridge, Collie Knox

Think Of All The Fun You're Missing

My Kind Of Boy

And Her Mother Came Too

The Oldest Game In The World

Night May Have It's Sadness

Rough Stuff

I've Never Been Kept Waiting

I Hate That Tune

There Are Times

A To Z

When I'm Dressed In Blue

I Don't Believe A Word Of It

Chez Patou

Tears

Puppets (Revue)

Vaudeville Theatre

First Night: January 2nd, 1924

Music by **Ivor Novello**

Lyrics by Dion Titheridge

And That's Not All

April's Lady

What Do You Mean

Same Old Moon

Raggedy Doll

Penelope

Barbary

Old Acquaintance Blues

She Needs Another Now

The House That Jack Built (Revue)

Adelphi Theatre

First Night: November 8th, 1929

Music by Ivor Novello, Vivian Ellis, Arthur Shwartz, Sydney Baynes

Lyrics by Donovan Parsons and Douglas Furber

The House We'd Build

At The Circus

Teardrops From Her Eyes

The Dowager fairy Queen

Ivor Novello

The Thought Never Entered My Head

Playing The Game

Ever So

There Must Be Something On My Mind

FILMS:

The Call Of The Blood (1920) Mercanton/ silent film

Miarka: Daughter Of The Bear (1920) Mercanton/ silent film

Carnival (1921) Alliance/ silent film

The Bohemian Girl (1922) Alliance/ silent film

The Man Without Desire (1923) Atlas Biocraft/ silent film

The White Rose (1923) Ideal/United Artistes/ silent film USA

Bonnie Prince Charlie (1923) Gaumont/ silent film

The Rat (1925) Gainsborough/ silent film UK

The Triumph Of The Rat (1926) Gainsborough/ silent film UK

The Lodger (1926) Gainsborough/ silent film UK

Downhill (1927) Gainsborough/ silent film UK

The Vortex (1928) Gainsborough/ silent film UK

The Constant Nymph (1928) Gainsborough/ silent film UK

The Gallant Hussar (1928) Gainsborough/ silent film UK

South Sea Bubble (1928) Gainsborough/ silent film UK

The Return Of The Rat (1928) Gainsborough UK

Symphony In Two Flats (1930) Gainsborough UK

Once A Lady (1931) Paramount/ Hollywood USA

The Lodger (1932) Twickenham/ UK

I Lived With You (1933) Twickenham/ UK

Sleeping Car (1933) Gaumont/ UK

Autumn Crocus (1934) Associated talking Pictures/ UK

PLAYS:

Debareu /Ambassadors Theatre 1921 *(Guitry/Granville-Barker)*

The Yellow Jacket / Kingsway Theatre 1922 *(Hazelton/Benrimo)*

Spanish Lovers / Kingsway Theatre 1922 *(Cordona)*

Enter Kiki / Playhouse Theatre 1923 *(Blow/Hoare)*

The Rat / Prince Of Wales Theatre 1924 *(Novello/Collier)*

Old Heidelberg / Garrick Theatre 1925 (Meyer-Forster/Bleichman)

Iris / Adelphi Theatre 1925 *(Pinero)*

The Firebrand / Wyndhams Theatre 1926 *(Mayer)*

Downhill / Queen's Theatre 1926 *(Novello/Collier)*

Lilliom / Duke Of York's Theatre 1926 *(Molnar)*

Sirocco / Daly's Theatre 1927 *(Coward)*

The Truth Game / Globe Theatre (now the Giulgud Theatre) 1928 *(Novello)*

The Truth Game (Broadway) / Ethel Barrymore Theatre 1930 *(Novello)*

Symphony In Two Flats / New Theatre 1929 *(Novello)*

Symphony In Two Flats (Broadway) Sam S Shubert Theatre 1930 *(Novello)*

I Lived With You / Prince Of Wales Theatre 1932 *(Novello)*

Party / Strand Theatre (now the Novello Theatre) 1932 *(Novello)*

Fresh Fields / Criterion Theatre 1933 *(Novello)*

Flies In The Sun / Playhouse Theatre 1933 *(Novello)*

Proscenium / Globe Theatre (now the Gielgud Theatre) 1933 *(Novello)*

The Sunshine Sisters / Queen's Theatre 1933 (Novello)

Murder In Mayfair / Globe Theatre (now the Giulgud Theatre) 1934 *(Novello)*

Full House / Theatre Royal Haymarket 1935 *(Novello)*

The Happy Hypocrite / His Majesty's Theatre 1936 *(Dane/Addinsell)*

Comedienne / Theatre Royal Haymarket 1938 *(Novello)*

Ladies Into Action / Lyric Theatre 1940 *(Novello)*

We Proudly Present / Duke Of York's Theatre 1947 *(Novello)*

Musicals:

Glamorous Night

Theatre Royal, Drury Lane

First Night: May 2nd, 1935

Book & Music: Ivor Novello

Lyrics: Christopher Hassall

Director: Leontine Sagan

Designed by Oliver Messel

Dances by Ralph Reader

Musical Director: Charles Prentice

Cast: *Ivor Novello, Mary Ellis, Barry Jones, Lyn Harding, Minnie Rayner, Elisabeth Welch, Olive Gilbert, Trefor Jones, Peter Graves, Victor Bogetti, Rudolph Brant, John Gatrell.*

Musical Numbers:

Suburbia

Her Majesty Miltza

Fold Your Wings

Glamorous Night

Shine Through My Dreams

When The Gypsy Played

Shanty Town

The Gypsy Wedding

March Of The Gypsies

The Girl I Knew

Ivor Novello

Singing Waltz

The Royal Wedding

Careless Rapture

Theatre Royal, Drury Lane

First Night: September 11th, 1936

Book & Music: Ivor Novello

Lyrics: Christopher Hassall

Director: Leontine Sagan

Designed by Alick Johnstone

Dances by Joan Davies and Anthony Tudor

Musical Director: Charles Prentice

Cast: *Ivor Novello, Dorothy Dickson, Zena Dare, Minnie Rayner, Ivan Samson, Olive Gilbert, Sybil Crawley, Eric Starling, Peter Graves, Nancy Pawley, Frederick Peisley, Olwen Brookes, Walter Crisham, Philip Friend, Gwen Floyd, Kenneth Howell, Enid Settle.*

Musical Numbers:

Thanks To Phylilida Frame

Singing Lesson

Music In May

Why Is There Ever Goodbye

Studio Duet

Wait For Me

Rose Ballet

Hi-Tie-Tiddly-Eye

Winnie, Get Off The Colonels Knee

Take A Trip To Hampstead

In Search of Ruritania

We Are The Wives

The Manchuko

Love Made The Song I Sing You

Chinese Procession

Temple Ballet

The Bridge Of Lovers

Crest Of The Wave

Theatre Royal, Drury Lane

First Night: September 1st, 1937

Book & Music: Ivor Novello

Lyrics: Christopher Hassall

Director: Leontine Sagan

Designed by Alick Johnstone

Dances by Ralph Reader

Ballet seq' by Lydia Soklova & Anthony Tudor

Musical Director: Charles Prentice

Cast: *Ivor Novello, Dorothy Dickson, Marie Lohr, Ena Burrill, Minnie Rayner, Peter Graves, Walter Crisham, Finaly Currie, Olive Gilbert, Reg Smith, Fred Hearne, Dorothy Batley, Renee Stocker, Jack Glyn, Aubrey Rose.*

Musical Numbers:

Rose Of England

Haven Of My Heart

Sarabande

Mazurka

Ivor Novello

Turbillon

Why Isn't It You

Nautical

If You Only Knew

March Of The Ancestors

Oh, Clementine

When Hollywood Plays

Christmas Carol

Used To You

The Dancing Years

Theatre Royal, Drury Lane

First Night: March 23rd, 1938

Book & Music: Ivor Novello

Lyrics: Christopher Hassall

Director: Leontine Sagan

Designed by Joseph Carl

Dances by Freddie Carpenter

Musical Director: Charles Prentice

Cast: *Ivor Novello, Mary Ellis, Roma Beaumont, Olive Gilbert, Anthony Nicholls, Minnie Rayner, Dunstan Hart, Peter Graves, Frances Clare, Muriel Barron, Hilary Allen, Fred Hearne, Harry Ferguson, Hilton Porter, Roger Parker, Edgar Elmes, John Palmer, Maria Rita, Patrick Ross, Hilary de Charville, Victor Raymond, Fred Nye.*

Musical Numbers:

Dawn Prelude

In Search of Ruritania

Uniform

Waltz Of My Heart

Masque Of Vienna 1911

The Wings Of Sleep

Lorelei

My Life Belongs To You

I Can Give You The Starlight

My Dearest Dear

Masque Of Vienna 1914

Primrose

In Praise Of Love

The Leap Year Waltz

Masque Of Vienna 1927

Memory Is My Happiness

When It's Spring In Vienna

Arc De Triomphe

Phoenix Theatre

First Night: November 9th, 1943

Book & Music: Ivor Novello

Lyrics: Christopher Hassall

Director: leonine Sagan

Designed by Joseph Carl

Ivor Novello

Dances by Keith Lester

Musical Director: Harry Acres

Cast: *Mary Ellis, Peter Graves, Raymond Lovell, Elisabeth Welch, Harcourt Williams, Gwen Floyd, Netta Westcott, Hilary Allen, Nesta Ross, Edgar Elmes, Harry Fergusson, Renee Crewe, Olive Gilbert.*

Musical Numbers:

Prelude

Shepherd Song

Man Of My Heart

Easy To Live With

I Wonder Why

Apache Ballet

Josephine

Waking Or Sleeping

Royal France

Paris Reminds Me Of You

Dark Music

The Phantom Court

Vision Duet

Jeanne d'Arc

France Will Rise Again

In Search of Ruritania

Perchance To Dream

Hippodrome Theatre

First Night: April 21st, 1945

Book, Lyrics & Music: Ivor Novello

Director: jack Minster

Designed by Joseph Carl

Dances by Frank Staff

Musical Director: Harry Acres

Cast: *Ivor Novello, Roma Beaumont, Muriel Barron, Robert Andrews, Margaret Rutherford, Olive Gilbert, Victor Bogetti, Anne Pinder, Dunstan Hart, harry Ferguson, Lawrence Drew, beryl Mariner, Roy Gunson, Gordon Duttson.*

Musical Numbers:

When The Gentlemen Get Together

Love Is My reason

The Meeting

The Path My Lady Walks

A Lady Went To market Fair

When I Curtsied To The King

Highwayman Love

The Triumph Of Spring

Autumn Lullaby

A Woman's Heart

We'll Gather Lilacs

The Victorian Wedding

The Glo-Glo

Ivor Novello

The Elopement

Ghost Finale

King's Rhapsody

Palace Theatre

First Night: September 15th, 1949

Book & Music: Ivor Novello

Lyrics: Christopher Hassall *(The Violin Began To Play: lyrics Novello)*

Director: Murray Mac Donald

Designed by Edward Delaney & Frederick Dawson

Dances by Pauline Grant

Musical Director: Harry Acres

Cast: *Ivor Novello, Vanessa Lee, Zena Dare, Phylis Dare, Robert Andrews, Olive Gilbert, Denis Martin, Michael Anthony, Victor Boggeti, Anne Pinder, John Palmer, Pamela Harrington, Wendy Warren, Eric Sutherland, Irene Claire, Ted Lane, Gordon Duttson.*

Musical Numbers:

The Dancing Lesson

Birthday Greetings

Someday My Heart Will Awake

National Anthem

Fly Home, Little Heart

Mountain Dove

If This Were Love

The Mayor Of Perpignan

The Gates Of Paradise

Take Your Girl

In Search of Ruritania

The Violin Began To Play

Muranian Rhapsody

Coronation Hymn

The Years Together

<u>Gay's The Word</u>

Saville Theatre

First Night: February 16th, 1951

Book & Music: Ivor Novello

Lyrics: Alan Melville

Director: Jack Hulbert

Designed by Edward Delaney & Berkley Sutcliffe

Dances by Irving Davies & Eunice Crowther

Musical Director: Harry Acres

Cast: *Cicely Courtneidge, Lizbeth Webb, Thorley Walters, Carl Jaffe, Dunstan Hart, Denis Val Norton, May Tomlin, John Wynyard, Maidie Andrews, Beryl Harrison, Molly Lumley, June Laverick, Susan Swinford, Hilary de Charville.*

Musical Numbers:

Ruritania

Everything Reminds Me Of You

It's Bound To Be Right On The Night

Father Thames

Teachers' Ballet

Finder, Please Return

An Englishman In Love

If Only He'd Looked My Way

Ivor Novello

Vitality

Teaching

Greek Dance

Sweet Thames

Gaiety Glad

A Matter Of Minutes

On Such A Night As This

Bees Are Buzzin

Further reading:

IVOR: *by Sandy Wilson*. Michael Joseph Publishing Ltd, London, 1975.

Those Dancing Years: *by Mary Ellis*. John Murray Publishers Ltd. London, 1982

The Story Of An Achievement: *by W. McQueen Pope*. Hutchinson Publishers Ltd, London, 1954.

Novello interview 1949: *by Elizabeth Frank*.

Sir Edward Marsh: *by Christopher Hassall*.Longmans, Green Ltd, London, 1959.

Oxford: *by James Morris*. Faber & Faber Publishing Ltd, London,1965.

A Tanners Worth of Tunes: Rediscovering the post-war British Musical *by Adrian Wright* / The Boydell Press, 2010.

The Oxford Handbook of the British Musical – *by Robert Gordon & Olaf Jubin* / Oxford University Press, published on 1 January 2017

Ivor Novello

Glamorous Night - Showcase

Theatre Royal, Drury Lane

May 8th, 1996

Producers: June Epstein & David Christy

Devised & Directed by David Christy

Musical Director: Derek Taverner

Cast: Fiona O'Neil, Richard Braebrook, Gia Frances, Peter McDermott

Tiffany Edwardes, Graham Bruce and students from The Royal Academy of Music.

Musical Numbers:

Glamorous Night

Fold Your Wings

Shanty Town

Shine Through My Dreams

Someday My Heart Will Awake

In Search of Ruritania

<u>*Glamorous Night - Stage Fair Presentation*</u>

Theatre Royal, Drury Lane

October 8th, 1996

Producers: June Epstein & David Christy

in Association with The Entertainment Business

Devised & Directed By David Christy and Gillian Gregory

Musical Director: Derek Taverner

Cast: Tiffany Edwardes and Graham Bruce

Musical Numbers:

Glamorous Night

Fold Your Wings

Shine Through My Dreams

Someday My Heart Will Awake.

50th Anniversay: Celebration Concert

Theatre Royal, Drury Lane

March 6th, 2001

Producers: Ivor Novello Appreciation Bureau

Devised & Directed by David Christy

Musical Director: Michael Topping

Cast: Michael Topping, Andy Simmons, Gia Frances, Sandra Watkins, Marie Sinnett, Christine Yates, Ruth Brown, Rachael Bowden, Colin Deveraux, Adam Goodman, Katie Haines, Claire Howard, Michael Howell, Lee Malcolmson, Gary Wright,

Musical Numbers:

Why Isn'y It You

And Her Mother Came Too!

Glamorous Night

Shine Through My Dreams

Shanty Town

I Can Give You The Starlight

Waltz Of My Heart

Wings Of Sleep

My Dearest Dear

Memory Is My Happiness

We'll Gather Lilacs

In Search of Ruritania

Love Is My reason

Someday My Heart Will Awake

The Violin Began To Play

Fly Home, Little Heart

Ruritania

Vitality

If Only He'd Looked My Way

Pray For Me

We'll Gather Lilacs (reprise)

Glamorous Night – Buxton 2008

Buxton Opera House

28 – 30 August 2008

Book: Ivor Novello. Lyrics: Christopher Hassall. Revised Libretto & Lyrics by: David Slattery-Christy.

By arrangement with Samuel French Ltd, London.

Producer: Present Company

Directed by: Jean Gemmell

Musical Director: Morris Fisher

Principal Cast: Sarah Potts (Militza); David Walters (Novello/Anthony); Richard Potts (Harry Tennent/King Steffan); Baron Lydyeff (Lee Stephens); Judith Hanson (Cleo Wellington); Andrew Lockwood (Lorenti)

Ladies & Gentlemen of the chorus.

Glamorous Night   The Cast

	Cabaret artist	Phil Birkett Colin Tarrant
Bill Baron Lydyeff	*Theatre Royal Director &* *Prime Minister*	Lee Stephens
Harry Tennant King Stefan	*Theatre Royal Manager &* *King of Krasnia*	Richard Potts
Ivor Novello Anthony Allen	*Composer &* *Journalist*	David Walters
Mario Landlord	*Ivy's Maître 'D &* *Innkeeper*	Albert Thomas
Boy Miss Davis Santiago Nico Militza Hajos Lorenti Phoebe Serg'e Lazlo Purser Cleo Wellington	 *Tour Guide* *Guard Captain* *Guard* *King's mistress* *Operatic tenor* *Militza's companion* *Militza's bodyguard* *Revolutionary* *SS Silver Star* *Lorenti's wife*	Harry Greatorex Celia Grantham Mike Spriggs Jim Blackmore Sarah Potts Andrew Lockwood Astrid Holford Chris Grantham James Ash Phil Lindsey Judith Hanson
The Operetta	*Queen* *Prince* *Princess*	Laura Taylor Andrew Lockwood Sarah Potts
Gypsy Wedding	*Queen* *Elder* *Bride* *Groom*	Laura Taylor Peter Gemmell Jayne Rawlinson Jon Morris
The Ball	*Princess* *Countess* *Duchess* *General* *Major Domo*	Christine Kilbourn Ann Morley Laura Taylor Colin Tarrant Mike Spriggs
Dancers Stephie Dennett Katie Lockwood	Louisa Hatton Danielle Roberts	Hannah Lockwood Bryony Thompson
Ladies & Gentlemen Hannah Atkins Trevor Davis Julie Fletcher Marcia Hewitt Sandra Tarrant	Mary Boocock Philip de Voil * Alison Greatorex Sue Spriggs Margaret Walker	James Davies Janette Faulkner * Steve Greatorex Martin Tailby _{Sings in concert only} *

BBC 4 & BBC Wales

The Handsomest Man in Britain - 2001

1/2 BBC Radio 2 – Keep The Home Fires Burning – Ivor Novello

Broadcast: Wednesday 8th October 2014.

Produced by Jonathon Mayo for BBC Radio 2

Presented by Don Black

Featuring: David Slattery-Christy, Ross Leadbetter, Simon Callow

Part 2

2/2 BBC Radio 2 - Friday Night is Music Night – Ivor Novello

Broadcast on 10 October 2014

Presented by Ken Bruce

Produced by BBC Radio 2

The BBC Concert Orchestra is conducted by Richard Balcombe with singers Wynne Evans, Sarah Fox, Charlotte Baptie and Lucy Williamson. The show is broadcast live from the Mermaid Theatre in London.

BBC Radio 3 - Composer of the Week – Ivor Novello

Broadcast on 26 to 30 December 2016 (5 one hour programmes)

Produced by Luke Whitlock for BBC Radio 3

Presented by Donald Macleod

Featuring: David Slattery-Christy, Rosy Runciman, William Differ. From Broadcasting House; Prince of Wales Theatre; Novello Theatre and Novello's old flat that is situated on top of the Novello Theatre at 11 Aldwych, London.

BBC Concert Orchestra & singers.

In Search of Ruritania

List of reviews/articles partially quoted in manuscript 'In Search of Ruritania'. With thanks to all the publishers for their kind permission.

Newspaper Articles:

Chapter 2 : SRING OF THE CAREER.

1. Daily telegraph 1911 - Review of Miss Evangeline Thomas recital at Royal Albert Hall.

2.

Chapter 3 : ROARING THROUGH THE 1920s

1. The Sunday Times 1919 - Review for 'Call Of The Blood' (film)

2. New York Tribune 1922 - Review for 'The Bohemian Girl (film)

3. New York Evening Mail 1922 - Review for 'The Bohemian Girl' (film)

4. The New York American 1922 - Gladys Coopers arrival in New York to marry Novello. (gossip)

5. The Times 1923 - Review for 'The White Rose' (film)

6. New York Evening Telegraph 1923 - Review for 'The White Rose' (film)

7. The Daily Telegraph 1923 - Review for 'Bonnie Prince Charlie' (film)

8. The Sunday Times 1922 - Review for 'The Yellow Jacket' (West End play)

9. The New Statesman 1922 - Review for 'Spanish Lovers' (West End play)

10. Daily Mirror 1923 - Review for 'Enter Kiki' (West End play)

11. The London Opinion 1924 - Review for 'The Rat' (Brighton play)

Chapter 4: NOEL, ALFRED & ELSIE

12. The Sunday Times 1925 - Review for 'Old Heidelberg' (West End play)

13. The Sunday Times 1926 - review for 'Lilliom' (West End play)

14. The Observer 1926 - Review for 'Down Hill' (West End play)

15. Theatre World 1928 - Review for 'The Truth Game' (West End play)

17. The Times 1928 - Review for 'The Truth Game' (West End play)

18. The Daily Telegraph 1929 - Review for 'Symphony In Two Flats' (West End play

19. The Times 1929 - Review for 'Symphony In Two Flats' (West End play)

Chapter 5: THE LAND THAT MIGHT HAVE BEEN

20. New York Times 1930 - Review for 'Symphony In Two Flats' (Broadway)

21. New York Theatre Magazine 1930 - review for 'The Truth Game' (Broadway)

22. New York Times 1930 - Review for 'The Truth Game' (Broadway)

23. Picturgoer Magazine 1931 - Review for 'Once A Lady' (film)

Chapter 7: A RUSSIAN ÉMIGRÉ & A GLAMOROUS FIGHT!

24. Film Weekly 1934 - Review for 'The Sleeping Car' (film)

25. The Times 1934 - review for 'I Lived With You' (film)

26. The Daily Telegraph 1935 - Review for 'Glamorous Night' (West End Musical)

27. The Observer 1935 - Review for 'Glamorous Night' (West End

Musical)

Chapter 8: *END OF AN ERA*

28. Evening Standard 1939 - Review for 'The Dancing Years' (West End Musical)

29. The News Chronicle 1939 - Review for 'The Dancing Years' (West End Musical)

30. Daily Mirror 1944 - Court report Novello's petrol offence.

31. Daily Sketch 1944 - Court report on Novello's sentence to prison.

32. The Sunday Times 1945 - review for 'Perchance To Dream' (West End musical)

33. The Observer 1949 - Review for 'King's Rhapsody' (West End musical)

34. The Sunday Times 1949 - Review for 'King's Rhapsody' (West End musical)

35. Evening Standard 1949 - Review for 'King's Rhapsody' (West End musical)

Other Credits:

Articles:

1. Ivor Novello by Elizabeth Frank : Courtesy of Maroussia Richardson

2. Rob Sedman, Lily Elsie Society

 "http://www.lily-elsie.com/"

3. Nicholas Gaze & Christopher Sansom,

Ivor Novello Appreciation Bureau

 "http://www.ivornovello.com/"

4. Matthew Lloyd

 "http://www.arthurlloyd.com/"

5. Dr. Robin Darwall-Smith, Magadalen College Archives, Oxford.

Picture Credits:

Front Cover : Courtesy of: Nick Gaze - Ivor Novello Appreciation Bureau / from Novello's personal collection.

Image: Bill Haines, Joan Crawford, Douglas Fairbanks Jnr and Ivor Novello at the premiere of Fairbank's film Union Station circa 1930. Copyright United Press International. Used with permission.

Section 1 Courtesy of: Nick Gaze - Ivor Novello Appreciation Bureau / from Novello's personal collection.

Magdalen College group: Courtesy of Magdalen College Archives, Oxford.

Lily Elsie/Novello: Courtesy of: Rob Sedman - Lily Elsie Society.

& David Slattery-Christy's & Novello's personal collection.

Section 2: David Slattery-Christy's & Novello's personal collection. Now displayed in the West End's new Novello Theatre. Lee Stephens for

Glamorous Night images featuring Sarah Potts, David Potts and David Walters – Buxton Opera House 2oo8.

Section 3: Novello Theatre, Aldwych, London. Copyright: Matthew Lloyd 2006. Gosford Park images copyright Capitol Films and Robert Altman – used with permission & David Slattery-Christy's & Novello's personal collection.

Every effort has been made to fulfil requirements with regard to reproducing copyright material. The author will be glad to rectify any ommissions at the earliest opportunity.

Elisabeth Welch, 99, Cabaret Hitmaker

By DOUGLAS MARTIN

Elisabeth Welch, an expatriate cabaret singer who mixed elegant phrasing and emotive power to craft extraordinary interpretations of the songs of America's Jazz Age and Britain's musical stage, died on Tuesday at a nursing home outside London. She was 99.

Like Josephine Baker and Mabel Mercer, Miss Welch was a black woman born at the beginning of the 20th century who made an exceptional singing career outside of the United States. In Paris and London she was the darling of cafe society and, of greater importance to her, of such composers as Cole Porter and Noël Coward.

Only when Miss Welch returned to perform in New York in 1980 after a half-century absence did Americans grasp the quality of her work and discover a living link with some of the great names of American musical theater. Her influence was enhanced by performing abilities that were substantially intact as an advanced age.

In 1980 she received excellent reviews for her role in "Black Broadway." In 1986 she was nominated for a Tony for her role in "Jerome Kern Goes to Hollywood" and won an Obie for her one-woman show, "Time to Start Living." In 1989 she charmed audiences at Weill Recital Hall.

Writing in The New York Post about her one-woman show, Clive Barnes called her an original. "With her sweetness, her gentility, arsenic-laced with a sense of roguish innuendo and pagan sensuality, she is like no one else," he wrote. "She has class, and class, and class. A saloon singer who would make any saloon into a salon."

In his review of the Kern show, Frank Rich of The New York Times urged readers to write their representatives in Congress demanding that she be detained in the United States "as a national resource too rare and précious for export."

Or perhaps too precious not to export. She sang in a Paris cabaret frequented by Gertrude Stein and in the surreal nightclubs of pre-Hitler Berlin. She introduced "Stormy Weather" to British audiences, stopping shows at the London Palladium, where 50 years later she would receive five standing ovations.

Elisabeth Welch was born in Manhattan on Feb. 27, 1904, though some accounts say 1908 and her age varied in interviews over the years. In an interview with The Associated Press on Feb. 1, 1986, she was said to be almost 77, which would mean she was born in 1909.

She was named after her mother, who was Scottish and spelled her name in the Scottish fashion. Her father, who descended from Africans and American Indians, was a coachman and later a gardener on an estate in Englewood, N.J.

She grew up in the area where Lincoln Center is now, which was then predominantly Irish. Her poor

Elisabeth Welch in 1986.

knew some in Paris. They make me cry."

Kathryn Crawford, a white actress, sang the song in Porter's revue. Critics were aghast that the wholesome-seeming young lady, dressed like a schoolgirl, sang such salacious stuff.

Porter, in a fury, left for Paris three days after the opening. The show's producers had meanwhile heard Miss Welch's more worldly rendition and hired her to replace Miss Crawford. Miss Welch insisted on apparel that an upmarket prostitute might fancy.

"I walked on in black satin and wore high patent-leather shoes with red heels," she said in an interview with The Associated Press in 1980. "I had a red maribou and a hat with an egret in it. The woman was very grand."

Porter was impressed when he met Miss Welch in Paris and asked her to appear in a show he was staging in London. She said yes. The show was "Nymph Errant," which starred Gertrude Lawrence. Porter wrote the song "Solomon" for Miss Welch, and the novelty tune became her signature.

While she waited for Porter's show to open in 1933, she sang in a London show called "Dark Doings," in which she introduced the song "Stormy Weather" to Britain.

She realized she had set a pattern, repeatedly singing what turned out to be a show's hit song, and often nothing else. She jokingly called herself "one-song Welch" and in 1935 again overwhelmed audiences with the song "Shantytown," which Ivor Novello, the star of prewar London musicals, wrote for her in his "Glamorous Night."

During World War II she entertained British troops with John Gielgud. In 1947 she brought "La Vie en Rose" to London, having heard Edith Piaf sing it in Paris.

Ms. Welch's decision to remain in Europe and make London her home may have resulted from a combination of her success there, her mother's Scottish and Irish ancestry and a visceral sense of belonging. Although American by birth, The Independent of London reported, she was British in thought and interest.

"I never had any feeling about being different from anybody else," The Independent quoted her as saying. "It equipped me to be an international person all my life."

Miss Welch said many times that she never had any particular plan for her life. She claimed to be as surprised as anybody when she turned up in New York as a new discovery in 1980.

"Things that have happened in my life just happened," she told The Times. "I never had any star that I strove toward."

SUPPORT THE FRESH AIR FUND

Miss Welch in Ivor Novello's "Glamorous Night" in 1935.

Wild" in 1923. She sang "Singing Charleston" to accompany the new dance, and in later years was often credited with having introduced the dance to the United States.

A brief marriage, when she was 18, ended in divorce, and she left no immediate survivors.

Using her nickname, Mr. Welch told his wife, "Girlie's on the boards, she's doomed." In anger, he left the family forever.

After high school she did social work for a settlement house while also appearing in popular all-black revues. She considered her real debut to be "Blackbirds of 1928," starring Bill (Bojangles) Robinson.

She was popular and accompanied the show to Paris, where it played the Moulin Rouge in 1929. She received her first favorable mentions in the press and appeared as a singer in chic nightclubs. Jean Patou, the designer, began giving her two dresses a year, in spring and fall.

In the summer of 1930 she was asked to come to New York to open a

Glamorous Night
A Musical Comedy

Original Book & Music
- Ivor Novello -
Lyrics by Christopher Hassall

Revised Libretto & Lyrics
David Slattery-Christy

Performance rights Samuel French Ltd, London

A

Agate, James 67,69,70,81,220
Altman, Robert 6,128,226,232,233,246,253, 255,256,257,259,263
Andrews, Robert 9,10,27,42,45,48,49,50,52,53,54, 56,57,58,59,61,70,72,75,78,79,81,88,101,108,115, 124,129,137,138,166,167,168,179,193,196,197,207, 216, 221,222,249,250,251,252
Arnold, Tom 224,251,252
Astaire, Adele 116
Astaire, Fred 116
Atterbury, John 238
Asquith, Margo 42,85

B

Baines, Sydney 92
Balaban, Bob 227
Balcon, Michael 64,75,76,93
Baron, Muriel 202
Batley, Dorothy 69
Beaton, Cecil 89,97
Beaumont, Binkie 173
Beaumont, Roma 245,263
Beaverbrook, Lord 70
Belasco, David 171
Benson, Anette 94
Berlin, Irving 248
Blakely, Claudia 231
Black, Don 5
Bloom, June 198
Boyer, Charles 80,
Braebrook, Richard 211
Braithwaite, Lillian 8,90,113
Brett, Jeremy 181
Brice, Fanny 112,113,115
Brooke, Rupert 39,41,42
Brown, Graham 87
Bruce, Graham 213
Bruce, Ken 5
Buchanan, Jack 46,53
Burns, Nica 211
Burke, Billy 112,113
Bushell, Anthony 94
Byam Shaw, Glen 89

C

Carrington, Desmond 244
Carroll, Madelaine 159
Caruso, Enrico 171
Chadwick, Spencer 24
Chamberlain, Joseph 190
Charlot, Andre 40,41
Chatterton, Ruth 118,119
Churston, Lady 51
Churchill, Lady Randolph 42,51
Churchill, Sir Winston 27,37,42,88,191,202,218
Codron, Maichael 211
Collier, Constance 52,61,62,63,71,76,81,87
Constable, Dora 206,216,217
Compton, Fay 161,162
Cooper, Lady Diana 51
Cooper, Gladys 51,52,54,56,57,60,71
Courtenidge, Cecily 225,241,248
Coward, Noel 45,46,51,65,72,73,74,79,81,82,87,88 114,129,133,160,168,181, 191,192,218,221
Crawford, Joan 110,115,116,120,133,135,136

D

Daly, John Augustine 24,
Dance, Charles 253
Daniels, Bebe 102
Dare, Phylis 223
Dare, Zena 104,106,108,164,165,218,223,252
Darwall Smith, Dr. Robin 95
Davies, David 15,19,20,27,29,47,121,122,124
Davies, Bette 172
Davies, Clara Novello 15,18,19,24,27,32,33,35,43, 45,47,48,49,71,72,105,122,124,166,204,221,
Dean, Basil 79,80
Devereaux, Colin 241,246,247,263
Dickson, Dorothy 102,103,189,190
Differ, William 239
Doble, Frances 73,74
Dudley, Lady 51
Duff, Lady Juliet 250,251
Du Maurier, Gerald 87,88
Duttson, Gordon 188,195,196,197,198,220,245,263

E
Eddy, Nelson 172
Edward VIII 35
Edwards, Tiffany 213
Edwardes, George 82,83
Ediss, Connie 24
Elsie, Lily 24,25,42,65,82,83,84,85,86,87,88,89,96,97,98,99,
Ellis, Mary 6,14,15,46,108,133,142,143,144,145,146,147,148,149,150,151,158,164,168,169,170,171,172,178,179,180,181,182,184,185,189,190,191,192,193,194,195,196,197,202,206,212,218,263
Ellis, Vivien 92
Ervine, St John 77

F
Fairbanks, Douglas Jnr. 115,116,120,126,133,136,162,262,263
Fellowes, Julian 252
Fontaine, Joan 80
Fontaine, Lynn 116
Florence, Evangeline 33
Ford, Lena Gilbert 37
Frances, Ghia 211,212,242,247
Frank, Elizabeth 161

G
Gable, Clark 162
Gambon, Michael 234
Garbo, Greta 82,120,121,133,136
Garrett, Lesley 219
Garrick, David 137
Gaze, Nicholas 132,182,240,242,255
Gielgud, John 17,79,172,173
Gilbert, Olive 106,108,109,133,147,177,182,183,220,221,223,224,249,250,251,255,261,
Gill, Tom 249,250
Graves, Robert 39,53
Gregory, Gillian 212,213
Griffith, D.W 53,54,56,57,64
Groves, Olive 255
Gordon, John 80
Grossmith, George 24

H
Hammerstein, Arthur 171,172,
Hammerstein, Oscar II 70,171,222
Hammond, Mary 211,242
Hassall, Christopher 164,165,166,172,173,174,208,219,223,240
Hassall, Nicholas 174,173,175,176
Hector, George 53
Hichens, Robert 49
Hickey, Brian G.L. 21,22,26
Hickey, Col. Michael 21,26
Hitchcock, Alfred 65,75,76,77,128
Hitler, Adolf 191,192,194,202
Hope, William 116
Hudson, Rock 56
Hulbert, Jack 92
Hume, Benita 90,93,94

J
Jacobs, David 211
Jeans, Isabel 160
Jeffries, Ellis 88
Jones, Barry 143
Jones, Trefor 147,156

K
Kern, Jerome 40
Kendell, William 69
Kennedy, Margaret 79
Kinsey, David 211

L
Lanchester, Elsa 80
Laughton, Charles 70,71
Lawrence, Gertrude 53
Lehar, Franz 83
Leigh, Vivien 17,108,133,180
Levy, David 246,253,255,256,257,259
Lillie, Beatrice 102
Lloyd Webber, Lord Andrew 69,208
Lucille, Lady Duff Gordon 84
Lunt, Alfred 116
Lupino, Ida 160

M

MacDonald, Kelly 228,238
Macdonald, Jeanette 172
Mackintosh, Sir Cameron 208,261,262
Macleod, Donald 5,6,7,139,239
Marsh, Sir Edward 37,38,39,40,41,42,43, 50,53,57, 62,65,70,72,74,75,81,88,129,163, 165,166,167,168,174, 189,191,192,217,219,254
Marsh, Mae 56
Mayer, Daniel 48
Mayer, Louis B 117,118
Mayo Jonathon 5
McDermot, Peter 211
Melville, Alan 249,250
Mercanton, Louis 48,49
Messell, Oliver 154,176,183
Monkman, Phyllis 8,15
Morgan 249,250,251
Morley, Sheridan 209
Moore, Lily 236,261
Miller, Gertie 24
Mirren, Dame Helen 258
Mundin, Herbert 53

N

Navarro, Ramon 128,
Nortcliff, Lynn 186,
Northam, Jeremy 128,227,230,231,254,256,258

O

Olivier, Laurence 17,108,135
O'neil, Fiona 211
Osborne, Lord 38
Osborne, Peter 252
O'shea, Tessie 241
Owen, Wilfred 39

P

Pankhurst, Emeline 69
Paxton, Betty 236,261
Payne, Edmund 24
Percival, Spencer 38,39
Phillipe, Ryan 227,234
Phipps, John 24
Pickford, Mary 115,116
Pollock, Elizabeth 53
Pope, Walter McQueen 22,214,215,218
Porter, Cole 248
Potts, Richard 157
Potts, Sarah 157
Power, Tyrone 133
Puccini, Giacomo 170

R

Ralph, George 90,
Rattigan, Terence 252
Raynor, Minnie 90,160,178,214
Reader, Ralph 176
Regent, Prince 38,40
Richardson, Ian 161,208
Roberts, John Varley 22,23,95
Rodgers, Richard 71,222,248
Rose, Billy 112,113
Rose, Richard 94
Ross, Herbert 53
Runciman, Rosy 5,139,239

S

Sagan, Leontine 178
Sassoon, Siegfried 39
Scott Thomas, Dame Kristen 227,229,234,235
Schartz, Arthur 92
Schubert, Sam. S. 111,113
Sealby, Mabel 89
Shakespeare, William 189
Simmonds, Andy 241,247,248
Sinatra, Frank 219
Sinnett, Marie 242,247
Smith, Dame Maggie 129,228,238,253,257
Streisand, Barbra 112
Summerville, Geraldine 234
Swanson, Gloria 34

T

Tennent, Harry 167,168,179
Terry, Ellen 52
Thalberg, Irving 116,118,119,120,121
Topping, Michael 241,245,247,248
Tree, Sir Herbert 37
Tree, Viola 37,87,89,90
Trevor, Ann 59,90

V

Valentino, Rudolfo 52
Victoria, Queen 20,35
Volpe, Frederick 89

W

Walters, Julie 209,210
Walton, Grace 214,215,216
Warren, Sir Thomas Herbert 18,19,21,22,29,95
Watkins, Sandra 242,247
Webb, Clifton 116
Welch, Elisabeth 6,140,141,152,153,177,178,206,211,212,218,242,247,263
Weldon, Duncan 211
Wellesly, Marquis 39
Walters, David 157
Walton, William 175
Whightman, Natasha 235
Wilde, Oscar 17
Williams, Kenneth 32
Williams, Simon 244,245
Williams, Lloyd 72,94
Wilson, Sandy 6,76,184,211,212
Wood, Victoria 209,210
Woodward, Edward 256
Wren, Sir Christopher 17

ABOUT THE AUTHOR

David Slattery-Christy

David was born in Oxford, England, in 1959. He graduated from London's City University with a BA (Hons) Degree in Journalism. In addition to this he has a Teaching Degree from Lancaster University [PGCE] and a Masters Degree (Dist) in the Arts from the University of Central Lancashire and continues his professional development by undertaking research and history courses at the University of Oxford. Prior to this he attended London Theatre Arts to study drama, and then worked extensively in the performing arts industry as a playwright, producer and director. His stage plays include the award winning Forever Nineteen, After The Tone and The Post Card - which enjoyed London and New York productions, as well as touring nationally in the United Kingdom. His involvement in adapting the libretto for Ivor Novello's 1935 musical Glamorous Night resulted in him directing the 50th Anniversary Concert to celebrate the life and work of Novello at the Theatre Royal, Drury Lane, in London's West End. Subsequently he has worked as the Ivor Novello Consultant on Julian Fellowes and Robert Altman's Oscar and BAFTA winning film Gosford Park, and contributed to the BBC Documentary on the life of Novello The Handsomest Man in Britain. For BBC Radio 3 Composer of Week on Ivor Novello he was script consultant and guest for the five hour programmes He is the author of In Search of Ruritania, a biography on Ivor Novello & Edwardian Beauty. Lily Elsie & The Merry Widow - the first biography of the elusive actress and singer who found fame in Lehar's The Merry Widow. He has written several plays, novels, biographies and screenplays.

Represented by Robert Smith Literary Agent, London.

Further information available at: www.christyplays.com

In Search of Ruritania

Ivor Novello

www.ingramcontent.com/pod-product-compliance
Lightning Source LLC
LaVergne TN
LVHW041957060526
838200LV00018B/375/J